DATE DUE

MAY 9 1985			
FEB 1 1 1987			
MAY 28 '98			

Distrust and Democracy

Distrust and Democracy

Political Distrust in Britain and America

VIVIEN HART

Lecturer in American Studies
University of Sussex

CAMBRIDGE UNIVERSITY PRESS

CAMBRIDGE

LONDON · NEW YORK · MELBOURNE

Published by the Syndics of the Cambridge University Press
The Pitt Building, Trumpington Street, Cambridge CB2 1RP
Bentley House, 200 Euston Road, London NW1 2DB
32 East 57th Street, New York, NY 10022, USA
296 Beaconsfield Parade, Middle Park, Melbourne 3206, Australia

© Cambridge University Press 1978

First published 1978

Printed in Great Britain by
Western Printing Services Ltd, Bristol

Library of Congress Cataloguing in Publication Data

Hart, Vivien.
Distrust and democracy.
Includes index.
1. Democracy. 2. Allegiance. 3. Representative
government and representation – Great Britain.
4. Representative government and representation –
United States. I. Title.
JC423.H368   321.8   77–84803
ISBN 0 521 21857 8

for my parents

Contents

List of tables and figures

Preface

There is one safeguard known generally to the wise, which is an advantage
and security to all, but especially to democracies as against despots. What
is it? Distrust.

Demosthenes, *Philippic 2*, sec. 24

The underlying preoccupation of this book is with the paradox
suggested by Demosthenes: that the philosophy of democracy, resting
upon confidence in the capacity of men to govern themselves, as well
as their right to do so, may depend for its fulfilment on a sustained
suspicion of the vulnerability of men and institutions to the temptations
of power. My immediate concern is with the politics of recent years in
Britain and the United States. In both countries, observers have noted
of late widespread misgivings among the general public about an
apparent contradiction between the professed ideals of democracy and
the day to day activities of government. Influential interpreters of such
public criticism have raised the alarm of a threat to orderly political
processes and a consequent and imminent crisis of the legitimacy of
political institutions.

It is this perception of a discrepancy between the ideals and realities
of the political process itself which I call political distrust. The roots of
political distrust lie in frustration at the practical failure of this political
process to meet the expectations and demands of citizens; fluctuations
in its intensity have been traced to the presence or absence of profound
issue grievances. This study, however, is not concerned with the causes
of distrust, but with its content and consequences: with what it means
to the distrustful themselves and with what it has meant and now
means for the politics of Britain and America. I stand against the most
frequent interpretation of distrust – that the critique of politics arises
from ignorance and results in alienation from the ideals of democracy.
The failure of the ordinary citizen to meet standards of eloquence,
logic or content imposed by intellectuals or practitioners of politics is
the wrong ground for dismissal. The proper question to ask is of the

internal consistency of political distrust – the consistency between the norms of the distrustful, the abuses they identify and the solutions which they propose – and its relation to their experience of the world. From thus respecting the terms of the distrustful themselves, a very different conclusion emerges: in both countries today, distrust is democratic and thoughtful, not an anti-democratic outburst of emotion, and is potentially constructive, threatening only to vested political interests. The distrustful are often inarticulate, and have certainly not solved the practical problems of the implementation of their ideals, but the validity and honesty of their position require that they be taken seriously.

The misinterpretation of the distrustful as anti-democratic has arisen both because of the political values and preferences of analysts and because of inadequacies in methodology and evidence. In particular, current events have generally been treated in isolation from history. This neglect is serious, not only because history may offer examples of distrust which further the understanding of the present, but because a historical sense may save the contemporary observer from reckless assertions of novelty, change or crisis. Such assertions have been commonplace recently; they are particularly astonishing in America, when that nation's past attitude to politics is borne in mind. For political folklore there has long held that politics is a tawdry and corrupting affair. Protective parents are a typical example, in their consistent and overwhelming rejection of politics as a dignified life's work for their offspring, because it is 'too corrupt', 'too crooked', or 'too hard to be honest'.[1] And this popular opinion is reflected again and again in major interpretations of American politics.

Thus, James Young derived from the writings of political observers and politicians themselves a picture of a 'culturally ingrained predisposition to view political power and politics as essentially evil' as early as the Era of Good Feelings.[2] Very shortly thereafter, Tocqueville suspected that this evaluation might be justified. His belief that 'one of the great advantages of universal suffrage is that it entrusts the direction of affairs to men who are worthy of the public confidence' was challenged by his discovery 'that mountebanks of all sorts are able to please the people'.[3] Lord Bryce observed that ' "Politician" is a term of reproach, not merely among the "superfine philosophers" of New England colleges, but among the better sort of citizens over the whole Union'.[4] ' "Low as a congressman" is a saying one often hears', Ostrogorski reported in 1902; he, like Tocqueville, found considerable justification for this reputation, but, predictably, concluded that structure, not human nature, was at the root of the debasement: 'It is the party Organization which has made possible this vast political corruption.'[5]

The clichés about politicians are an easy way for the inarticulate to express their feelings; deeper probing of these feelings uncovers assessments of the political system as elitist, corrupt, unresponsive, inaccessible, partial to influential groups, and unrepresentative. Yet, curiously, history also suggests that profound doubts about politics have been matched by an equally continuous tradition of the proud affirmation of American democracy. This found recent expression, for example, in the spontaneous answers of a large sample of American citizens to the question, 'Speaking generally, what are the things about this country that you are most proud of?'

> Eighty-five per cent of the American respondents cited some feature of the American government or political tradition – the Constitution, political freedom, democracy, and the like – as compared with 46 per cent for the British, 7 per cent for the Germans, 3 per cent for the Italians, and 30 per cent for the Mexicans.[6]

Perhaps the paradoxical combination of political doubt and political pride in American culture can be seen as the reflection in popular attitudes of the national ambivalence between high ideals and realism about human nature. The tenth paper of *The Federalist* is a classic expression of this ambivalence, with its recognition of the fallibility of human reason and its commitment to democracy tempered by the recognition that 'Enlightened statesmen will not always be at the helm.'[7] Certainly, both hopes and fears are reflected in the lofty aims and careful checks and balances of the American constitution.

Alternatively, perhaps the apparent incongruity can be explained away. One source of information about the incidence of distrustfulness has been studies putting forward a theory of political stratification. High levels of cynicism in the general citizenry seemed one of a group of characteristics from which a composite picture was drawn of the 'mass' as ignorant, incoherent and apathetic about political affairs and profoundly demoralised by feelings of powerlessness and misanthropy. By this theory, inconsistency lies in the untrained or disturbed minds of the populace rather than in the complexity and contradictions of their political environment. Of course, even supposing that the inconsistency could thus be removed from cultural and social to psychological realms, the attitudes would remain deserving of investigation.

However untrained the minds, the existence of a sizeable body of citizens who perceive a substantial discrepancy between culturally accepted ideals and actual facts cannot be without significance for the polity.

One sure challenge to tendencies towards psychological reductionism is to examine comparative evidence of cultural variations; the rarity of such comparisons is a further weakness of the literature on political distrust. It is ironic that the study quoted above shows only half as many Britons as Americans expressing pride in their political system, for a dominant theme of comparisons between the two countries has been the contrast between deferential, accepting Britons and critical Americans:

> Britons are deferential to a ruling elite not only because of ingrained social attitudes but also because they believe that the ruling elite is honest and doing the best it can...Americans are considerably less trusting than Britons of those who govern on their behalf...They tend to feel that those who go into politics or even the civil service may have some admirable motives but probably also some less admirable ones.[8]

And, buttressed in their position by the *Oxford English Dictionary*, which makes special reference to the United States when it records the derogatory connotations of 'politician', the British have tended themselves to make somewhat condescending comparisons. Yet, their apparent combination of higher trust with lower pride seems as paradoxical as the American pattern. Furthermore, British complacency has been threatened recently by suggestions of fundamental change. A study of British schoolchildren found a 'substantial "anarchist" minority',[9] and one national opinion poll has reported that only 4 per cent of adults now give Members of Parliament first place for trustworthiness among a choice of public and professional figures.[10] As in the United States, prominent office-holders may be becoming the public scapegoats for a considerable disaffection with political processes. At any rate, the British case, by offering both a striking contrast to the consistent American history and, apparently, a recent and dramatic change, promises a double advantage in providing a comparison with the United States.

In this book, then, I examine both contemporary and historical evidence of the incidence of distrust in these two polities. Studies of these attitudes have too often been systematically descriptive but have then gone on to cry wolf, threatening crises of legitimacy and democracy on no more than intuitive grounds. But the descriptive statistics tell nothing more than the existence of a mood. We cannot be sure that this is new or traditional without historical investigation. Nor can we infer that dire, or any particular, consequences will follow, without considering what other conditions may affect the outcome and what national characteristics might inhibit or encourage actions or structure the direction that they take.

The questions I ask thus include: what is distrust, and against what is it directed? Is it really increasing in either Britain or America, or are academic studies simply noticing now what was there but disregarded before? Or, if there is indeed a new mood of disenchantment, what then? Is democratic government threatened by a massive withdrawal into apathy, or by revolt? Or may distrust make a positive contribution within the conventions of the polity which it criticises? And do the striking similarities in attitudes expressed recently by both Britons and Americans justify the assumption that similar consequences will follow in both countries?

The first chapter is mainly definitional. In it, I isolate the crucial characteristics of political distrust, introducing the particular form which it takes in the Anglo-American democracies and distinguishing it from the variety and confusion of studies over the last two decades which have been concerned with phenomena such as political aliena-tion, anomie, cynicism and inefficacy. A close acquaintance with the concept is essential for understanding the choice of evidence and the argument of the substantive chapters which follow, but readers without experience of the voluminous conceptual and empirical literature on political attitudes may wish to avoid the latter part of the chapter, which examines in more detail the relation of the language and values of social science to previous interpretations of distrust.

Chapter 2 uses recent evidence of the incidence and content of political distrust to clarify its meaning today, to suggest what may be its consequences and to question the conventional wisdom of the differences between the political cultures of Britain and America. My analysis of an unpublished survey of the political attitudes of teenagers in Britain and America both corrects some previous impressions of the meaning of distrust and demonstrates the subtle differences between the two nations which appear when criticisms of government are related to the ideals of the critics instead of being treated in isolation. The consequences of distrust are importantly shaped by the responses of the powerful: in both Britain and America governments have recently taken official note of the discontent of their citizens and the second part of this chapter examines the findings of a study made in Britain for the Royal Commission on the Constitution and comparable research commissioned by a sub-committee of the United States Senate. Both governments appear substantially more complacent about the state of the nation than are their citizens.

Such studies of a single moment, however, suggest important lines of enquiry to which they can provide no answers. Chapters 3 and 4 attempt, in a very limited way, to demonstrate the kind of historical evidence which deepens our understanding of the present and enables statements about development and change. Each chapter is a case study, of Populism in Kansas in the early months of 1890 and of Radical Liberalism in Birmingham during the reform debates of 1883–4, of a moment at which public rhetoric was uncannily similar to much that has been heard and labelled as distrust recently. Whether such superficial impressions of similarity are accurate is as questionable in these cases as in the present. My enquiry is into whether authentic public discontent lay behind the headlines, what was the pattern of beliefs about politics and criticisms by ordinary citizens, and what, if anything, came of their complaints.

Finally, in Chapter 5, I reconsider the state of politics in Britain and America today, comparing the present with the past and the experience of each country with the other. The British today have become more like the Americans. In the nineteenth century the contrast was clear – Americans were both idealistic and critical, the British unconcerned and accepting. Now a critique in similar terms is made in both countries and indeed in some respects is more serious in Britain. But I shall argue that in crucial ways the British are still more like their nineteenth century ancestors than they are like Americans. Because these crucial ways bear particularly upon the consequences of distrust, we should not expect a convergence in the form or content of British and American democracy. But we should expect and demand from the polity an openness to this critical and idealistic distrust; citizens who are not easily fooled are surely 'an advantage and security to all'.

This study began life as a doctoral dissertation for the Department of Government of Harvard University and in that form was awarded the University's DeLancey K. Jay prize. It has been revised and shortened, but not significantly altered in its argument, for publication. In the course of research and writing, help and constructive criticism have come from too many quarters to acknowledge individually. Needless to say, the responsibility for the end-product is all my own, but I am grateful to the anonymous many as well as to the few whose particular contributions demand mention here: Nelson Rosenbaum, of the Urban Institute in Washington, D.C., generously gave me a free hand with his survey data; the Research Directors of Harris Polls in London and New York provided much useful information; the staff of the Kansas State Historical Society were a great help with the research on Populism; Professor Bruce Graham and Eugene Lewis made detailed comments on the whole manuscript and improved it greatly; the Department of Government of Harvard University gave a grant for data analysis and their Travelling Fellowship enabled me to visit Topeka and Birmingham; on the administrative side, the School of English and American Studies of the University of Sussex gave clerical help, Michael Timms deciphered and typed most of the manuscript at least twice and Caroline Fisher and Paul Simpson helped in various ways.

My debt to Professor Samuel H. Beer of Harvard University is of a different order. It is not only for the judicious alternation of threats and encouragement which pushed the dissertation to completion under his supervision. His insistence on asking big and basic questions about politics and his conception of the breadth of evidence and the range of disciplines which must contribute to even the beginnings of answers have been formative influences on this book.

University of Sussex V. H.
April 1977

1. Alienation and distrust

Soothsaying is a favourite sport of political observers. Recently, an augury of the collapse of western democracy has been seen in the vociferous rejection of governments by their publics, in just those countries where its future had previously seemed most assured. The accumulating evidence from the behaviour of British and American electorates in the 1960s ranged through unprecedented volatility, a decline in the numbers bothering to vote at all, and at the extreme, a rejection of democratic procedures in favour of destructive forms of direct action. At one end of the scale, this threatening behaviour was apparently supported by attitudes of carping criticism and unthinking suspicion, at the other by hostile and uncompromising ideologies.

The legitimacy granted to any particular administration by citizens of a democracy will rest in part upon the benefits it is credited with producing. A means of expressing and responding to such disaffection is built into the institutions in the periodic opportunity to 'throw the rascals out' or to declare for preferred alternatives. But in the long run the legitimacy of the polity depends on a more permanent assent to the forms of institutions and the principles which guide them; people will accept policies with which they disagree and the neglect of their own priorities, provided that they believe decisions have been reached by democratic processes. Once this is doubted, and if channels of access and control seem to be closed, a problem of a different order arises. A new uncertainty, and even fear, complicates the situation; for those who suddenly doubt the system because their habitual confidence is upset, for those in politics because the security of normal partisan alternations in power is threatened, and for both sides because there is no automatic method for resolving the problem.

From a position of detachment the solution might seem obvious. Where a government stands accused it can investigate the charges and reform procedures which have failed to meet the public criteria for democracy. But governments are not noted for humility; in fact it seems as likely that the problem will be made more intractable by declarations of innocence from institutions dedicated to maintaining business as usual. In America, where the alarm was raised earliest, this reaction certainly came promptly. But it was not quite as brazen a neglect of public sensibilities as might be thought; it was justified by the presentation and analysis of the situation by the same social scientists who first charted the rise of public discontent. The authority of their identification of a 'crisis of democracy' rested on the assumptions that their evidence was accurate and complete and that their analytical framework was neutral as a basis for evaluating the condition and allocating responsibility.

It is my contention that understanding of an important and immediate issue in the politics of America and Britain has been clouded by an uncritical acceptance of these two assumptions. In fact, the evidence has been incomplete and sometimes even misleading, and the analysis prejudicial. That which I call political distrust is, in a democracy, an unfavourable evaluation of the processes of their polity based upon the perception by citizens of a discrepancy between the actual operation of the political system and the democratic norms publicly accepted as its standards. In contrast to the most prominent reaction, I believe that the position of the great majority of people expressing discontent with politics has been one of serious and reasoned criticism, derived from a belief in and an understanding of the norms of democratic politics. Furthermore, their behaviour has been democratic – the great majority have nothing in common with the few who have attempted to force their views on society or who have withdrawn altogether from politics.

There is no disagreement that substantial numbers of people in both Britain and America now disparage politics. The disagreement is over the significance of this fact – over what political distrust means for those who express it and over what it means, and whether it means the same, for each of these polities. One national difference is immediately evident from the existing literature on distrust: it has been a much more recent development in Britain, or at least has only recently received attention there. The British preoccupation with the nature of deference in politics may have been indirectly relevant, for the discovery of escalating distrust is the obverse of evidence of the recent decline in deference.[1] But, whatever the reasons, now that attention in Britain has turned to the presence of political distrust it has been directed by theories and investigated by methods taken straight from the longer experience of America.[2] For this reason, the critical discussion of theories and conclusions in this chapter will be concerned almost entirely with material by and about Americans. The grounds on which these are found inappropriate are equally valid in the British case.

Political distrust has been recorded and analysed under many labels: political cynicism, disenchantment, dysphoria, incivility, normlessness and scepticism, to name but a few. To add to the variety, a number of studies of political powerlessness, inefficacy and futility identify the identical phenomenon or a very close relation. The inventive terminology, however, conceals two crucial areas of agreement: in conceptual discussion, most authors relate their favoured label to the root concepts of alienation or (sometimes and) anomie; in their conclusions, most authors find these critical attitudes and their consequences harmful to democracy. Their prior assumptions, their particular definitions and their facts combine to make this conclusion inevitable.

Research proceeded from the assumption that the ordinary person was incapable of consistent, effective and democratic participation. During the 1950s empirical studies supporting this assumption had become available from all sides. Students of right wing politics in postwar America found substantial evidence of anti-democratic tendencies, if not an authentic fascist streak, in both its rhetoric and its social bases of support.[3] Social psychology located the sources of such attitudes deep in the personality and predicted their distribution primarily among the lower classes.[4] The result of elaborate surveys of political attitudes was the discovery of a great gulf, in both the comprehension and application of democratic principles, between an educated elite and the population at large.[5] Only voting studies offered a faint, if cynical, hope in this bleak prospect, for they confirmed the more deplorable traits of a large proportion of the electorate, but simultaneously identified these same people as the least likely to participate in politics.[6]

This damning evidence, however, brought social scientists into conflict with the basic premise of modern citizenship – that it is active and participatory. The kind of participation required need not be democratic – in the fascist state, for example, the citizen is called upon only to endorse the symbols or decisions of the regime after the event. The characteristics of the mass of citizens, however, suggested a double jeopardy – that they might give such responsive endorsement too willingly, and that, from the same lack of reason and moderation, they would be unable to fulfil the heavier demands of democratic participation. For in modern theories of democracy, both individualist and collectivist, participation requires initiative and decision and is the essential basis of political freedom: 'Man can realize his political freedom only through his own action, by determining the aim and method of political power...Thus the democratic political system is the only one which institutionalizes the activist element of political freedom.'[7] Social science appeared to have discovered that man was inherently incapable of realising his own political freedom.

The resolution of this incompatibility was found through a reconsideration of the meaning of 'his own action'. It was not even necessary to denigrate the common man to prove that this could not be taken literally. Full direct democracy was simply impractical for organisational reasons in large, complex and technologically-advanced societies. With this point conceded, it became somewhat arbitrary at what level of 'his own action' the line should be drawn to define democratic politics. So democracy became 'a social mechanism which permits the largest possible part of the population to influence major decisions by choosing among contenders for political office'.[8] The line was drawn at the level which the mass public was believed capable of reaching – it would be presented with regular, carefully defined choices. The democratic citizen was to have his opportunity to participate, but under conditions which would minimise the likelihood of the unleashing of his worst tendencies.

Democratic politics on this model will work, however, only if two conditions are met. The first is that those who, of necessity, are more deeply and continuously involved in politics do not share the attributes of the masses. Fortunately this appeared to be no problem; parallel research into the political elite had found reassuring evidence of 'their stronger approval of democratic ideas, their greater tolerance and regard for proper procedures and citizen rights, their superior understanding and acceptance of the "rules of the game", and their more affirmative attitudes toward the political system in general'.[9]

The second requirement for this institutional democracy is that the masses accept the definition and are content with the limited participation which it permits. As perhaps the most influential theorists of this position put it, once democracy is defined to fit the realities of the modern world and the modern citizen, a delicate balance is required in practice: 'the democratic citizen is called on to pursue contradictory goals: he must be active, yet passive; involved, yet not too involved; influential, yet deferential'.[10] As the argument goes, this subtle position seems to be achieved in Britain and America by the civic culture – a political culture which decently covers the distasteful inherent psychological and intellectual failings of the masses with internalised attitudes about democratic government and the role of the citizen. These attitudes may be directly supportive of 'democratic elitism', but in any case their effect is so precisely because the citizens do not properly understand the contradictions of their position. Thus, in their confusion, some opt for one goal or the other, preserving the polity from the twin evils of too much involvement and too little. Equally functional is the alternative response: 'certain *inconsistencies in the attitudes of an individual* make it possible for him to pursue these seemingly conflicting goals at the same time'.[11] Furthermore, in addition to its own moderate and democratic instincts, the elite is checked in its activity by the thought that unresponsiveness to the needs and wishes of the people might focus all this confused and undirected energy; consistent attitudes in the public, with behaviour brought into line with them, would end the stability of the system. Central to the theory of the civic culture is the 'democratic myth of citizen competence';[12] ironically, it appears that if it were to be put to the test the stability of these democracies would collapse. If this seems a poor substitute for the notion of democratic participation as the road to human freedom, then its proponents would surely defend the modest conclusions of realism as preferable to fruitless idealism.

Clearly, political distrust is not the position of the integrated member of the civic culture; distrust typically assesses the political system as elitist, corrupt, unresponsive, inaccessible, partial to influential groups, and unrepresentative. But what if this assessment is accurate? The possibility that the democratic balance might have been shattered by the political elite and not by the distrustful public was neglected. What scholars knew of the nature of the mass and the elite made it improbable to them. The assumption that the civic culture was the basis for stable democracy defined such criticism from the public, accurate or not, as a destabilising factor: 'if some relatively severe dissatisfaction with government occurs, the individual will be motivated to think about the topic', with alarming consequences.[13] And, thus led to conclude that distrust was both misguided and anti-democratic, it was easily and indiscriminately labelled as alienation or anomie – words whose current meaning confirmed that political distrust was a problem and that the problem was located in the minds of the distrustful.

It caricatures the truth only slightly, then, to summarise the picture of political distrust derived from these assumptions about the proper nature of politics and the actual nature of ordinary people thus: distrust, or rather let us say alienation, is the criticism of modern democratic politics by its citizens; it must be ill-founded, because of the inherent limitations of these citizens and because the political elite is both superior in capacity and practical in its recognition of the need for responsiveness; it is anti-democratic because democracy depends upon respect for the wisdom of elected officials and because the stability and thus the survival of democracy requires a passive public, allowing substantial latitude to these officials; alienation stirs the minds of the general public – it follows that they may also be stirred to action; and because that action is likely to be irrational and because the system has a limited capacity to absorb action, it can only be destructive.

There are at least four important criticisms to be made of this version of political distrust: its facts are open to question; its definition of democracy is open to question; the equation with alienation and anomie requires explanation; and its assumption of a simple causal relationship between attitudes and behaviour is not one which psychologists or social scientists have generally supported with any degree of confidence. The main purpose of this book is to justify criticism on all these counts by offering some additional and some different evidence of political distrust itself. But, because it is not simply a question of gathering more and better evidence but of finding the most appropriate concepts and categories with which to organise the evidence, in this chapter I give further attention to the difficulties in the theory of 'political alienation'. Three of the four criticisms I have raised will first receive a relatively brief review; my main concern will, then, be to consider the significance of the association of political distrust with alienation. The implications of this association have generally been overlooked, but go far to explain the central and general error of this literature in defining distrust as necessarily a problem, and a problem with its source and solution in the minds of the distrustful.[14]

The fact of an inherently incapable populace has been challenged from more than one direction. Later studies have shown both that the evidence itself was not always reliable and that, to the extent that it was an accurate picture, it was also a time-bound picture of the unusually placid politics of the Eisenhower era. The masses had been condemned first for their lack of a consistent structure of beliefs related to, and compatible with, each other, and then for their inability to apply this rag bag of general principles to particular issues or cases. Critics argue, on the other hand, that the research methods required of respondents the ability to articulate complex beliefs, but that this is not necessarily a correlate of the possession of beliefs; that with a different criterion of consistency (the maintenance of a pattern over time rather than the possession of a particular pattern at any one time) the masses score well; that if members of the political elite are grouped according to levels of education they prove no more coherent than matching groups of the public; and that the questions had been biased towards the particular political expertise of the elite – questions more suited to the experience of the public (allocating responsibility and perceiving appropriate action on everyday problems for example) produced intelligent and accurate responses.[15]

The gist of most of these corrective studies was that the understanding of the ordinary citizen might be different from that of the elite but was not thereby necessarily less coherent or democratic. The political elite is not necessarily coterminous with an upper class but will tend to be drawn from the higher levels of society; studies of class-based differences in culture in both America and Britain confirm a general difference in the mode of expression, similar to that found in political matters: 'The public's belief structure does not differ generally from that of the leaders. Certainly the structuring of beliefs by citizens seems more a product of their personal perceptions, compared with the abstractions of leaders, but both evidence a meaningful constraint among beliefs.'[16]

These are corrections applicable to the 1950s as much as to the present. They imply also that differences are due more to social attributes than to inherent limitations and thus that social change might be expected to lead to changing patterns of political beliefs. In particular, a rise in educational levels or an increase in upward social mobility would be expected to bring more people into the category of abstract thinkers. By 1972, at least the rise in educational levels had taken place, and achievement had risen too on measures of attitude consistency: 'the average American citizen from 1964 onward displays a level of attitude consistency similar to and in some areas exceeding that of congressional candidates just a few years earlier'.[17] But, closer inspection showed that the increase in consistency could not be attributed entirely to the rise in education; something other than 'permanent personal characteristics or the ability to obtain and utilize contextual knowledge' evidently affected people's political sensibilities.[18] Election studies provided a plausible answer: the electoral politics of the 1960s was marked by an increasing sense of urgency about substantial issues, expressed by a public which was well-informed where it was concerned.[19] In other words, if people feel that politics is important they will give the attention necessary to clarify their positions on principles and issues.[20] This discovery forced a fundamental change in approach to political distrust: 'what appear to be deeply ingrained personality characteristics based on a culture of poverty, may often be a realistic assessment that there are no institutional avenues of protest'.[21] And this was further supported by evidence that those who were disenchanted with politics were also notable for the high level of their ideological constraint.[22]

If the public's less abstract view of democracy is accepted as valid, then perhaps there are other respects in which the institutional definition of democracy is too restricted. The crucial disagreement here is over how much and what kind of participation makes a polity democratic. The social scientists I have described (and will refer to collectively as the school of democratic elitism) surely reduced participation to an absolute minimum. Their justification for this reduction was the requirements of the system, for stability and efficiency. At the opposite end of the spectrum are those who would maximise participation, within such constraints as are forced by the sheer size of modern polities, from a belief that participation is a value in itself. Regardless of any evidence of human incapacity or threat of the loss of efficiency, their argument holds that 'democracy is a soul satisfying thing' – an end in itself and not simply a mechanism for the efficient making of decisions.[23]

There is relatively little direct evidence of the meaning of democracy to the ordinary citizen – not least because researchers do not look for something they do not expect to exist. Indirectly, though, democratic standards can be inferred from the consistent criticisms reported in the literature on political alienation. Substantial numbers repeatedly agree that politicians are dishonest, lacking in ability, motivated by self-interest, the tools of special interests and out of touch and unconcerned with the views of the electorate. There is equal consistency in criticisms of bias and partiality towards big interests at the expense of the public good, the lack of attention to the people's wishes (and the lack of account taken of them in decision making even when they are ascertained) and the feeling that, while there are no channels of influence or even of communication upwards from the electorate to their representatives, communication downwards is used by the government to manipulate the electorate.[24] The public, clearly, are demanding more than the replacement of existing personnel with a wise and honest elite. They are demanding a greater degree of communication together with enactment of their own demands – and something more than the occasional opportunity to vote, for they consistently deplore that there is no way but voting to express their dismay.

Whether or not the position of the democratic elitists is too far to the non-participatory end of this scale to be acceptable as democracy depends very much upon where the judge of this point stands himself. It was certainly novel in the extent to which it excluded active involvement by the citizens, and there are strong precedents for arguing that it thereby lost essential qualities; as early critics of the new position pointed out: 'Classical democracy was *not* defined institutionally as a "system of decision-making"...democracy in the traditional sense involves...political equality, active consent about the form of government and the "rules of the game", widespread discussion and participation.'[25] But this is not, in any case, a philosophical debate without political consequences. The definition of the democratic elitists did carry the authority of academic approval and claimed a scientific basis and there is ample evidence of its influence on official responses to dissent in America. The same science appeared to show that where citizens accepted that definition of democracy they did so without understanding it – and implied that understanding would be a threat to the polity. Indeed it would be a threat, but to the *status quo*, if their definition of democracy proved different. Under such circumstances, what grounds are there for choosing between the alternative definitions?

Certainly, the public held a political philosophy which placed a much greater emphasis on participation than did democratic elitism. To the extent that this was recognised by the experts as having any intellectual standing, it was still not accepted as 'democratic'. Participation was not one of the 'necessary conditions' for democracy, Robert Dahl once wrote, because it was not 'what we call democracy' and because what we did call democracy could be seen to be working.[26] What it was, such writers decided, was populism, assuredly at that time a pejorative label. In an analysis of this alternative philosophy, Edward Shils presented populism as the opposite of civility and of that 'pluralistic moderation' which he saw as the essence of stable democracy; from his description a certain kinship with political distrust appears:

> Distrust of professional and party politicians, impatience with the traditional legal and political institutions which intervene between the people's

desires and their execution by their elected representatives, belief in the moral superiority of the people, and a suspicion of privacy and withdrawal from the common culture.[27]

One might wonder what is so distasteful in the American context about something which is said to have 'grown out of the excesses of equality, of a critical attitude towards authority, of the self-esteem of the ordinary people', even if one sympathises with the origin of the condemnation in reaction to the presumed roots of McCarthyism.[28] The sentiments sound more suited to Lord North than to a twentieth century commentator. It did not help that populism was seen as radical, hence automatically incompatible with pluralist politics: 'It is radical in the fundamental distrust of the dominant institutions and authorities of modern society. . .rejection of the ordinary matter-of-fact, un-dramatic, unsystematic outlook of day-to-day politics.'[29] Once again, the assumption is that the system is working well, a beneficent and responsible elite is in control and the conditions of democracy are being fulfilled. Democratic elitists must blame the distrustful, for they cannot blame the system.

Clearly, as political distrust increased it reinforced the public disagreement on the nature of democratic politics. The democratic elitists recognised the philosophical disagreement and argued against it when they did not simply dismiss it. The general public recognised the disagreement in practice and continued to protest, unconvinced by assurances that their suspicions were unfounded. Both positions have strengths and weaknesses, which they sometimes hold in common.

In terms of practical politics, if not of philosophy, it seems reasonable to take constraining facts into account in a discussion of ideals of government. But present conditions are not necessarily a permanent fact of life and the factual premises of the democratic elitists have been shown by the passage of time to be irrelevant. There are, most certainly, potential problems in implementing any form of democratic government, but in neither of these cases do we *know* that the ideal is an impossibility.

Nor can either position be rejected on grounds of its internal logic. In placing complaints in line with their norms, and solutions with their ideals, the general public have at least equal standing with the democratic elitists. They complain of elitism, corruption, lack of responsiveness, inaccessibility and partiality; they demand equality, honesty, communication and public control.

By a long and honourable tradition, these demands would be seen as for democracy, not against it. Indeed, in his discussion of varieties of democratic theory, Robert Dahl does accord 'populistic democracy' this standing, though by damning it with faint praise he implies that there is 'good' and 'bad' democracy – a novel twist to the argument. He admits that 'running through the whole history of democratic theories is the identification of "democracy" with political equality, popular sovereignty, and rule by majorities'. Indeed it is a trend for which he finds distinguished authorities – Aristotle, Locke, Rousseau, Jefferson, Lincoln and de Tocqueville.[30]

It is understandable that the problem of reconciling the rights of minorities with majority rule should loom particularly large at a time when the majority were feared so greatly for their apparent insensitivity to democratic tolerance. But, with the arguable exception of Rousseau, these authorities have not depended on an impractical notion of full direct democracy, nor a totalitarian equation of state and society, nor yet a political primitivism assuming 'a healing of the breach between men and their nature by simplicity, spontaneity, and elementary, ascetic, and largely agrarian virtue'.[31] Their accusers have invented straw men, with extreme and mystical tendencies.

'Populistic democracy' (whose synonym of radical democracy I shall prefer as perhaps rousing less emotional associations), has indeed been preoccupied with the role of 'the people'. For radical democrats, the polity is 'a body of individuals bound together and guided forward by a unified and authoritative will...forming the ultimate and only sovereign'.[32] But the historical effort of radical democrats can be seen 'in the reality of innumerable political mechanisms and devices ranging from the referendum and the election, the mandate, the initiative and the recall, through town meetings, plebiscites', all concerned with 'the conception and praxis of the involvement of the people in the governing of their own lives, however ineffective the achievement'.[33] Such measures hardly suggest totalitarianism, nor the perils of a mass society without intermediary organisations which were conjured up by the democratic elitists. Instead, they reinforce the point that the debate over the significance of distrust is a confrontation of two different conceptions of both the theory and the practice of democracy, but hinging around degrees of participation rather than any absolute opposition. The idea of democracy is full of confusion and ambiguity – if the same is true of the political ideals of the ordinary citizen then he is no more culpable in this respect than the philosopher or politician.

A similar judgement of equal culpability on both sides is the least that is fair to the distrustful in respect of their actions. The tendency for it to be harder to be consistent in the application than the assertion of abstract principles has been widely found. At its most obvious, the prophetic motto of John Mitchell, Attorney General of the Nixon administration – 'Watch what we do, not what we say' – is a reminder that this may be a common human failing and not a particular property of the lower orders.

Abstract ideals of democracy simply do not give clear guidance on the means of application. Neither can there be an automatic assumption that actions do simply follow from ideals. Few would deny that they may do so, under certain conditions. But few would wish to be more specific in predicting the general relationship between attitudes and actions. The psychological mechanisms are still little understood, any more than is the interaction between society and the individual.[34]

Other things being equal, the standard studies of political participation have found it most likely among people of high political interest, high levels of political information, high political efficacy, high socio-economic status, a high expectation of rewards from political activity and where a relative freedom from other social pressures allows undistracted involvement.[35] Complaints about politics in the 1950s seemed mainly to come from people scoring low on all these measures, whose most pressing concerns were the immediate needs of day to day existence.

To those who feared it, the saving grace of political distrust seemed to be this association with those social groups traditionally least likely to act upon their grievances. We now know that a good many of the assumptions made about the man in the street in the 1950s were inaccurate. But in any case, the social location of the distrustful has changed since then. By the early 1970s they were to be found throughout society, but disproportionately in those groups with a propensity to high political participation.[36]

Furthermore, other things are not equal. One of the factors apparently connected with the rise in interest and understanding of political issues was the changing political environment. It would not be surprising if this also had a direct effect upon the propensity of people to take action, independent of the effect of social position. Similarly, to the extent that norms are more clearly understood, they may, depending upon their content, give a further direct incentive to action. The theorists of *The civic culture* hoped that people would believe that they could influence politics but that they would not test that proposition. Later, William Gamson argued that the optimum conditions for the mobilisation of citizens to action would be where two cognitive elements, based upon knowledge of oneself and of the polity, were combined: the belief that personal influence was possible, and the perception that it was necessary.[37] That a third condition may be added is clear from the example of radical democracy: this contributes a normative element – the perception of a right and a duty to act regardless of the difficulties. Whether all three conditions do occur together and whether their effects are as predicted remain questions in need of empirical investigation. They add further complexity to the understanding of the causes of political behaviour, neither replacing nor removing any of the multiplicity of conceivable circumstances which may be involved.

Each of these questions of fact, definition and consequence is matched in the specific case of the association of political distrust with alienation and anomie. Despite their different pedigrees, the terms have been used inconsistently, interchangeably and even as categories of the other. That their recent use in a political context refers to political distrust is clear from many definitions, of which the following are typical: Murray Levin described the 'alienated' as people who 'feel angry, resentful, hopeless and politically powerless, people who have come to believe that voting is meaningless and useless. . .people who believe in the democratic ideals of majority rule and responsible government, but who feel that the realities of political life contradict the ideal';[38] Inkeles has defined 'political anomie' as the perception of politicians failing in their obligations to 'pay attention to the common man, serve the public rather than their own careers, and keep their campaign promises after elections'.[39]

The choice of labels is not a trivial matter. Such terms have 'theoretical roots', as Ada Finifter remarked, choosing normlessness as her label because it 'has theoretical ties in the alienation framework and in the Durkheim–Merton inspired theories of anomie'.[40] This may, as she suggests, be an advantage, but only if political distrust can appropriately be related to the theoretical roots of both alienation and anomie, or even of one or the other. In fact, there are two flaws in this association: the current political discontent is inappropriately labelled in this way even by present social science usage; and these current meanings have themselves little connection with the classic definitions of Marx and Durkheim, and the implications of those meanings for politics.

One characteristic of the recent use of these terms has been a confusion of slightly different meanings and uncertainty about the extent to which these complement or contradict each other. Notably, there has been a steadily changing position on whether there is a simple and single condition or a multiplicity of specific varieties of alienation. The starting point for understanding the recent intellectual history of the concept is an article 'On the meaning of alienation' published by Melvin Seeman in 1959.[41] It was important as the first synthesis of many separate pieces of research, and for its own conclusions, which summarised the essential points of the modern concept: alienation was a useful inclusive term for a series of related 'meanings of alienation' – normlessness, meaninglessness, powerlessness, social isolation and self-estrangement; alienation existed with reference to the social or political world, but was itself a psychological condition, characterised by low expectancies of control of the social environment and of relations with this environment, or by low expectancies of rewards from social action. But Seeman offered no empirical validation of the connection between his meanings of alienation; he simply assumed that the evidence which he ordered in this way had a common element, and that this was alienation.

Subsequent research has gradually disaggregated Seeman's unifying concept, in two ways. Attitudes towards politics have been separated from those with other social referents. Then, the attitudes themselves within each distinctive area were first seen as comprising a set of several dimensions, not necessarily of fixed relationship to each other, and later as a series of independent conditions.[42] Indeed, alienation as a general term had become virtually useless; it embraced a multiplicity of specific conditions whose only common ground was the vaguest notion of a loss of autonomy or identity in the face of mass society. Almost any subjective sense of unease or discontent could be thrown into the category, and, judging by the indexes of social science literature, sooner or later did acquire this indiscriminate label.

Studies of political alienation have been somewhat more specific. First, they combined or linked three of Seeman's five meanings: powerlessness, meaninglessness and normlessness.[43] Together these imply that the individual feels that he has little influence over political outcomes, is unclear as to what he should believe about politics and lacks authoritative standards for political behaviour, a combination which some early studies suggested were both positively correlated with each other and apparently most commonly found among the socially inadequate.

With the discovery that even these three dimensions did not necessarily occur or vary together, a more modest combination was brought into play. It seemed at least plausible that two identifiable sets of political attitudes, namely powerlessness (or the feeling of personal inefficacy in political action) and normlessness (or the loss of trust in socially approved ways of political action) were closely connected.[44] A low estimation of the possibility of participating effectively oneself and a perceived general breakdown of expected patterns of political behaviour intuitively seem two sides of the same coin, the latter perhaps explaining and making tolerable the former to the subject: the same conclusion of a failure of democratic politics reached by judging and blaming in the one case oneself and in the other the system.

Yet further conceptual confusion exists. Parallel to, but separate from, the treatment of two distinct but related dimensions of political alienation, there has developed a considerable body of literature on a concept of 'political efficacy'. In its negative form of inefficacy this apparently united powerlessness and normlessness. The source of this concept was in the University of Michigan Survey Research Center's long-term studies of electoral behaviour; its survival must in part be due to the unusual advantages of continuity of a scale which had been in use for more than fifteen years before serious evidence began to accumulate suggesting its duality. The Efficacy Scale first appeared in the Michigan study of the 1952 presidential election: efficacy was defined as 'the feeling that individual political action does have, or can have, an impact upon the political process'.[45] It is not surprising that efficacy and trust were here regarded as a single concept, since this definition was based on a scale of five questions in which the two were inextricably combined. Respondents, for example, were asked to agree or disagree with the statement: 'I don't think public officials care much about what people like me think.' There is no certain way of distinguishing answers which evaluate 'people like me' from those which are judgements of the system − 'public officials'.

Not only is this the same concept as the definition of political alienation as powerlessness plus normlessness, but it has been subject to the same criticism, that it has united two political attributes which should be given separate status. Indeed, it has now been similarly admitted that the scale has lost the unidimensionality which was asserted in 1952: 'It is useful conceptually to partition gross feelings of political efficacy as we have measured them over the years into at least two components, which might be more precisely labelled "personal feelings of political competence" and "trust in system responsiveness".[46] In fact the two bodies of literature should be regarded as complementary, for they have been looking at two stages of the same development. The social psychologists have called it alienation and treated it as a dependent variable, investigating its psychological roots and social correlates. Meanwhile political scientists have labelled it inefficacy and have concentrated upon it as an independent variable, looking particularly at its incidence and political consequences.

These concepts of alienation and inefficacy provide an object lesson in the value of comparative perspectives. The coupling of a sense of powerlessness with a loss of faith in the political system makes sense where the norms of the system raise expectations that it should be otherwise. But the apparent capacity of the British to combine happily a sense of powerlessness with an amazing trust in their government has long been taken for granted.[47] It would be hard to evolve a theory combining the two dimensions in this way in a context where the American state of 'alienation' appears to be a comfortable state of integration. The point which this comparative perspective makes is not simply that these concepts were culture-bound, but that the reason was that their authors ignored the relevance of their subjects' norms. Needless to say, this was the more easily done when those norms were believed characterised by confusion and irrelevance. But it might be expected that the acknowledgement of evaluation of the political system as a separate phenomenon would have rectified this omission. For surely the subject's evaluation of the system cannot be studied without attention to the standards by which he makes his judgement? Yet attention remained with the critical attitudes themselves, treated as a psychological state apparently divorced from both norms and actual political conditions.

Nonetheless, recent definitions have both been more modest and more sophisticated than the early theories of political alienation. The more cautious argument has been that the two dimensions of powerlessness and normlessness do not necessarily occur or vary together or have the same consequences, although they are often found simultaneously and can then usefully be treated together. This more complex approach is well illustrated in a discussion by William A. Gamson: he confirms that political discontent normally has two evaluative components – of the self and of the system, and adds that the specific target of criticism may be any particular aspect of politics. Thus the distrustful citizen might criticise his own political role or the institutions of politics or both, and in addition might criticise, for example, either or both of the electoral system and the policy making process. The consequences of political distrust may vary with those differences in social position and political capacities on which the standard account depended in concluding that, generally, distrust resulted in apathy. They may also vary according to the particular combination of criticisms and targets which are found in any particular case – common sense suggesting, for example, that some targets will be more easily attacked than others.[48]

Recently, a variety of evidence has challenged even Gamson's more conditional model of alienation and its consequences. Studies of political socialisation have found that either trust or distrust developed much earlier in children's development than did any sense of efficacy; thus the two appear to have different roots.[49] In a different approach to the roots of these attitudes, psychologists have suggested that diffuse social trust and general personal efficacy appear to be discrete attitudes; they have evidence of a positive correlation between each of these and their political equivalents.[50] Powerlessness and normlessness appear also to have different, and not necessarily connected consequences: it may be that while efficacy does affect participation, trust does not.[51] And several studies of local referenda have reported that, again, trust does not directly affect participation, but that the strongly distrustful are most likely to vote 'No', regardless of the issue.[52] Powerlessness and normlessness, efficacy and trust, now appear most probably to be separate conditions, whose interaction and consequences will depend upon both their content and their context.

So, from Seeman's first multidimensional concept of alienation, the field has come right round to the point where the existence of those dimensions is substantiated by the empirical evidence, but they have the status of independent phenomena. They are not simply subsidiary parts of any identifiable larger complex, under whose aegis predictable inter-relations of the parts can be found. If the term alienation must be retained, then there are not one but a number of distinct alienations.

What these political alienations do all have in common is, first, that each is a conscious state of discontent. The datum is the content of minds. External circumstances, structures or events, may optionally be drawn upon in explanations of the condition, but are not an essential part of the condition itself. If the condition is then evaluated as a problem, the consequence is that solutions must be found in changing a state of mind – with no necessary implication that this, in turn, depends upon changing a state of society. Political alienations are also apparently an unusually self-contained set of attitudes, having reference to politics alone, without predictable relationships to other social or psychological attributes.

Political anomie, though sometimes used as a synonym for alienation, generally differs from it in being identified as an inextricable part of a single complex of more general social attitudes. This is partly a product of the universally used definition of anomie in an attitude scale constructed by Srole; this contains one statement on politics together with four of general social reference whose tenor is of despair and pessimism.[53] It was assumed in the definition that misanthropy, despondency over the future and a sense of helplessness and loss of control over every aspect of life would have their effect on politics too. While the legitimacy of the combination has from time to time been challenged, unlike alienation, tests continue to support the unity of this concept of anomie.[54] In addition, while political alienation evidently has no invariable relation with other social and psychological attributes, anomie does appear to be consistently found with low socio-economic status, physical isolation, membership of minority groups and some psychological dysfunctions.[55]

The politically distrustful are not necessarily anomic, but it seems that the anomic always manifest some element of political distrust. The common element is the loss of a sense of autonomy and identity; the difference is that for the anomic this is comprehensive, whereas political alienation is restricted to the specialised autonomy and identity of the citizen. It is not only important for descriptive accuracy to distinguish these two groups of people. The difference is also crucial in estimating the consequences of political discontent. It is generally claimed in theory, and the evidence of psychological and social correlates enhances the probability, that the behavioural consequences of anomie will be apathy. Some authors explicitly use alienation to imply 'active rejection' and anomie to imply passivity.[56] Exactly what forms of behaviour will follow from political alienation have been no more satisfactorily established in general theoretical terms than have the bounds of the concept itself; outcomes seem to depend very much on other attributes of the alienated, on alternative opportunities for action, and on variables like political culture and the political atmosphere of the time. By contrast, the literature on anomie and politics mentions only one likely intervening variable between anomie and apathy, namely the presence of charismatic or fascist-style movements of political protest. The 'normal' reaction of the anomic is apathy, but it is argued that their sense of despair, helplessness and indirection make them also uniquely vulnerable to anti-democratic appeals.[57]

The anomic are the classic citizens of the mass society theory, cut loose from the small-scale and comprehensible traditional community which gave them well-defined and limited roles to play, isolated and confused in the vastness and impersonality of a technological society. This anomie is a separate concept from alienation, distinguished by diffuseness rather than specificity, by being composed of integrally combined rather than related characteristics and by having a single and direct relationship to behavioural consequences under all but a particular set of exceptional circumstances. And anomie is an entirely inappropriate label for political distrust. Those who are critical of politics are not necessarily misanthropists, nor do they necessarily feel powerless. Normlessness is often used as a synonym for anomie, but the distrustful do not lack norms; the only normlessness involved is that which they see in politics.

Nor does political alienation seem to fit the case of distrust. It has been intended simply as a statement of fact: certain specified individuals or groups feel powerless in themselves or feel dissatisfied with politics. But if this is political alienation, it is *not* political distrust. Political distrust cannot be understood as a purely internal, psychological state, which neither subject nor observer need relate to political conditions or norms. It is clear from much of the evidence of these studies that the alienated themselves did not just feel powerless; they felt *wrongly* powerless. They did not just dislike politics; they felt that politics *should* be different. If it seems obvious that a feeling of dissatisfaction cannot exist without some sense of an alternative condition, then it must be remembered that the definition required just that neutrality of both subject and observer. In his original statement, Seeman acknowledged the descent of his concept from Marx and Durkheim, but claimed in his own favour that he had avoided the 'critical, polemic element' of the originals. He specifically eliminated not only any editorial judgement by the observer but even by the alienated: 'the observer's *judgement* of that situation against some ethical standard' and the 'individual's sense of a *discrepancy* between his expectations for control and his desire for control' were equally irrelevant.[58]

While the evidence bursts the bounds of the definition of alienation by containing an integral element of evaluation by the alienated, the social scientists' use of the concept also fails to meet their own standard of neutrality. Indeed, not only are the current meanings of alienation and anomie inappropriate to the study of distrust but they differ so substantially in ideology from the classic terms that the claimed derivation is entirely misleading. A comparison with these classic meanings is instructive, not as a pointless search for the impossible dream of total detachment in the social sciences, but because it reveals most clearly the theory within whose context the modern terms become emotionally loaded and evaluative.

The context from which both Marx and Durkheim developed their concepts was the same; the inspiration came from their experience and observation of industrial society. This, indeed, they share with the latter-day mass society theorists whose influence on the recent concepts has been substantial. The common concern was to characterise the changes in social relations brought about by industrialisation, urbanisation and the communications revolution. They found lives fragmented into specialised functions, impersonal authority, secular norms of efficiency in place of mutuality, mobility and consequently rootlessness, a broadened range of relationships but a loss of depth and permanence. Paradoxically, as man's technical ability to control his environment increased, an expansion of the scale and complexity of social institutions occurred which seemed to put them beyond the comprehension and control of any individual.

But Marx and Durkheim explicitly went beyond neutral descriptions to make strong moral judgements about the conditions they described. They saw alienation and anomie as structural conditions, with dependent psychological consequences. They identified their presence by examination of social structures, whereas modern work identifies conscious feelings of depersonalisation, indirection, rootlessness and so on and then labels these alienation or anomie. And Marx and Durkheim looked to the release from this condition in radical structural change.

Alienation, as Marx described it, had four distinguishable aspects: 'alienated man, alienated labour, alienated life, and estranged man'.[59] All these may be subsumed in the general definition that man is in various ways diminished against his full potential. Thus, man is creative; but his creations come to control him and dispel his natural spontaneity. Further, the act of production has become a means to other ends, not a satisfaction in itself. Man should be free and self-directed; but his life has become subservient to external constraints.

Man should be social; yet he is isolated from other men by those same social circumstances which prevent fulfilment of his individual potential. So 'each man is alienated from others, and. . .each of the others is likewise alienated from human life'.[60]

Marx described alienation in economic terms, since it was there, in the fundamental structures of society, that all its forms originated. Since these structures are the basis of all social relations, the fact of alienation permeates all human life. Man is as fragmented and powerless in his political as his economic role, but the political cannot be treated as separate and self-contained. To understand politics requires understanding of the material relationships of the members of the polity, and there will be no escape from political alienation without the 'positive supercession of private property. . .and thus the return of man from religion, the family, the State, etc., to his *human*, i.e. social life'.[61]

Political alienation was unaffected by the principles introduced by the emerging democratic theory of the enlightenment, which promised a universalism and equality in political life in vivid contrast with the particularism and inequality of bourgeois economic life. Marx examined the *Declaration of the Rights of Man and of the Citizen*, and concluded that, although it summarised the partial advance made by men in perceiving the possibility of political equality, it illustrated well how the bourgeois state fragmented personality into worker and citizen. The citizen role became a mere subsidiary means for the preservation of economic man: 'He lives in the *political community*, where he regards himself as a *communal being*, and in *civil society* where he acts simply as a *private individual*, treats other men as means, degrades himself to the role of a mere means, and becomes the plaything of alien powers.'[62] Thus any attempt to escape from political alienation by a purely political route, such as the participatory citizenship of radical democrats, would lead only to an illusory emancipation. The democratic state had freed itself from particularistic religious and economic distinctions by establishing political equality, but had failed to, and indeed could not, free the whole of human life from their stranglehold.

Liberal individualist democracy thus perpetuated political alienation, and Marx would not have recognised as any more adequate the alternative propounded by some collectivist theorists of democracy, of the total immersion of man in the political community as the basis of all other human relationships. There is an important difference here between Marx, some recent political philosophy, and empirical social science in both definition and prognosis. Neumann, for example, joined Marx in seeing both individualist and collectivist democracy as forms of political alienation. But he differed from Marx in arguing that the realities of the institutional requirements of self-government, regardless of any conceivable change in fundamental economic structures, made it inevitable that 'no matter what the form of government, political power will always be alienated'.[63] Thus, philosophies of political alienation find that there will always be some residue in modern societies. Neumann's alienation retains the structural roots which Marx gave it, whereas the operational definitions of social scientists have both rooted it in people's minds and allowed an optimism about its elimination. They define it against a limited standard of participatory citizenship which is, for the philosophers, itself alienation. For the empiricists, some personal political activity and a sense of control which need not even be realistic are not a route towards the diminution of alienation, they are freedom from alienation.

A further difference in the meaning of alienation is apparent from Marx's account of its history. For Marx, alienation was not only a property of modernity, although there it reached the peak of intensity. He argued that all men had been alienated from their true nature since the earliest moments of the organisation of production: 'As long as a cleavage exists between the particular and the common interest, as long therefore as activity is not voluntarily, but naturally, divided, man's own deed becomes an alien power opposed to him, which enslaves him instead of being controlled by him.'[64] This is a healthy corrective to the tendency to see the pre-modern era as a golden age. Marx was under no illusion that the dismal grind of the medieval peasant was any more humanly fulfilling than the intense exploitation which the factory worker suffered. The security and sense of control often attributed to men in the tight, local communities of pre-industrial Europe were as fraudulent as the material benefits of technology, when weighed against what men might be.

The universality of alienation as defined against the observer's ideal of human nature or society is not the case with the effect on alienation of the subject's own ideals. The fatalism or religious faith of the medieval peasant were explanations of situations of powerlessness which he did not expect to control. Both the progress of science and the norms of modern society lead modern man to expect to be able to control, and to regard it as right that he should control, his social environment. By Seeman's definition of powerlessness ('*the expectancy or probability held by the individual that his own behaviour cannot determine the occurrence of outcomes, or reinforcements, he seeks*') as well as by Marx's external standard of judgement, both situations are alienation.[65] But as subjective feelings, the former of acceptance, the latter of wrongful deprivation, they are qualitatively different, a distinction lost to both theorists but potentially crucial for understanding their consequences.

But if Marx did not conceive the necessity of an internal standard of judgement for the alienated, indeed did not require it to be a conscious feeling, he was perfectly clear about the existence and content of an external standard of judgement. Marxian alienation is always alienation *from* something valued – from specific aspects of life, the self, human nature. It cannot be understood as a self-contained or neutral descriptive term, but rests firmly on his optimistic theory of the perfectibility of man; in the words of Steven Lukes, on the belief that 'man is still an angel, rational and good, who requires a good and rational society in which to develop his essential nature'.[66]

For Marx, universal alienation had no *direct* consequences in action. It was the contributory, but immediate and comprehensible, facts of exploitation and deprivation which generated class consciousness and built the conditions for radical change. This distinction emphasises again the fact that his alienation was not simply a feeling of discontent or despair; it was a universal of the human condition under defined structural circumstances, shared by the happy and prosperous as well as the disillusioned and deprived. Though man himself had originally produced the means of his own alienation, it was an involuntary condition, and no amount of individual adjustment or resignation would end it. Only the dialectical process of structural change would eventually free men.

The sense of active rejection, by which some modern definitions distinguish alienation from anomie, actually comes from the literature of anomie, particularly from Robert Merton's 'rebellion' option of adaptation to normative disjunction. The modern concepts of alienation and anomie can be used to distinguish two different psychological conditions, but the theoretical discussions of the concepts tend to muddy the distinction, not least because both have in common certain major premises which also differentiate them from the classic terms. Thus the modern concept of anomie too is a psychological condition with no necessary relation to structure, and it is claimed to be neutral while actually taking an evaluative position. Durkheim's anomie shared the structural source and critical intention of Marx's alienation, but the details were very different.

Durkheim's view of man was quite opposite from that of Marx. It was pessimistic, and had much in common with earlier, 'conservative' political theorists such as Hobbes and Burke. This similarity lay in the claim that under no social circumstances could men achieve, by their own resources alone, the self-control necessary to make social life possible, let alone fulfilling. But Durkheim placed his faith neither in a Hobbesian sovereign nor in a wise elite, but in the integrating and controlling power of society, operating through the collective conscience. While this was evidently not envisaged as a force altogether external to men, it was far from the optimism for autonomy expressed by Marx as he talked of creativity, spontaneity and self-fulfilment. Durkheim's men escaped the anarchy of human impulses by submersion in a regulatory social order: Marx's men freed their creativity and natural social instincts by submersion in a liberating social order.

In terms very similar to those of Hobbes, Durkheim started with the proposition that the human species was distinguished from the animal orders by the power of reflection, and was thus able 'to imagine other ends than those implicit in its physical nature'.[67] But this capacity, once set in motion, quickly exceeded any individual's ability to achieve his desires. Unfortunately, 'nothing appears in man's organic nor in his psychological constitution which sets a limit to such tendencies'.[68] Left to himself, he exhibited exactly the same 'perpetuall and restlesse desire' of the natural man described by Hobbes.[69] Hobbes' man, however, through a process of reasoning, reached a compromise alternative to the destructive situation of individual striving, in which his hope seemed to have the best chance of fulfilment. Durkheim, on the other hand, saw this individual desire as internally destructive rather than fought out through external competition and compromise. Hence the reaction was rather different: 'To pursue a goal which is by definition unobtainable is to condemn oneself to a state of perpetual unhappiness.'[70] The consequence for Durkheim's man was that he was 'stopped in his tracks' by the inevitable realisation of the futility of his efforts.[71] Weariness brought disillusionment. He neither reasoned nor carried on the struggle – he lost his hope: Men 'are wearied, as it were, at the end of a long course, and thus become incapable of energetic reaction'.[72] And, in fine contrast to the Hobbesian man, whose particular desires were all subsumed in the desire to live, and who formed a social contract to better his chance of survival, the only solution Durkheim's man seemed capable of unaided was suicide.

This is the source of the consistently reiterated connection of anomie with hopelessness and despair, and with apathy. Aside from suicide, anomie will only be escaped when desire is restrained. Since men are themselves incapable of such restraint 'they must receive it from an authority which they respect, to which they yield spontaneously'.[73] The form of this solution did not follow simply from the steps of reasoning to this point – it reintroduced the theory of social structure: 'Either directly and as a whole, or through the agency of one of its organs, *society* alone can play this moderating role; for it is the only moral power superior to the individual, the authority of which it accepts.'[74] Anomie, though reflected in a psychological state, was really a failure of social structure.

Durkheim did not suggest a Hobbesian state of nature in which all men were anomic, followed by a once for all solution in structural reform. The incidence of anomie fluctuated, its peaks and dips following the strength and consistency of the directive social structure. Anomie was not solely a property of modernity, but it was in modern society that it reached pathological levels, and for the same reason it would never be entirely eliminated. Some anomie was 'normal in a society where perfection and progress are part of its constitution', but it was 'only wholesome as long as it is not preponderant'.[75] But the dramatic acceleration of change in modern societies created new life-situations before norms could be institutionalised to match them; this was the situation which Durkheim called a 'state of de-regulation' or anomie.[76] And the philosophy of modern industrial society was one of individualism and progress – norms which seemed to him functional to industrial growth but contrary to human needs. A society which established for its members the goals of perfection, progress or success was offering them the very infinite and empty goals that their natural imagination and desire constructed. There was no limit to hope and there were no means of regulating competition or reconciling conflict.

Durkheim thus escaped a definition that equated fatalism with resented powerlessness, for structural failure caused the situation in both cases, but also provided the human expectations which distinguish the two. Thus the medieval peasant was the archetype of the non-anomic man: tightly integrated into a stable social structure, where his relationships were direct, intimate and predictable and his aspirations restricted to the appropriate limits of his station in life. He neither had

nor expected control of his destiny. So Durkheim's solution for industrial society lay in structural change, which would to some extent
reconstitute this cocooning and reassuring social situation. He saw that,
in the modern world, economic concerns were dominant, and so
proposed intermediate economic organisations between the individual
and the distant and incomprehensible whole: occupational groups
where workers and bosses would share a community based on their
common and major interest. Durkheim not only believed that needs
from the most individual to the most general would be met by these
groups but that human nature would not be freed but transformed by
the consequent integration and discipline. For from such groups would
come 'a warmth which animates its members, making them intensely
human, destroying their egotisms'.[77] Not, as for Marx, that the good-
ness of man would survive despite the corruption of human institutions,
but that the evil of man could be overcome by the right institutions.

For Durkheim, as Marx, political anomie was not a separable state
but a manifestation of the more general social condition. Indeed, the
scale of modern political institutions and the expectations of personal
control given by democratic theory were a perfect case of an anomic
situation. But, whereas for Marx social change would eventually
eliminate all aspects of alienation, Durkheim shared Neumann's position that political anomie seemed inevitable. Participatory citizenship
was no solution at all, for men would always feel estranged and helpless
when they contemplated distant social institutions such as the state:
'Whatever connection there may be between our daily tasks and the
whole of public life, it is too indirect for us to feel it keenly and constantly.'[78]

Durkheim's concept of anomie is closer in this respect to the modern
meanings of both alienation and anomie than was Marx's alienation.
But this similarity is superficial; for they are fundamentally different in
the explanatory theories which account for the existence of anomie and
point to the responsibility and the palliatives. In fact, in its development, the concept has undergone a transformation of the same kind as
did the concept of alienation. In both cases, this transformation is the
source of the evaluative bias which does in fact characterise the
allegedly neutral modern concepts. The literature of both is not simply
descriptive of a condition; it is condemnatory of the psychological
state and supportive of the social and political context in which it is
found.

The crucial changes in the meaning of anomie were made in the influential essays on the concept by Robert Merton. First, Merton differed from Durkheim in taking the structural inequalities and normative individualism of modern society for granted. His example was of American society and the American Dream of achievement and success, in which 'there is no final stopping point' – exactly the empty and infinite goals which are the source of anomie.[79] But for Merton the state of anomie came not from society's infinite goals but from the recognition by many people of their technical incapacity to begin to reach them by legitimate means. His second innovation was his solution to anomie. This was still to involve the disciplining power of society, but no longer implemented through structural change to create realistic goals for life. The need was for society 'to provide the intensive disciplining required if an individual is to retain intact a goal that remains elusively beyond reach'. The point for Merton, was to 'examine the varying adaptations *to* anomie'.[80]

The problem of anomie, then, had become the psychological condition resulting from the gap between goals and the possibility of achieving them. The solution now lay in making this incompatibility tolerable through psychological adjustment, not through reducing the gap. Merton's discussion still retained the source of the problem in social structure even though the solution was not; his concept had other points in common with Durkheim, in the description of a state of hopeless despair, the diffuse social focus of the attitudes and the passive reaction of the individuals involved. But later writers have abandoned the structural source of anomie altogether – it has become normlessness, the complete detachment from a sense of place in society and the concomitant ideals and expectations.

Alienation and anomie as modern, empirical social science defines them have little to do with the classic meanings of those terms. They have become definitions of psychological conditions, identifiable only in the consciousness of the subject, whereas for Marx and Durkheim they were conditions of the social structure, identified by objective indicators. They have become narrowly focused sets of attitudes, referring to politics without connection with other social conditions, whereas for Marx and Durkheim they were an integral part of a social theory. But the most important point to arise from this comparison of the old and the new concepts, is that they have failed to establish the one difference which they themselves have claimed from the 'theoretical roots' of alienation and anomie: they are no more free from an evaluative position than were the classic terms. But the 'critical, polemic

element' is now very different. Both old and new concepts defined
alienation and anomie as destructive, the old of people, the new of the
political system; both deplored them, but the old concepts for their
effect on humanity, the new for their effect on the system. The theory
has been turned from a profoundly radical critique of the social order
for its destructive effect on human nature, to a profoundly conservative
defence of the social order against the destructive effect on it of human
nature. The solution no longer lies in fundamental social change to
allow the fullest development of man but in controlling man in order
to maintain society as it is.

Political distrust – the unfavourable evaluation of politics by citizens
who see a discrepancy between the ideal and the reality – is not alienation or anomie. It differs from the classic terms of Marx and Durkheim
in being a subjective condition. It differs from the recent uses of these
terms by involving the subject's norms, as well as his perceptions of
politics, as an integral part of the condition. Indeed, little remains of
the original accumulation of support for a political alienation grounded
in ignorance and threatening to democracy. Both the current meanings
and the tradition of alienation and anomie are inappropriate; the facts
which devalued the arguments of the distrustful are questionable; the
theory of democracy which condemned the alienated is no sounder
than their own; the consequences remain problematic, but at least in the
light of the revision of theory and fact cannot simply be assumed to be
alarming.

The process of criticism of past interpretations of the evidence has
clarified the nature of political distrust. The essential point is that it is
subjective *and* evaluative; by definition the condition combines both
normative and cognitive elements – it is the discrepancy between these
two which measures the depth or intensity of distrust. This was the
element omitted in Seeman's typology in the language of expectancies;
it is not just a question of low expectancies (of control, of prediction,
of attaining rewards), but of low expectancies *relative to normative
standards*. The medieval peasant or the deferential working class
conservative in Britain had low expectancies of control – they were not
distrustful, because their political beliefs endorsed this humble position.

The norms themselves thus become an important variable, which is
an added advantage if the notion of discrepancy is applied to cross-
national comparisons of distrust. Given the possibility of variation in
both individual perceptions of the actual conditions of politics and the

normative standards held, it follows that: the levels of criticism of politics in two countries may be different – as goes the conventional wisdom about the difference between Britain and the United States; or levels of criticism may be the same, as some recent findings have suggested; but also, whatever the relative levels of criticism may be, the discrepancy between these and the ideals, i.e. the actual amount of distrust, may vary with variations in the ideals held. Political distrust is a relational concept, with both sides of the relationship potentially variable. In virtually all the classic and modern usages of alienation and anomie, whether the standard of evaluation is implicit or explicit, assumed to be of the observer or of the subject, it has been taken as a fixed datum: *this*, for example, is the nature of man, therefore the discrepant facts demonstrate alienation; or *this* is democracy, therefore the facts prove alienation from it.

While distrust does share the notion of wrongful deprivation which is surely intrinsic to the idea of alienation, and while discrepancy has also now been claimed as the essential quality of every particular alienation, this present difference is a further ground, if one is needed, for avoiding the term altogether. 'Alienation' is both too inclusive and too loaded with past confusions to demarcate the very precise and limited condition of political distrust.

The persistent search for a single, inclusive meaning for alienation has thrown up one further possibility which, though it does not re-instate distrust as a variant of alienation, does point to the need for one further refinement in its definition: variously described as separation or loss or estrangement, this characterisation of alienation identifies again a subjective feeling of dissatisfaction. But from what are the distrustful estranged? It used to be assumed that they were indeed estranged, from the democratic norms of the polity. But from their point of view this is not true – the distrustful in Britain or America see themselves as democrats in a democratic polity, integrated into its norms and 'estranged' only from its current condition. Again, the inclusion of the norms of the subjects in the field of investigation pro-vides an important correction to the common assumptions about the nature of political discontent. If discontent in itself is assumed to be anti-democratic, regardless of its content, two very different categories of complainants may be thrown indiscriminately together. There is little in common between those who reject the norms of democratic politics and ground their discontent upon some alternative philosophy and those who judge their polity in the name of democracy and reject only its violation in practice. If alienation is estrangement, then it is the former group who are alienated, for their rejection of democratic politics is permanent and profound; the rejection of the distrustful is temporary and remediable.

The concept of political distrust as discrepancy has, of course, no necessary connection with democracy; it is equally applicable to the analysis of disaffection with the reality, within the normative tradition of any type of polity. But political distrust in the democracies of Britain and America is the concern of this study, and it may be that there is a particular confusion in the concept of democracy which makes this final definitional problem unique to democratic politics. For it is already clear that there is a disagreement about what constitutes democratic norms. The dispute is in the open in the American literature, where the radical democracy of the distrustful conflicts with the democratic elitism of scholars and politicians; if the recent evidence is right in finding the same radical democracy among the distrustful in Britain, the disagreement is as great with the formal basis of the government there in parliamentary democracy. In both cases, some middle ground is called for between complete agreement and complete disagreement, between the blanket acceptance of the democratic norms of the most powerful groups in society and the deviant (in the sense of rejection of democracy) norms of those who are entirely estranged from the polity. The answer lies in expanding the unhelpful dichotomy of dominant and deviant norms into a tripartite scheme, whose terminology I borrow from Frank Parkin:

> (1) The *dominant* value system, the social source of which is the major institutional order...
> (2) The *subordinate* value system...This is a moral framework which promotes *accommodative* responses...
> (3) *The radical* value system...This is a moral framework which promotes an *oppositional* interpretation.[81]

A definition of political distrust which carries no particular implication of the nature of the beliefs involved, but which differentiates those who are essentially, but not uncritically, integrated into their polities from those who reject them is then possible: political distrust is an unfavourable evaluation of the condition of their polity, derived by citizens from their perceptions of a discrepancy between the present reality of politics and dominant or subordinate, but not radical, norms for its operation.

This definition of distrust is based on an alternative interpretation of existing evidence; the implication of what we know already is that distrust may be informed, guided by norms, and unthreatening to democracy. However, it has also been argued in this chapter that the existing evidence is inadequate to prove either its own case or mine. The chapters which follow will attempt to test the validity of this interpretation with new and more adequate evidence.

2. Two views of political distrust

Recently, the commonplace understanding of differences between the politics of Britain and America has been overturned by the probing of survey research into the incidence of political distrust. Once, it seemed, everybody knew that Britain was a stable country. Its citizens' respect for parliamentary democracy and contentment with incremental social change contrasted with restless criticism of their government by Americans, periodic outbursts of anti-democratic hysteria and a constant expectation of rapid and infinite progress. The turmoil of American politics in the 1960s, as prosperity failed to solve social and moral dilemmas, apparently confirmed this contrast, for British government continued to grapple with economic decline unhindered by serious political unrest. Until, suddenly, a time bomb was discovered which threatened to demolish the foundation of respect and contentment upon which British government apparently had rested. British teenagers, soon to become British voters, massively rejected existing government and, even more fundamentally, questioned the usefulness and benevolence of any government. The confident judgement of 1968, that 'Americans are considerably less trusting than Britons of those that govern on their behalf', became the opposite by 1971: 'More than simply drawing even, the British may soon surpass Americans in this particular competition.'[1] And a past which had always been taken for granted suddenly seemed idyllic by contrast with a dismaying and uncertain future.

The conclusion which followed these new findings, by Jack Dennis and colleagues, is worth quoting at length, for it raises many of the problems which I shall examine in the central chapters of this study:

> However firm our beliefs and how much traditional wisdom gives us to understand that the British system is stable, we may nonetheless profit by calling into question such cherished assumptions. Britain has indeed enjoyed remarkable progress and steady evolution of her political order. The bedrock of this happy constancy has been formed in a homogeneous political

culture and wide public regard for strong government. To ask then, if in some brief span, forces of rapid transformation could upset such ultra-stability is virtually to ask the unaskable. But this is precisely the question we must pose at this time. Can the continuity of this system be maintained in the indefinite, or even into the relatively near, future?[2]

Puzzling aspects of this conclusion become doubly so if the comparative context of this analysis of British political developments is borne in mind. Judgements of the present and jeremiads about the future are contrasted with a picture of Americans 'typically well-disposed' towards nation and government.[3] Implicitly, then, the authors also bring into question the conventional wisdom of an American political culture of relatively tenuous active commitment to the ways of democratic government. Even if this is not their intention, how can their gloomy prediction for British politics be squared with the facts of the long survival of the American polity, with distrust a recurrent part of its tradition?

The reconciliation of such contradictions may be achieved by questioning the relevance and the accuracy of the evidence from which they arise. Clearly, a comparison of attitudes between the two nations in the conventional terms (deferential versus distrustful or subject versus participant) is an over-simplification at best. But the conventional wisdom may be on stronger ground in comparing behaviour than attitudes. The archives of American politics overflow with evidence of the public expression of disrespect for its leaders, dislike of its parties, disgust with its electoral system. Outsiders as candidates, efforts to form third parties, innovations in methods of public control of politics, have mostly failed to achieve their aims, but nonetheless have been repeatedly offered. There are relatively few such events in British political history – political behaviour has been largely conventional and acquiescent, just as the standard expectation goes. But to argue that this hard evidence of political action necessarily reflects parallel differences in political attitudes would be to make the unwarranted general assumption that there is a simple and direct relationship between attitudes and behaviour. Such appears, indeed, to be the reasoning of Dennis's study, which leaps to the conclusion that what is newly articulated must be newly present and also immediately reflected in new actions.

The methodological problem of verifying the existence of attitudes where logically appropriate verbalising or actions do not exist is, of course, enormous. In this case, it is not Dennis's choice of methodology which is at fault, but his use of it. He makes a comparison between the present, for which he has data on attitudes unrelated to behaviour, with the past, for which he has unverified impressions of behaviour without an attempt to probe deeper for attitudes. The attitude survey at its worst may be accused of stimulating ideas where none existed before and thus creating the phenomenon which it claims merely to discover. Certainly, if a past devoid of political distrust is assumed, one may well ask whether its sudden appearance was more than co-incidentally simultaneous with the descent on Britain of squadrons of American academics with American preoccupations. But the attitude survey is also the best tool we have for probing such 'invisible' parts of the political world. Its techniques, by now, are refined and varied enough to avoid the obvious pitfalls; its bad reputation comes as much from the misuse of the evidence gathered by its means as from inherent faults in the whole enterprise.

The British polity has overtly been deferential, but this does not, then, eliminate the possibility that critical attitudes have been held, yet have remained private. Both structural and cultural inhibitions may contribute to the difference between holding attitudes, expressing them openly and acting upon them. They will act as both external and internal constraints. External constraints may be much more subtle than formal legal restrictions through systems of censorship or other means of directly acknowledging and suppressing criticism. There are less immediately coercive limitations, such as the political education of citizens into the perception of a limited number of legitimate modes of political action, and the actual availability of channels for expression and action, including the accessibility of organisations, institutions, personnel and the media. The effect of such factors may be inhibiting, whether or not the intention originally was thus. There are internal constraints too, different in nature (begging the question of whether both sources and intention of political culture are ultimately the same as those of the external constraints of education and opportunity). Internalised language and norms may provide powerful inhibitions against the articulation of vaguely felt discontent. This is not only a difficulty for those with a limited grasp of language – a study of members of the British political elite showed the effect on even the most educated and experienced: 'A few British respondents seemed to be reaching for a conception of democracy that would give them some critical leverage.' A Member of Parliament simply gave up trying to convey the constructive criticism he wanted to make, and the author commented sympathetically: 'His culture simply does not provide him with conceptual tools for thinking about that different, more democratic kind of society that he wanted. Knowing "how we do things here" is not enough if you want to do them differently.'[4] Equally, it is easy to conceive of a pattern of political norms which would inhibit the expression of criticism – the conventional wisdom for Britain suggests relatively low expectations of direct participation and high tolerance of elitism in government, which might well result in even the critical Briton being less vocal and less assertive in action than his American counterpart. Finally, in addition to the acculturation of the individual, there will be other personal restraints stemming from both psychological and cultural attributes, a crucial factor being the sense of political efficacy.

While factors constraining, or equally encouraging, the expression of political distrust may thus be structural, cultural or individual, it is the cultural with which this book is particularly concerned. Of the three, political culture has been the most neglected, partly because of the prominence in recent social science of theories which have seen it as simply derivative, on the one hand from structural sources, on the other from psychological, and therefore of no independent explanatory value. It is also the least amenable to systematic investigation, given the difficulties already suggested of the accurate communication of what is in the minds of the populace. But my own findings, I hope, will make a case for the importance of attempting to solve the methodological problems which block the understanding of political culture, and for political culture itself as an independent factor with significance for political behaviour. The declarations about the past, present and future of the British polity which I quoted above offer an object lesson in the mistakes which can follow from the neglect of political culture.

Not the least controversial of the conclusions reached by Dennis is that of the 'remarkable progress' of the British political order; only if the prime criterion of success is stability can this be accepted without qualification. Success is then explained by the nature of the British political culture: 'The bedrock of this happy constancy has been formed in a homogeneous political culture and wide public regard for strong government.' But, where is the support for this statement? Much of the evidence of the attitudes of the British towards politics comes from attitude surveys, presenting two immediate problems: first that many such surveys have been very blunt instruments for investigating complex and often ill-articulated attitudes, and second that surveys are anyway a relatively recent invention, giving at best some indication of conditions since the Second World War. Earlier evidence which might support such a sweeping historical statement is mostly indirect, from the scattered observations of journalists, academics or interested politicians, and so even less adequate. Furthermore, while the notion of homogeneity has certainly been part of the conventional picture of British politics, even this inadequate body of evidence provides little support for it. Some research has led to the conclusion that political stratification is the major characteristic of British political culture: an elite which comprehends and endorses democracy sustains democratic government with the assent but not the commitment of the majority.[5] Political stratification may also simply be the political effect of social stratification, if the political elite is coterminous with a social class. In the explanation of political *behaviour* class has constantly been used as a most powerful explanatory factor, accounting for variety. It has been a curiously neglected point that class might equally be used to identify variety in political *culture*. Then again, nationalisms within the United Kingdom are hardly new; while their existence does not preclude cultural agreement at the most general level on the notion of democratic government, it does further destroy the notion of an entirely 'homogeneous political culture'.

The 'bedrock of this happy constancy' is thus open to question on several grounds, and so must be the assumption of the content of this political culture. Once again, we simply do not know enough to make such sweeping assertions. If the conclusions of any of the proponents of a theory of political stratification are correct then the 'wide regard for strong government' may more accurately be wide *acceptance* of strong government – a crucial difference between legitimacy and realism. Certainly, there are some historical indications that this may be so, for example in Pelling's findings of the resentment of Victorian workers against government where it impinged on their lives and their indifference to it where it did not.[6]

Similar criticisms can be applied to the alarming predictions for the future of British politics, with its continuity shattered by 'forces of rapid transformation'. The unmediated impact of political culture on political events is again assumed, and so is the continuity of an uncritical culture through history. Again, there is some evidence to suggest the opposite – for example in one of the classic sources for the theme of stability in Britain. In their study of *The civic culture*, Gabriel Almond and Sidney Verba concluded that Britain boasted the ideal civic culture, 'the one most congruent with a stable, democratic system', with expectations of participation in government muted by the survival of traditional parochial perceptions and the acceptance of authority.[7] Yet this reassuring picture is threatened, both by the authors' general theory of cultural change and by parts of their own evidence. Their theory is of a linear development through three types – from a parochial to a subject and thence to a participant political culture. Most advanced in this scheme is America, where 'there tends to be too much weight placed on the participant role'.[8] The inference must be that differences between Britain and America are simply the products of the different timing of their development, with no reason inherent in British conditions why the participant component of its culture should not increase. Instead of reading the study as a gratifying picture of a secure Britain, it might be taken as a prophecy of precisely the dissatisfaction which, a decade later, Dennis claimed to find. For *The civic culture* evidence itself gives no unqualified cause for complacency that participation would be uncritical. Compared with 85 per cent of American respondents, only 46 per cent of the British expressed spontaneous pride in their political institutions; among those in each country who were highly educated and ranked as particularly competent politically the figures were higher but the gap even wider – 95 per cent in America to 52 per cent in Britain expressing such pride.[9] The authors' belief that political competence would tend to go along with a belief in both the duty and the possibility to participate in government was not sustained by their own evidence for Britain, where greater competence was as likely to go along with the desire to participate and the perception of the impossibility of actually doing so – surely creating a decided potential for disaffection with politics. Indeed, an early translation of this hidden potential into the kind of direct action and idealistic third party challenge more characteristic of the United States may have been in events such as the Campaign for Nuclear Disarmament of the 1950s and the revival of hopes for a viable Liberal Party with the Orpington by-election victory of 1959. Both were particularly strongly supported by young, politically aware, competent and critical activists.[10]

The authors of these studies fail to observe the limitations of their methodology. A single attitude survey is time-bound, however sophisticated in eliciting appropriate information. Its findings may at best show significant relationships in the present, but predictions from it are surely only possible with some understanding of the past. And hearsay about the past has often gained authority simply from having been around for a long time, whereas the standards for accepting historical evidence should be as rigorous as those for the present. There is a failure to recognise the problematic nature of the relationships assumed, and a failure to understand the complex nature of the political culture discussed. Nonetheless, these studies have raised important questions about the nature and significance of political culture. And if better answers are needed, they are not easily come by, for in practice neither the ideal methodology for the present nor such rigorous evidence from the past has been discovered.

By studying the content and impact of one group of political attitudes, political distrust, in more detail, this book tries to take a step towards identifying unavoidable limitations on understanding as well as finding more substantial answers to the questions. The evidence of this chapter is from two recent attitude surveys; there will follow two historical case studies – attempts to piece together the evidence of potentially comparable episodes and to examine them for precedents which might illuminate the present.

The view from below

In 1972, cross-sections of the adolescent populations of London and Boston were asked the same extensive series of questions about their political beliefs. The samples were large, and both socially and educationally representative of their age group.[11] The survey, taken by Nelson Rosenbaum, provides an unusual opportunity for a controlled comparison of political attitudes between Britain and America, during a period of allegedly critical change in both countries. Because the teenagers were given the opportunity to express both their beliefs about governments and their criticisms of them, the findings provide fresh and appropriate evidence about political distrust.

The fact that the survey was of teenagers has the advantage of providing somewhat of a replication of the research by Dennis and thus a direct challenge of his interpretations from a comparable base. It has also the obvious disadvantage of revealing the attitudes of a group who have not yet become official participants in politics, whose views have thus not yet been challenged by the personal experience of exercising their democratic rights. However, research in political socialisation has tended to suggest that the fundamental 'commitment to, and identification with, the political system and its dominant values'

is formed in a child's early years and remains remarkably stable thereafter.[12] And, furthermore, children appear to have a very accurate
perception of the impact of government actions on their own lives;
indeed they make shrewd political judgements and are quick to relate
the formal instruction of civics lessons and their normative commitment to the experiences of adults within their purview. Robert Coles
talked with poor and minority children, and with white children suddenly exposed to racial tension over the bussing issue in South Boston,
and concluded that 'unforgettable events in the lives of children very
definitely help to shape their attitudes towards their nation and its
political authority'. For example, 'a black child of eight, in rural
Mississippi or in a northern ghetto, an Indian or Chicano or Appalach-
ian child, can sound like a disillusioned old radical: 'down with the
system, because it's a thoroughly unjust one, for all that one hears in
school'.[13] From Greenstein to Coles, the literature on children's trust in
government charts the same decline as does the literature on adults:[14]
the children's views are not so much different as more outspoken, but
both are reactions to the same experience of the world.

At first glance, Rosenbaum's data seem to sustain the argument that
British teenagers are more distrustful of their government than are
Americans, though by the narrowest of margins. Table 1 summarises
the responses to a direct question. Table 2 shows that the British also
feel more strongly about the actual performance of their government
and are more divided between disapproval and approval. Those who
clearly disapprove are, however, a larger group than their American
counterparts. More general support for the institutions of government
is measured in Table 3: again the British give markedly less support
than the Americans, but the contrast is far less dramatic than appeared
in Dennis's data, with a gap of only 9 per cent here as opposed to
31 per cent between the national totals disagreeing with his proposition.

A closer look at the basis for these conclusions, however, suggests a
number of problems which limit the value of such statements, whether
of the circumstances of each country individually or of comparisons
between them. On the methodological side, here is a demonstration
that if survey questions need not lead the respondent, they often do:
unless one assumes a dramatic fading away of disagreement in the few
years between the two surveys, much of the difference shown in Table 3
must surely be derived from the different statements presented, with
Dennis's dogmatic proposition receiving a far less equivocal response.
If dogma can thus breed dogma, ambiguity will also provide nothing

Table 1. *How much do you think the government in Washington/London can be trusted to do what is right?*

	UK	US
Don't know	8%	9%
Never	9%	6%
Sometimes	43%	34%
Most times	35%	41%
Always	5%	11%
	100%	101%*
N	(943)	(987)

* Numbers in all tables have been rounded to the nearest percentage point and so will not always add exactly to 100%.

Table 2. *In general, how well do you think the federal/British government meets the needs of the people in its actions and policies?*

	UK	US
Not at all	5%	5%
Not well	22%	15%
Somewhat	40%	55%
Quite well	29%	23%
Very well	3	3
	99%	101%
N	(927)	(975)

Table 3. *Some people say that the American/British form of government is the best and should be copied by other nations. What is your feeling about this?*

	UK	Dennis UK sample*	US
Strongly agree	5%	15%	14%
Agree	32%	22%	35%
Don't know	27%	13%	26%
Disagree	23%	26%	19%
Strongly disagree	11%	26%	6%
	98%	102%	100%
N	(934)	(933)	(977)

* Adapted from Dennis, 'Support for nation and government', Table 3, p. 32. The statement presented for agreement was 'The British system of government is one that all countries should have'. I have combined their figures for the age groups 11–17 and rounded them to the nearest percentage point.

but ambiguous evidence. 'To trust', in this study and in others, has been given a highly specific and technical meaning. In colloquial usage there is no such refinement – the meaning to survey respondents may vary according to context or national practice. Confusion between respondent and academic interpreter in this case is most likely to arise over two common usages of the term: to trust, as the *Oxford English Dictionary* puts it, as 'to have faith or confidence *that* something desired is, or will be, the case', and alternatively as having straightforward faith or confidence *in* government. The first is expectation of how things will be, the second a commitment based on norms. Thus Tables 1 and 2 may as well present a prospective and a retrospective judgement of the same empirically based expectation of performance as the contrast between diffuse faith and specific judgement which my first glance suggested.

A check on whether the intentions of the respondents have been accurately received must come from a far more detailed analysis of norms and judgements, which can also increase the validity of cross-national comparisons of such data. The cliché that Americans and Britons are two nations separated by their use of a common language conveys the warning that meanings may also differ between the two samples. The problem is compounded by the probability that not only language, but the norms themselves against which judgements are reached, will differ between nations. Here the theoretical elegance of a definition of alienation or distrust as a discrepancy – a relational concept which assumes both variable norms and variable judgements – resolves the methodological difficulties also. Nations can be compared in terms of the gap between their own norms and judgements, regardless of possible differences in both norms and language.

The content of ideals cannot simply be taken for granted. Nordlinger, for example, reported that British workers felt that they had little say in government, but then it transpired that they did not think that they should have much say, and were, after all, relatively content with the situation.[15] Similarly, the 63 per cent of young Britons in Rosenbaum's survey who thought that more Members of Parliament were stupid than were smart may have shared a long standing British doubt: 'Men as different as Lord Salisbury and Ernest Bevin have used the term "clever" as one of abuse. Mark Abrams found in a survey that only 17 per cent of those interviewed thought cleverness a desirable characteristic in party leaders.'[16] In both cases it seems likely that identical questions yielding identical responses in America would actually have represented far greater dissatisfaction. Nor can the investigator's own standards be imposed upon his subjects. Dennis, for example, assumed that 'willingness to criticize one's leaders' presented a threat to the stability of democracy.[17] Yet 79 per cent of Rosenbaum's British sample and 78 per cent of his Americans saw this as being a democratic duty: 'Every person has a duty to criticize the government when it does something wrong even if the matter does not concern him directly.'

Rosenbaum's survey does escape some of these problems. While he did not ask precisely matched questions about norms of government and perceptions of its current condition, his data do allow a more rough and ready matching of the two and thus a comparative estimate of the intensity of distrust. The respondents were presented with two series of statements for their agreement or disagreement. The first set revealed their standards for democratic government, the second their assessment of the actual operation of government by a mixture of criteria of democracy and efficiency. From their responses a rough and ready index of discrepancy has been constructed. Nine of the statements on ideals and seven of those assessing reality have responses whose scores can be assigned numerical values: in the case of ideals a higher score, and a higher mean value for the nine answers, indicates a higher democratic standard for government (with democracy arbitrarily defined from these statements as centring around equality of access to and participation in decision making, with shared responsibility rather than delegation to an elite); for the second set of answers a higher score represents a higher level of satisfaction with the operation of government.[18] Table 4 reports the mean scores for each country on both sets of statements.

The mean score overall (based on a scale from 1 to 5) indicates a lower level of democratic expectation in Britain than in the United States – 3.386 against 3.684 – but a higher level of satisfaction among the British – 2.899 as against 2.851. These differences are certainly not striking, either between countries on individual questions or between the national totals. But the difference between the two countries recorded in Table 1 is reversed by this measure: when distrust is measured as discrepancy, the Americans, with higher expectations and lower assessments, show the greater distrust – 0.833 points against 0.487 points for the British.

But a summary measure of this kind, for all its advantages, also involves a substantial loss of detailed information. Contained within

Table 4. *Mean scores of responses to questions on ideals of government and perception of its actual mode of operation*

	UK mean	US mean
Democratic ideals		
Intelligent only should vote	2.756	2.763
A few able people have to run government	2.312	3.036
Should leave politics to the politicians	3.475	4.069
Don't care about methods, only results	3.425	3.875
Have a duty to criticise the government	4.045	4.037
Need proper education for public office	3.520	3.579
Individual's vote not very important	3.877	3.988
Chance for all to participate in decisions	4.369	4.479
Duty to stay informed about government	2.701	3.336
Mean level of expectations:	3.386	3.684
Assessment of actual operation of government		
Attention paid by government to people	3.447	3.277
People in government smart or stupid*	2.157	2.232
How much say do people have in government	2.383	2.568
How much of our taxes wasted by government	2.726	2.478
Government would help me if needed	2.903	2.937
People in government honest with public	3.348	3.100
MP's voting influenced by people	3.331	3.365
Mean level of satisfaction:	2.899	2.851
Discrepancy between mean level of expectation and mean level of satisfaction:	0.487	0.833

Note: Responses were coded into 5 values except for the statement marked * which has only 3. The statements on ideals had been coded 1–5 and those on realities 0–4; I have raised all values of the latter by one point so that the gap between the two should not be artificially inflated.

Table 4 are indications of differences between Britons and Americans over the finer details. The differences in democratic ideals are all in the same direction; if 'democracy' is envisaged to include varying degrees of direct and equal participation in government, then the ideals of the Americans can all be placed further towards the participatory and egalitarian end of the spectrum. The statements tapping ideals included references to meritocratic criteria for electors and representatives, participation through voting and more generally in decision making, and on the balance between means and ends and the duties of the citizen. The mean scores for the British sample show them in every case as more elitist and less participatory. The difference from the Americans is sometimes exceedingly small, but always in the same direction. This is exactly what studies of the traditional British understanding of parliamentary democracy would lead us to expect: by comparison with the Americans, the British are more inclined to support representative than direct democracy, liberal than radical ideals of government. Like the adults of Almond and Verba's study – the generation of their parents – their active and participatory ideals appear to be moderated by the simultaneous presence of 'subject orientations'.

Almond and Verba saw as linked attributes of British political culture 'deferential and subject orientations'.[19] A contented subject orientation is made possible where deference to the competence and character of leaders instils trust that there can be responsible rule without the active check and control of sustained citizen participation: 'the sense of trust in the political elite – the belief that they are not alien and extractive forces, but part of the same political community – makes citizens willing to turn over power to them'.[20] Their study was less of the citizen's assessment of the political elite and institutions than of himself as political actor and beneficiary, but the general satisfaction with politics which they found certainly appeared to betoken the presence of such trust in institutions. Rosenbaum's survey throws new light on the nature of deference in British political culture.

Among Almond and Verba's adult Britons, 83 per cent expected that they would get equal treatment in dealings with government officials, and the figure was the same for their American sample.[21] Table 5 suggests that there has been substantial change since then in

Table 5. *Do you think that officials in the federal/British government give everyone an even break or do you think they give special favours and privileges to some people?*

	UK	US
Don't know	27%	16%
Give favours	55%	72%
Treat evenly	18%	12%
	100%	100%
N	(950)	(990)

both countries. The British now see more equity in government dealings with citizens than do the Americans, but the overall decline is striking. That confidence would later be enhanced by adult experience with government, to raise it to anywhere near the 83 per cent level, seems most unlikely. Where differences in the incidence of distrust between adults and children have been found, the level has always been higher among adults – a fact normally assumed to be the product of greater political experience.[22] Certainly, teenagers in Rosenbaum's study tended to be more distrustful the greater their political experience.

The deferential and subject orientations of the British in *The civic culture* did not spring from any sense of their own incompetence in political affairs: 'exposure to politics, interest, involvement, and a sense of competence are relatively high'.[23] As much as 57 per cent felt confident of some capacity to act in both local and national affairs; only 19 per cent lacked such confidence entirely. The change in the assessment of government by young Britons in the 1970s appears not to have come from any drastic change in their sense of subjective competence, which might still be described as 'relatively high' by the measure reported in Table 6. There are, however, some clues to other

Table 6. *Generally speaking, how well prepared do you think people like your parents and yourself are to participate in the political activity and decision making in our society?*

	UK	US
Not at all	5%	4%
Not well	25%	16%
Somewhat	40%	43%
Well	26%	29%
Very well	5%	8%
	101%	100%
N	(901)	(970)

changes, which might have contributed to this newly critical assessment, to be found in the second half of Table 4, among the particular points upon which the British sample are most critical. It may be deduced from these that, while the British still give more support to representative government than direct democracy by comparison with the Americans, this may be more a pragmatic acceptance of inevitabilities than a normative commitment. From their answers to these seven items, together with three similar judgemental questions not used in Table 4, the British seem the very antithesis of the deferential subjects we used to know and love.[24] When asked about the calibre of their governors, 63 per cent of them felt that 'some of them don't seem to know what they are doing', against 55 per cent of the traditionally disrespectful Americans. Nor did they hold notably high hopes of personal assistance from the government: their responses are reported in Table 7 and in this case again they were less positive than the Americans.

Table 7. *Suppose you or your family needed help with some problem from the British govern- ment – for example, a tax question or a housing matter. How much do you think you could rely on the government to provide the help you needed?*

	Don't know	Never	Some- times	Most times	Always	
UK	11%	20%	44%	19%	7%	= 101% (N = 939)

The most interesting group of criticisms has to do with participation in the making of political decisions. The British thought that their Members of Parliament paid less attention to them in deciding which way to vote in Parliament: 35 per cent thought that they paid none or not much attention, compared to 26 per cent of Americans of their Congressmen. And 61 per cent of the British, compared to 52 per cent of the Americans, thought that 'people like themselves' had no say, or not much, in what the government did. Given their apparent lesser sympathy for the ideals of direct democracy, both points might be dismissed as no evidence of complaint by the British. But the national difference revealed in Table 8 is instructive: a full 67 per cent of the British thought that they *should* have more say; the Americans were markedly more content with their opportunities. Yet, as Table 9 shows, this same critical group of young Britons also agreed quite strongly that government will always be elitist. Taken together, these observa- tions and beliefs suggest that this final conclusion may be reached in a spirit of resignation, or even of cynicism, but hardly from contentment, let alone from enthusiasm. Even were they to trust, that is to expect, that the actions of government would often be to their benefit, there appears not to be a basic trust, or faith, in their government among these British teenagers.

The cases in which the young Americans were more critical overlap slightly with the British complaints: on another question on the atten- tion given by government to the views of the people they were less inclined to believe that this was substantial (48 per cent against 54 per cent of the British) with rather more of them uncertain how to answer. But the rest of their more critical scores were of a different kind: more thought that their government gave favours (America 72 per cent, Britain 55 per cent); that it wasted tax money (Waste a lot – America

Table 8. *How much say do you think people like your parents and yourself should have about what the government does?*

	UK	US
Don't know	12%	11%
Less	1%	5%
Same	20%	26%
More	67%	58%
	100%	100%
N	(929)	(968)

Table 9. *Despite all the talk about democracy, it will always be necessary to have a few able people in the government actually running things*

	UK	US
Strongly agree	20%	12%
Agree	44%	29%
Don't know	24%	21%
Disagree	7%	20%
Strongly disagree	5%	19%
	100%	101%
N	(962)	(993)

42 per cent, Britain 26 per cent); that government personnel were not honest in their dealings with the public (Most/almost all honest – America 40 per cent, Britain 60 per cent); and that government was effectively in the hands of big interests (America 46 per cent, Britain 26 per cent).

These two sets of criticisms suggest rather different patterns of complaint. The Americans were more concerned with the output of government – that it was biased, often wasteful, and that the individual was on the receiving end of dishonest treatment. All these are criticisms which are directed primarily towards administrative problems. The British criticisms go deeper, beyond a perception of injustice in the final output of government, to the way in which its decisions have been reached. Tables 1 and 2 indicated that the British seemed both somewhat less willing to trust their government and somewhat less satisfied with its outputs; when it comes down to more specific criticisms, it is the lack of trust, not the inadequacy of policies, which is the greatest preoccupation. If the British feel less distrustful by the summary measure of Table 4, nonetheless their discontent appears potentially the more serious for the political system. For their criticisms cannot be met simply by the tightening of procedures and a change of faces in the government. The British pragmatically accept elitism in government in practice, but not without limits, for they also demand a greater degree of participation than they presently feel they have. They are still far from being idealist radical democrats, calling for the overthrow of traditional processes of parliamentary government, but their criticisms challenge the principle of delegated authority and require change and innovation in institutions if they are to be met.

The question of whether the political system will respond to the discontents of its members directs attention to the consequences of political distrust in these polities. First, however, one or two general comments are in order. The information from Rosenbaum's survey does not demolish the picture presented by Dennis and his colleagues, but it does moderate it considerably. One possibility is that Dennis took his survey at a time of unusually high disaffection with politics among young people. In the case of American youth, for example, it may be that the growing sense of a credibility gap between citizens and government and the mounting protest over the Vietnam War in the mid-1960s are enough to account for the higher disaffection then. The schoolchildren of Rosenbaum's sample were answering their questions without the shadow of the draft, apparently near to peace with Vietnam and just before the Watergate scandals began to be uncovered. But even so, among adults in America distrust and criticism of government continued to increase steadily right up to 1972. No such plausible grounds for the decline of trust present themselves for the British sample; as the *Annual Register* opened its review of events in Britain: 'An atmosphere of bitterness, lawlessness, and, at times, even violence permeated British society in the early months of 1972.'[25] Constitutional questions were at the heart of many of the major issues of these months, as miners and railwaymen struck and gained massive pay rises from government, dockers defied the National Industrial Relations Court, the Irish question was exacerbated by bombings in England and the abrupt introduction of direct rule from Westminster, Parliament tensely debated the EEC bill following the signing of the Treaty of Accession, with political parties divided on the issue, and, of course, sterling declined. The different context of the two surveys suggests little to qualify the explanation of their differences as a product of the different tone of questioning, with Dennis's stronger statements resulting in a picture in black and white instead of the shades of grey which the more detailed and more subtle questioning of Rosenbaum produced.

While little can yet be said about the past history of political distrust, these surveys may yet offer some insight into the likely consequences of the situation which they describe. Dennis, it will be remembered, anticipated disaster, asking: 'Can the continuity of this system be maintained in the indefinite, or even into the relatively near future?' He wisely disclaimed prophetic vision, but nonetheless made an easy jump from discussing the presence of critical attitudes to assuming that they will have some effect upon the political system. His respondents might feel reassured, since this is exactly what they do not believe. But many independent factors may intervene between the presence of critical attitudes and political change: some constraints upon critical individuals were suggested earlier, but in addition much will depend on the responsiveness of political institutions themselves. Thus the complex combinations of institutional inertia, human accident, historical situation, and so forth which bear upon institutional behaviour become relevant here too. I will return to the responses of government to political distrust later in this chapter; first I will examine the evidence of Rosenbaum's survey for contributions to an understanding of the consequences of the distrust he describes.

The limited conceptual apparatus of the average citizen means that he is most likely to think about his rights in politics in the highly simplified common currency of his political culture – which makes it easier for the American spontaneously to voice complaints about participation than for the Briton, who lacks any powerful mythology of the independent rights and sovereignty of the people. The attitude survey must tread a fine line in such circumstances, between putting ideas into heads which were free of them before and providing the language to express thoughts which were there but struggling for expression. If feelings of political distrust have indeed spontaneously crystallised in people's minds, then whether anything more comes of them and what form the expression of people's feelings is likely to take depends also on what channels they perceive as being available for their communications. Tables 10 through 13 compare the perceptions of Rosenbaum's two groups of teenagers on this point. The British believed more strongly that the only way they could participate in politics was through voting, and they also believed more strongly that this was an effective mode of communication with the government.

Similarly, they had a stronger confidence in the effectiveness of political parties and of the press and television as channels for their views. So, although their demand for more participation was stronger than that of the Americans, and in the context of parliamentary government

Table 10. *Some people say that voting is the only way a citizen can have any say about the way the (federal) government runs things. What do you think?*

	UK	US
Strongly agree	19%	13%
Agree	39%	34%
Don't know	11%	16%
Disagree	23%	26%
Strongly disagree	8%	10%
	100%	99%
N	(941)	(987)

Table 11. *How effective do you think elections are in making the British/federal government pay attention to the wishes of the people?*

	UK	US
Don't know	7%	12%
Not at all	5%	3%
Not much	24%	23%
Much	38%	47%
Very much	27%	15%
	101%	100%
N	(939)	(978)

Table 12. *How much do you feel that the political parties help in making the British/federal government respond to the wishes of the people?*

	UK	US
Don't know	17%	17%
Not at all	5%	5%
Not much	25%	30%
Much	42%	40%
Very much	12%	8%
	101%	100%
N	(951)	(987)

Table 13. *To what extent do you think that the newspapers, magazines and television help in making the British/federal government respond to the wishes of the people?*

	UK	US
Don't know	8%	9%
Not at all	5%	3%
Not much	25%	25%
Much	39%	48%
Very much	24%	14%
	101%	99%
N	(932)	(971)

apparently more radical, they were more hopeful of obtaining a response through traditional channels.

There was no follow-up question for those of either nationality who believed that voting was not the only way for a citizen to share in decisions, so we do not know what the greater number of young Americans who felt this way may have had in mind.[26] But, given their lesser confidence in traditional ways, we might expect them to be more ready to act through demonstrations, community pressure groups and so forth. Certainly they had had more experience of this kind of activity: 37 per cent of Americans, compared to 21 per cent of the British, had contacted the media, joined a non-partisan organisation with political involvement, or attended some kind of rally.

If the distrust of the British was in itself more radical, it seems it may be less so in its immediate consequences, since their faith in constitutional political action was stronger. But as this generation of young Britons reaches adulthood, perhaps their experience as voters will undermine this confidence, just as the lesser confidence of Americans in these methods is coupled with greater experience of partisan as well as non-partisan activity: 49 per cent, compared with 26 per cent of the British, said that they had campaigned, worked for a party or attended a party meeting.

Meanwhile, if today's adults match these children in their faith in the power of the vote as well as their disillusion with government, then it is not so surprising that they turned out massively to vote in the 1974 parliamentary elections. But Table 14 shows that the distrustful came disproportionately from that 40 per cent of the British sample who claimed independence of party affiliation or didn't know where they stood. In 1974 the Liberal Party evidently appeared to such

Table 14. *Party affiliation and distrustfulness in the British sample*

	Party preference:				
	Cons	Lab	Lib	Ind	Don't know
Distrust:					
High	22%	48%	40%	63%	52%
Medium	66%	45%	51%	34%	42%
Low	12%	7%	9%	3%	6%
	100%	100%	100%	100%	100%
N	(206)	(321)	(87)	(132)	(180)

people, as well as to the disaffected with party labels, a credible option for the exercise of their only effective political weapon, the vote.[27] If future elections offer no credible option, will they turn negatively to abstention, or vote for the lesser evil, or will they open their minds, as some Americans in this sample seem to be doing, to other ways of exerting political influence? The survey data and recent events leave this question open.

But the likelihood of action following from the presence of attitudes depends on more than the availability of institutional channels for expression; behaviour, as well as the expression of views, is influenced by cultural factors. For example, although the British had greater confidence in and placed their hope in action through voting, they were less likely than the Americans to express a strong sense of their duty to do so. The Americans felt more strongly that the individual's vote did matter (America 71 per cent, Britain 65 per cent). When asked if they agreed with the statement that 'Every person should devote himself to staying informed about politics and government even if it means giving up some spare time', 55 per cent of the Americans agreed, against only 35 per cent of the British. The differences in actual electoral turnout (between 54.5 per cent of the American electorate in 1972 and 78.8 per cent of the British in February, 1974) suggest that the possession of such a sense of duty will not necessarily nudge a voter into action. But in this sample the common-sense expectation did hold: in Britain there was a positive correlation of 0.387 between summary measures of a sense of civic duty and levels of political activity, and in America of 0.311.

A psychological attribute which has been given prominence in studies of the roots of political action is the subjective sense of political efficacy of the individual. Table 6 showed one measure of how well prepared for effective political activity the samples felt, and Table 15 adds another. Again, the differences are not striking, but the Americans do appear to have a somewhat higher confidence in their own preparation for participation. In the 1950s, when political distrust tended to be

Table 15. *How well do you feel you understand the important issues of politics and government which confront our society?*

	UK	US
Not at all	9%	6%
Not well	35%	23%
Somewhat	29%	42%
Quite well	24%	22%
Very well	3%	7%
	100%	100%
N	(931)	(977)

confused with anomie, it was commonly assumed that it would inevitably be demoralising and would lead to apathy and withdrawal. The discovery that it might exist in combination with a high sense of efficacy led to the formulation of what has regrettably been labelled the 'mistrustful–efficacious hypothesis': 'a combination of high sense of political efficacy and low political trust is the optimum combination for mobilization – a belief that influence is both possible and necessary'.[28] Some analyses of American data have failed to support this hypothesis: among the highly efficacious, those who were also highly distrustful participated less than those who scored low on distrust.[29] In other words, distrust did seem to lead to withdrawal, regardless of its relation to efficacy. Table 16 shows the results of a similar analysis of Rosenbaum's data. Since 'a high sense of political efficacy' is a rather rare characteristic, the numbers involved are small and the results therefore need to be treated with caution, but they strongly suggest that in this sample the highly competent politically who were also distrustful were more active than the highly competent and trustful.

However, the highly competent altogether were only 21 per cent of the American sample and 15 per cent of the British, and the highly distrustful and active only a small part of this group. Though percentages disguise the fact that in the nation at large this is actually a large number of individuals seeking reform towards their democratic ideals, and though the active, competent and distrustful one or two per cent are likely to wield an influence disproportionate to their numbers, still the potential effect of those few has to be set against the likely behaviour of the majority of the distrustful. For the bulk of the distrustful in both countries the relationship is the opposite of the group just described. For those of both low and medium competence, attitudes of high distrust go with low levels of political activity.

Table 16

(a) *The effect of distrust on activity among the highly competent in America**

	Distrust of government:		
	Low	Medium	High
Activity:			
Low	58.3%	48.5%	17.4%
Medium	16.7%	24.2%	39.1%
High	25.0%	27.3%	43.5%
	100.0%	100.0%	100.0%
N	(12)	(33)	(23)

(b) *The effect of distrust on activity among the highly competent in Britain.**

	Distrust of government:		
	Low	Medium	High
Activity:			
Low	80.0%	55.6%	26.7%
Medium	20.0%	33.3%	60.0%
High	–	11.1%	13.3%
	100.0%	100.0%	100.0%
N	(5)	(9)	(15)

* Competence index combines scores on questions reported in Tables 6 and 15. Index of distrust combines scores on questions reported in Tables 1 and 7 and a question on the honesty of people running government. Activity index additive of reported participation through media or in party, campaign or meetings.

A sense of civic duty, which independently appeared quite strongly related to political activism, appears rather less effective in overriding the generally depressant effect of distrust upon activism than was political efficacy. As Table 17 shows, among those with a high sense of civic duty the highly distrustful were somewhat more active than those of low or medium distrust. But in this case the majority of all three groups were disinclined to action, perhaps because it is this sense of civic duty which is most directly mocked by the realities perceived by the distrustful.

Table 17

(a) *The effect of distrust on activity among those with a high sense of civic duty in America**

	Distrust of government:		
	Low	Medium	High
Activity:			
Low	74.2%	56.8%	54.2%
Medium	16.1%	26.0%	30.6%
High	9.7%	17.2%	15.3%
	100.0%	100.0%	100.1%
N	(31)	(169)	(144)

(b) *The effect of distrust on activity among those with a high sense of civic duty in Britain*

	Distrust of government:		
	Low	Medium	High
Activity:			
Low	81.3%	71.9%	58.7%
Medium	6.3%	20.2%	27.2%
High	12.5%	7.9%	14.1%
	100.1%	100.0%	100.0%
N	(16)	(89)	(92)

* Civic duty index combines scores on questions on duty to vote and to stay informed and on leaving politics to the politicians.

Sociological characteristics are related directly to levels of political participation, in addition to the indirect effect which they have through the kind of subjective characteristics discussed above. They must therefore be considered in their own right when debating the consequences of distrust in a polity. To the extent that the distribution of the distrustful in society is disproportionately in one social group, or that they are untypical in education levels, we may expect their levels of political activity to be skewed in the same direction. In this sample, as in others, the variables with the strongest relationship with levels of participation

were the not unrelated ones of socio-economic status and education.[30]
Table 18 shows that both were positively related to levels of participation. But it also shows that neither status nor education had any
relationship to distrust, except that in America there was a slight
tendency for distrust to be moderated by higher educational achievement. Distrust was thus rather evenly spread across all classes and
educational levels in each nation; in addition it had itself almost no
direct relationship with political activism: the correlation between
distrust and activism in Britain was $+0.085$ and in America only
-0.042. Something other than simply social position affects the potential for activism of the distrustful. And clearly the subjective sense of
political efficacy is one such factor.

Table 18. *Correlation matrices of social and political variables for Britain and the United
States*

	Distrust	Political competence	Participation
UK			
Status	−0.059	0.180†	0.178†
Education	−0.092*	0.250†	0.287†
US			
Status	−0.009	0.209†	0.277†
Education	−0.146†	0.358†	0.465†

* Significant at the 0.01 level.
† Significant at the 0.001 level.
Unmarked correlations not significant.
Status measured by father's occupation; education by respondent's educational
environment and performance; participation is a measure of reported interest and
involvement in discussion.

The distrustful are not disproportionately drawn from any social
group, but their even spread across both nations means that it is the
larger lower classes who furnish the greater numbers. Thus, the bulk
of the distrustful not only are socially disadvantaged but feel politically
disadvantaged. The prospects for a mighty movement, rising up in the
name of democratic ideals to reclaim lost political rights, seems remote
on this evidence. It seems particularly remote in Britain, where there
has not been innovative political activity comparable with the surge of
third party attempts, primary challenges, community politics, direct
action and so on which occurred simultaneously with the rise of political distrust in the United States during the 1960s. But the details of
Rosenbaum's survey suggest that this vacuum of action in Britain

should not be taken as evidence that distrust there is a phony mood, stimulated simply by academic inquiries. Its consequences may be, as yet, uncertain, but the mood is very real to substantial numbers of people in Britain. It is more than simple assent to suggestions – it comprises a coherently related set of propositions about what politics should be and assessments of what politics actually is. But if people are able to articulate this mood in response to questioning, it is a far harder step to take effective action, for this involves conceiving possible lines of action which are new to the polity and foreign to the formal theory of parliamentary sovereignty. And indeed the picture is not one of a total vacuum; there are signs of activity, often following American examples, which would begin to answer some of the complaints of the distrustful. Even if devolution, parliamentary and electoral reform, the reduction of government secrecy, the revitalisation of local politics, industrial democracy and so on come to nothing immediately, the debates on their merits do involve an education in the possibility of new political relationships and thus weaken the inhibitions of a limiting political culture.

Whether such innovations would threaten democracy or refresh it remains to be seen, but there is hope in these data to set against Dennis's pessimism. The distrustful do espouse democratic values – it is not results at any price but democratic modes of government which they say they want to see. If the majority of the distrustful show little propensity to spontaneous political initiative, their openness to responsive action if a lead were given is another matter. Those with the necessary resources to give immediate effect to such a lead, are of course, the governments of the two nations. The extent to which they will be prepared to reform themselves will depend in part on their perception of the seriousness and justification of grievances among their citizens. It is the government view of political distrust to which I turn next.

The view from above

The last few years have seen an outpouring of diagnoses and prognostications concerning the confidence of the ordinary citizens of Britain and America in their governments. This has become headline news – 'Put Not Your Trust in Presidents. . .' and the subject matter of exhortatory editorials.[31] The real state of our knowledge, however, was revealed one month in 1973 with the publication in Britain, almost simultaneously and with major publicity, of surveys on the question taken for the BBC and Independent Television. The *Sunday Times*, joint sponsor of the BBC poll, headlined its report 'MPs, the untrusted men who don't run Britain'; but the Granada/ITV poll told quite a different story – indeed 'the results of the poll were something of a blow for the Granada team...as they had originally intended to set their discussion of Parliamentary reform within the context of public disaffection with MPs. But the poll had failed to demonstrate the extent of disaffection they expected.'[32] Only 4 per cent of the BBC sample put Members of Parliament first when ranking the trustworthiness of the holders of prominent public and professional positions, whereas, faced with a similar list, 41 per cent of the Granada sample declared them 'very valuable' to the community.[33]

Clearly, the Watergate affair in America and the stormy politics and crisis economics of Britain in the 1970s gave good and immediate grounds for doubting the capacity of politicians and institutions. But evidence for the United States suggests that the Watergate revelations must have come as a confirmation of distrust, hardly as its cause. There was a steep rise in its incidence, from the relatively low levels of the late 1950s, beginning around the year 1964; it was no coincidence that this was the time that the concept of the 'credibility gap' acquired currency.[34] There is no such solid evidence for Britain. But there are scattered hints that distrust may have been a latent feature, at least of the working class political culture, long before it became public and the subject of systematic measurement. A Mass Observation study, published in 1948, made a familiar point, even implying the rise of a new phenomenon:

> In the political sphere, as in other spheres, people are losing faith in the goodwill and potentialities of authorities. 'Whatever you do you get the same thing.' It does not mean that they are apathetic in their minds, that they don't *care* what happens. Probably more care today than ever before. But they feel they're out of the picture, that all the great hierarchies of organisation by which lives are increasingly ordered aren't really *concerned* with them and their wants and needs...It is not chiefly that people are losing faith in ideals and objectives, but that they are losing hope of the capacity and desire of those in prominent positions to help realise those desires. Apathy is the apathy of frustration more than of thoughtlessness.[35]

But, regardless of the problems of scrupulous measurement and of the lingering doubt that surveys may be creating the mood that they measure, there may be a substantial impact on the polity if such attitudes are publicly *believed* to be escalating and reaching serious proportions. The alarm of an academic is open to criticism based on an adequate demonstration of the facts. But the alarm of political leaders or of citizens is liable to be a causal factor in political events, regardless of the accuracy of its factual basis. Recently these attitudes have been elevated from the subject matter of sensational television or academic excitement to certification in both countries as an official problem; this gives particular importance to the findings of two surveys with eminent public sponsorship.[36]

In Britain, the Royal Commission on the Constitution was established in 1969, primarily in response to the demands of the Scots, Welsh and Irish for devolution or independence. In the opening pages of its report (the Kilbrandon Report) a broader question was raised: 'In Scotland and Wales the desire for more participation might be bolstered by the fact of nationhood, but it was claimed that the sense of alienation and frustration which gave rise to that idea existed everywhere, and that the basic need was for people in Britain as a whole to win back power from London.'[37] The Commission started from a position of uncertainty about the depth of this discontent. It recognised two possibilities, of which the second would be immeasurably more serious in its implications: either 'dissatisfaction with the current performance of the government in office – part of the ebb and flow of politics – or from resentment at the remoteness and inaccessibility of government in general, reflecting a need for government at all levels to be more sensitive and responsive to personal needs and feelings'.[38] As part of its inquiry, it commissioned a nationwide attitude survey to investigate the themes of participation, nationalism and devolution; the brief on participation focused precisely on that gap between political ideals and political realities which I have defined as distrust.[39]

In 1973, a subcommittee of the United States Senate Committee on Government Operations commissioned an attitude survey which was to be: 'A study to measure public perception of the responsiveness of government at the Federal, State and local levels and to explore ways to increase the responsiveness and efficiency of government at all levels.'[40] Where the Kilbrandon Commission had been a response to perceptions of crisis, the Senate survey was part of a continuing concern with government operations and also a Congressional response to a Presidential initiative:

> In his domestic program called 'The New Federalism' which he sent to Congress this year, the President has further challenged the Congress to re-examine and re-evaluate the roles that... governments do and should play in our domestic system.

To meet that challenge, we believed it appropriate to go to the American people...to get their views about how government at all levels is working and can work.[41]

As with Kilbrandon, built into the Senate brief is a concern with both dimensions of distrustful attitudes: evaluations of the reality of politics and examination of the standards for an ideal polity held by the citizens. While the two surveys are not directly comparable in the questions which they ask, an examination of their published findings does offer some comparative insights into the condition of distrust, the possibility of a 'crisis of legitimacy' in each of these countries in the early 1970s, and the seriousness of the governmental response. The form of both surveys allows a rough estimate of the intensity of political distrust to be made. Taking the British evidence first, I shall examine the criticisms and the ideals of the respondents and compare these two aspects for the symmetry and logic which distinguish distrust from unfocused and random darts aimed at the political system.

A measure of the general level of dissatisfaction with government in Britain is given in Table 19.[42] The small group of 'Don't knows' were

Table 19. *Which of these statements best expresses your opinion on the present system of running Britain?**

Weighted base: all informants	(4,982)
'Works extremely well and could not be improved'	5%
'Could be improved in small ways but mainly works well'	43%
'Could be improved quite a lot'	35%
'Needs a great deal of improvement'	14%
'Don't know'	4%

* *Source:* Kilbrandon Commission, *Research Papers* 7, p. 1.

disproportionately from the elderly and the less educated. But dissatisfaction was found rather evenly across different demographic groups: 'The young, professional people and those with more education tended overall to be a little more dissatisfied with the way things are run than other sections of the population but the differences are small.'[43]

Interesting in its implications for the consequences of this dissatisfaction is the fact that it was found to occur virtually independently of other 'political' variables – of interest and involvement in politics (slightly more of the dissatisfied – 53 per cent – were involved in political activity than of the satisfied – 47 per cent),[44] of knowledge about politics and of general political comprehension.[45]

Dissatisfaction was apparently not a product of unfortunate direct experience of government – again its incidence was quite even across those who had and those who had not had direct contact with government, and 'in as far as this gives rise to a sense of grievance, it is at a broad and abstract level rather than a sentiment based on concrete experience'.[46]

When 49 per cent of the population are prepared to agree that their government could do with quite a lot, if not a great deal, of improvement, it might be argued that a crisis level of support for political institutions had been reached. Without closer examination, however, such interpretation can only be a matter of opinion, as the majority report of the Commission admitted in finding the evidence reassuring:

> We do not wish to give the impression that we have found evidence of seething discontent throughout the land. We have not. Although the people of Great Britain have less attachment to their system of government than in the past, in our opinion it cannot be said that they are seriously dissatisfied with it.[47]

Leaving aside for the moment their entirely unfounded historical assertion, there is some evidence in the research report which may contribute to a less opinionated assessment of the significance of the basic finding.

The dissatisfaction uncovered can, for a start, not be dismissed as simply the grumbling of twentieth-century man, captured by the idea that constant change is valuable in itself. There was almost no relationship between dissatisfaction and a favourable attitude towards social change in general; indeed there was a slight association between conservatism and dissatisfaction.[48] This suggests that the survey is tapping a specifically political feeling rather than a general social *malaise*; the political ideals against which the system is found wanting and the nature of the reforms which the dissatisfied feel will meet their complaints should then throw further light on its meaning.

There are no matching questions on assessments and ideals from which to calculate an index of discrepancy, but several questions are phrased in such a way that their answers can be taken as implying discrepancy between reality and idealism.[49] The report constructs from these an index of 'Powerlessness in the face of government' which clearly measures evaluations of the system and not of the respondent's personal capability;[50] thus it presents a view of what the system should be, as well as a statement of what it is actually perceived to be. Figure 1 shows that feelings of powerlessness predominated in the sample.

Powerlessness proved to be somewhat stronger among the young,

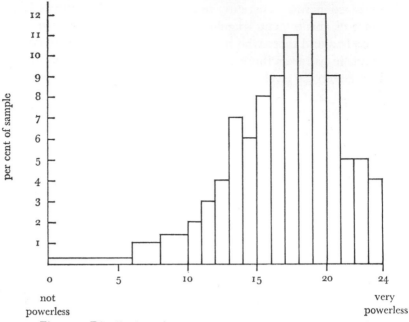

Figure 1. Distribution of powerlessness in the Kilbrandon sample

the less educated and the working class.[51] But its most interesting relationship was with the feeling of dissatisfaction with the system of governing Britain, summarised in Table 20. This relationship is the essence of distrust: those who were dissatisfied with the system of governing Britain were also those who felt that it was not meeting their standards of openness and accessibility – that government was secretive and unresponsive to the people and their representatives. The

Table 20. *Dissatisfaction in Britain with how things are run, by feeling of powerlessness in the face of government* *

	Total	Very powerless	Fairly powerless	Not really powerless	Not at all powerless
Weighted base: all informants	(4,892)	(1,125)	(1,588)	(1,107)	(1,072)
Dissatisfaction with the way things are run:					
Dissatisfied	38%	51%	38%	34%	28%
Fairly satisfied	33%	30%	33%	34%	34%
Very satisfied	29%	19%	29%	32%	38%

* *Source:* Kilbrandon Commission, *Research Papers* 7, p. 21.

dissatisfaction was not just a diffuse feeling of discontent but was derived from the perception of a gulf between government as it is and government as it should be.

The presence of distrust is clear; its content and rationality remain to be examined. The evidence is severely limited on these points by the narrowness of the brief given by the Kilbrandon Commission; it asked only about participation, responsiveness and secrecy, not about other related aspects of criticism, such as corruption, bias and elitism.[52] The strongest agreement with statements in the powerlessness scale was to two items on communication: 'The council should take more notice of the views of the people who live in the area' (73 per cent Strongly agree), and 'It's too difficult for ordinary people to make their views known to the government about things that affect them' (52 per cent Strongly agree).[53] From these two figures the report deduces that: 'What people seem to be feeling a need for is not simply more opportunity to make their views known to those in government (important though that is); the man in the street considers that his rulers should be more positively concerned to know what his problems and views are.'[54] This conclusion, however, reads a proposal into what is actually only a critical statement; there is no logical reason, though there is a cultural reason in the harmony of this suggestion with traditional parliamentary democracy, why the solution to a felt lack of communication should be greater attentiveness by the rulers rather than greater direct participation by the ruled. That the former alternative is what the respondents actually had in mind is not so obvious from the suggestions for reforms which they endorsed.

There was widespread concern not only for better communication by the government but for more participation within the decision-making process. The official report chose to give only the former attention; its interest is justified by the endorsement by 57 per cent of the sample of the proposal 'for the government to take more trouble to understand the region's special needs'.[55] But its neglect of the demand for participation is not justified. For example, 50 per cent endorsed a proposal 'to allow each Member of Parliament to have more influence over what the government does in the region'. In the light of other replies this actually implies greater involvement of citizens, for MPs, unlike councils and civil servants, are seen as responsive and accessible to popular views and as having too little power over government decisions.[56] The official report also plays down the importance of substantial numbers thinking that there should be more opportunity for ordinary people to get on to the council.[57] Furthermore, the general endorsement of greater devolution of government power to regional authorities was not only on the grounds of efficiency, but also because it would make greater participation in decisions possible to the citizen: 81 per cent agreed that 'the needs of the people would be looked after much better' and 76 per cent that 'the ordinary man could have more say in deciding what is done in the region'.[58]

A memorandum of dissent by Lord Crowther-Hunt and Professor Alan Peacock took issue with the main report: 'The combined evidence of our witnesses and various surveys of public opinion reveal a widespread and grave disquiet about our system of government today.'[59] Its further analysis of the Commission's survey concentrated on 'whether or not there was a frustrated demand for greater participation in the processes of government'.[60] The dissenters concluded that the sentiments of the 'powerless' group of respondents were much more subtle than a simple feeling that they were not being kept informed: the survey, they suggested, showed a 'widespread and justifiable belief that the country is becoming less democratic, that we the people, have not enough say in, and influence on government, that we have too little power in the face of government and that the government has become too centralised and congested'.[61]

The powerless, who I have identified in this case as the distrustful, had a coherent analysis of political failings rather than a gut feeling of discontent. This is confirmed by the findings of the report that their support for solutions to the problem of both secrecy and unresponsiveness was stronger than the average, just as was their discontent.[62] Both the powerless and those dissatisfied with 'the way things are run' wanted to see more extensive changes in the political system than did the contented in both categories.[63] And when the indices of powerlessness and dissatisfaction are combined, giving categories from those satisfied on both counts to those both dissatisfied and feeling powerless, there is a steady matching increase in the numbers endorsing the radical proposals of almost or complete devolution – only 27 per cent of the contented against 55 per cent of the distrustful.[64] It is true that this latter group are only about 11 per cent of the total (570 out of 4,892). But in national terms this is a sizeable number of people who both feel deeply discontented with the current operation of their political system and perceive a radical solution, which they expect to increase both their policy satisfaction and the achievement of a level of direct participation nearer their own ideal.

The consequences of the presence of this disaffection in British politics will depend upon two factors: the likelihood of the distrustful taking action and the response of the government. It is, of course, entirely possible that the distrustful will confine their activities to grumbling to their neighbours, or to passing interviewers, or that the government will conclude that nothing need be done.

There is some evidence in the past political behaviour of the distrustful group on the first point, for those who have already been active are more likely to be so again. 79 per cent of the entire sample claimed to have voted in the recent General Election; the non-voters' reasons for staying away from the polls were principally very practical ones, though a total of 9 per cent of the sample gave reasons such as 'None of them is any good so why bother' which suggest disaffection from the current political system.[65] Table 21 shows the relationship of

Table 21. *Index of interest and involvement by index of dissatisfaction in Britain**

	Total	Very satisfied	Fairly satisfied	Not very satisfied
Weighted base: all informants	(4,892)	(1,425)	(1,609)	(1,858)
'Very' and 'fairly' informed	50%	48%	50%	53%
'Not much' and 'Not at all' involved	50%	52%	50%	47%

* *Source:* Kilbrandon Commission, *Research Papers 7*, p. 8.

expressed interest and involvement in politics with dissatisfaction. The official report concluded that this 'indicates that the kind of dissatisfaction and feeling for change in the way things are run that we measured does not necessarily lead on to interest and involvement in political and community affairs but can be associated with a completely passive and uninterested attitude'.[66] It can indeed, but this table shows that while there is only a slight relationship, it is in the direction of a *positive* association between dissatisfaction and interest and involvement. The assumption of the direction of causation is also unwarranted – it is as possible that disaffection follows from greater involvement as the reverse. The evidence also suggests that a substantial number, perhaps about half, of the 55 per cent who are dissatisfied with the political system, have some past experience of political action – thus some at least of the distrustful may be considered to have a higher than average propensity to take political action in pursuit of political change.

Predicting future action is a hazardous business, but one of the more reliable indicators has been an individual's sense of political self-confidence or of his own efficacy. The definition of efficacy in the Kilbrandon survey requires an extraordinarily high standard of the citizen, namely that he feels capable of doing the job of a local councillor.[67] There is obviously a vast difference between feeling confident of one's ability as a citizen and as a representative, and the conclusion that 'the majority of the sample had a rather low level of confidence in their political capability' seems rather unkind, and hardly to do justice to the facts.[68] As the Minority Report points out:

> It is worth noting that 26 per cent thought they could do as good a job as the average councillor...But in absolute numbers, 'only a quarter' represents about 10 million people aged 18 and over. And when this is set against the fact that...there are less than 25,000 councillors...then those who believe they could do as good a job as a local councillor are far in excess of the opportunities available.[69]

This quarter of the sample tended to be more highly educated than the average and more comprehending of the issues touched upon by the questionnaire – attributes offering hope that those who may act may act appropriately.[70]

However, the survey finds no relationship between efficacy and dissatisfaction:

> This means that someone who feels that he himself would not be capable of understanding and coping with the problems that those in government deal with does not *necessarily* feel that the ordinary man's views and needs are insufficiently taken into account by those in government, though they may do.[71]

While those who had specific grievances against government bodies and felt politically effective had in the past taken action more often than the average, those who felt generally powerless or dissatisfied and effective had taken action no more often than the average.[72] Thus the distrustful demonstrate no overwhelming propensity to action; but it has not been demonstrated that they will not act. It is possible that there may be a concealed relationship in this data of the type found in the Rosenbaum sample: there the mean concealed the fact that the highly distrustful had a greater than average propensity to act and the remainder of the distrustful a lower propensity. Given that the highly distrustful in the Kilbrandon sample share with the Rosenbaum sample the characteristics of greater past involvement, higher education and greater comprehension of the problems, it seems probable that there is a sizeable group who feel strongly and have the expertise and motivation to do something about their discontent. That their discontent and their solutions are logically related is recognised by the survey report itself:

> The picture that emerges is one that seems to begin to make a pattern; those who are dissatisfied with the way things are run at present, who feel that the views of people like themselves are ignored and who are concerned and interested in political and community affairs are those who show most interest in devolution to more regional responsibility. But whereas those who are particularly involved in political and community activity are interested in a moderate degree of change, those who feel dissatisfied with the way things are run and those who feel powerless in the face of government tend to choose the more extreme options.[73]

What kind of action they will take must remain an open question. The final alarm of the Minority Report seems uncalled for, on the basis of the evidence at hand:

> In any event, the resulting sense of powerlessness contributes to the growing alienation from our peaceful, constitutional political processes. The danger is that this will push us along the road to direct action – possibly violent action – when people and groups believe they have no other alternative to secure what they feel are their just demands; there is already obvious evidence that this is the road we are beginning to travel.[74]

The evidence of this survey suggests that people want more say in the democratic process and more devolution of power to the level at which they feel some confidence of obtaining access to the making of decisions. The direct action by students and unions which presumably contributed to this gloomy forecast may or may not have been generated by the distrustful. The declining electoral turnout, which the minority memorandum emphasised, has been reversed in the two elections of 1974 and the referendum of 1975.[75] When people are concerned, they vote. At any rate, it seems more plausible to question whether those who want more democracy and are committed to participation are likely, except in the last resort, to turn to undemocratic processes to gain their point. There is nothing in this survey to suggest that the last resort has been reached.

The dissatisfaction revealed is not, though, what the report described as 'part of the ebb and flow of politics' – discontent with the government of the day and with specific policies or actions taken by that government. It is disaffection which may well have been generated by such complaints, but has escalated to a more abstract concern with the ways in which policies are determined and implemented – with the nature of democratic government. It is thus less easily satisfied, but still the evidence suggests that change need not be too radical; the demand is for more participation but the most extreme solutions were rejected by a majority of the sample, and notably by the better informed and involved among them. Indeed, there was fear of too radical a change, on the grounds that it might diminish the benefits received from government. Concern with outputs seems to lie not far below the democratic critique of these citizens. Only 10 per cent wanted devolution if it meant that people would actually be worse off, and, while 48 per cent wanted to see regional decisions taken by people elected locally, a close 45 per cent preferred people appointed for their special expertise.[76]

For people in power, the dilemma is how best to decide whether a 55 per cent rate of dissatisfaction is serious and whether it suggests a desire for extensive reform or a cautious wish for change provided it comes without cost. The alternative interpretations of the dissenting memorandum and the official report confirm the point that a survey which is neither longitudinal nor comparative offers no grounds for making such decisions. The dissent does indeed acknowledge this, adding a small amount of trend data before reaching the conclusion that the evidence is disquieting and does demand action:

> It is therefore, crucial to the health of the body politic that we should provide the institutional changes...If we believe in democracy, this must mean seeking to involve more people in the governmental and political process...It must mean, too, providing adequate means for the redress of individual grievances...we must also seek to devise means of lightening the load on our central institution of government...If any believe that the 'communications gap' can be bridged by exhortation alone, and without institutional change, then they show a touching faith in the natural behaviour of governments which flies in the face of all historical and contemporary evidence.[77]

The conclusions of the main report are rather different. They are justified in their conclusion that: 'Whatever its precise nature and strength may be, the desire for increased participation and communication has not yet crystallised into general support for a particular set of constitutional proposals.'[78] But they are patronising, and also inaccurate in their identification of discontent as primarily concerned with outputs:

The wishes of the people are the most important consideration to be taken into account. As we noted in our discussion of alleged defects, most people understandably have no very clear idea of the changes needed to remedy them. They expect certain results from government. If their expectations are not met they complain. . .But the basic structure of government is largely taken for granted. When things go wrong the pressure is for a new government rather than for a change in the system. And many of those who do favour some kind of constitutional reform tend not to have thought out very carefully the changes they would like to see.[79]

Given the attitude that the discontent is rather superficial and ignorant, it is not surprising that their recommendation was so much less drastic than that of the dissenters:

The principle of democracy – government by the people – must be preserved and fostered; elected representatives of the people must have real control. Where day-to-day control is impracticable, there should be a chain of accountability leading back to the elected representatives.[80]

This is indeed a modest notion of government by the people; whether it is an adequate one to satisfy the British people is an unresolved but crucial question.

The survey commissioned by the United States Senate raises many of the same problems. It opened with a finding of similar levels of general dissatisfaction to those in Britain: 55 per cent of the sample felt 'alienated and powerless', a steep rise from a level of only 29 per cent in 1966. Table 22 analyses the content of this discontent; while it does

Table 22. *Trend in alienation and powerlessness felt by the American people**

	1973	1972	1971	1968	1966	Change 1966–73
Agree with statement						
The rich get rich and the poor get poorer	76%	68%	62%	54%	45%	+31
What you think doesn't count much anymore	61%	53%	44%	42%	37%	+24
People running the country don't really care what happens to you	55%	50%	41%	36%	26%	+29
Feel left out of things going on around you	29%	25%	20%	12%	9%	+20
Average feeling alienated and powerless	55%	49%	42%	36%	29%	+26

* *Source:* US Senate, *Confidence and Concern,* I, p. 30.

not only measure political feelings, it does suggest that these were people who wanted more than economic equality. They wanted attention given to their views, involvement in government and responsiveness from it – a different standard of democratic government from that which they saw being practised. This feeling was remarkably evenly distributed over races, religions, age groups and educational levels, with the single exception that the college-educated felt less powerless on each of the items – a reversal of the British pattern which might have significance for the consequences of distrust.[81] The combination of dissatisfaction with a sense of failure in terms of political norms is borne out by further evidence in the report, picturesquely summarised: 'In the forest of the disenchanted, there are actually sturdy trees of faith and traditional trust. Americans who evidence doubt about the quality of both life and political leadership nonetheless believe strongly that government can work and should continue an active, innovative role in society.'[82]

Why then are so many discontented and what specific norms and violations do they identify? It is clear that, in America too, political distrust originated in policy or output discontent. Those who felt that the quality of life in the last decade had improved held strongly positive attitudes to the government.[83] But it was more than a grumble about benefits missed, for there is evidence here of a critical analysis of the way that benefits are allocated and decisions reached.

There is, first, criticism directed against the incumbents of political positions. The survey asked two matched sets of questions, appraising the actual qualities of elected officials and asking what qualities those in government should have. In Table 23, constructed from the replies, the larger the discrepancy figure the greater the perception of distance between ideal and reality; the ranked order is by the size of the discrepancy while the percentage mentioning each item suggests which were of the most widespread concern. That the widest gulf concerns the honesty of politicians may perhaps be explained by the fact that the survey was taken in June, 1973, in the thick of the televised Senate Watergate hearings. But the most frequently mentioned critical qualities cannot be explained away so easily – that promises are made but broken and that politicians are out for themselves. Evidently much would be achieved by having a different kind of man in office and indeed 40 per cent of the respondents assented to this suggestion for making the government work better.[84]

But disaffection was directed beyond incumbents, to the structures of government also: 48 per cent preferred the suggested alternative road to improvement, namely 'should tight checks be set up by legislators, courts and citizen groups to watch government closely?'[85] And though 40 per cent thought that electing good or honest leaders would improve matters, this was not a call for the politics of personality — for a leader to set the world to rights. For far fewer, only 27 per cent,

Table 23. *Qualities which best describe actual and ideal elected American officials**

Quality	Actual	Ideal	Discrepancy
Honest	13	66	53
Make promises that are never kept	42	0	42
Dedicated to hard work	22	56	34
Out for themselves	29	1	28
Want to help people	25	51	26
Courageous	12	35	23
Only want power	22	1	21
Tell it like it is	3	23	20
Efficient	8	24	16
Corrupt	17	1	16
Bureaucratic	16	1	15
Intelligent, bright	27	41	14
Care about freedom	14	28	14
Play it safe	15	2	13
Creative, imaginative	2	12	10
Making red tape	11	1	10

* *Source:* Extracted from US Senate, *Confidence and Concern,* 1, pp. 307 and 311.

thought that if good leaders were elected the institution of further checks would then be unnecessary.[86] Structural reform was regarded as essential as well, on the principle of checks and balances, particularly to ensure greater responsiveness of the government to its citizens.[87]

The main criticisms of the structures of government were summarised by the comment of a store owner in Ashland, Kentucky: 'People now want some changes made, but nothing good comes out. The laws are all written for the rich and the people who know the right people.'[88] Government here means the federal government; though confidence in state and local government was also found to have declined in recent years the withdrawal of support was relatively slight. This difference cannot be written off as simply another reaction to Watergate, since people proved shrewd and accurate at assigning blame for different problems to the appropriate branch of government and found federal government failing on a range of accurately attributed responsibilities.[89]

The Senate report contains a discrepancy index based on questions which listed a series of attributes and asked first whether the federal government possessed them and then whether their attainment was believed possible.[90] Table 24 reports the discrepancies perceived, the

Table 24. *Attributes the American public and leaders feel the federal government lacks today and the possibility of having them**

	Gap: Realities below Ideals	
	Public	Leaders
Leaders genuinely working for peace	−32	−15
Public officials really care about the people	−54	−35
Most public officials dedicated to helping the country	−50	−33
The good of the country is placed above special interests	−61	−61
Government is the most exciting place to work	−50	−36
The best people are attracted to serve in public life	−63	−65
Leaders come up with solutions to inflation that work	−69	−68
Corruption and payoffs almost never take place	−52	−43

* *Source*, US Senate, *Confidence and Concern*, i, p. 142.

negative figures indicating in every case that actual conditions are seen as falling short of possible conditions. The leaders, a sample of elected officials from every level of government, show a somewhat different pattern of responses from that of the general public, tending to acknowledge the existence of problems but to regard them less seriously. Fewer leaders felt that there was something deeply wrong in America and more (52 per cent compared with 37 per cent of the public) were prepared to regard the current state of affairs as quite normal;[91] their reasons were different too – both groups agreed that there were too many corrupt leaders but, for the rest, the leaders placed heavy emphasis on the apathy of the people or even their moral decline, a lack of respect for social institutions, and the belief that crises are inherent in a democracy.[92] This gap between assessments was supported by their general view of the last decade, for 61 per cent of the leaders thought that the quality of life had improved and only 20 per cent that it had deteriorated, against 35 per cent and 45 per cent respectively of the public.[93]

These differences are significant for the likelihood of action on the part of both government and citizens. The leaders did recognise the existence of discontent, but clearly regarded it as far less serious than did the citizens; it is then less likely that they will feel it necessary to take action – particularly since they put so much of the blame on the public. They, more than the public, believed that the solution was to 'put the right people in and trust them', and they were more sceptical about the necessity and the effectiveness of checks and scrutiny, believing that most officials were more knowledgeable than the public anyway and that 'checking is ineffective'.[94] But as the report concluded, in a passage of comment: 'Given the public mood against secrecy and the powerful desire on the part of the public to share in governmental decision-making, leaders will have a hard time taking such a case to the American people in today's climate.'[95] On the other hand, effective public action may well be inhibited by the same problem noted in Britain – that public opinion has not crystallised around any particular solution. In their answers to an open-ended question, those who had identified the state of politics as a serious social problem were unable to produce any very clear remedy: most agreement was on the need for stricter laws against corruption in government and on campaign finance, a substantial number suggested electing officials who care, and some without being more specific as to how, suggested that people should participate more.[96]

One of the weakest parts of the survey is the attempt to meet the brief from the Senate of exploring 'ways to increase the responsiveness and efficiency of government at all levels'.[97] The two solutions to dissatisfaction with incumbents were precise if limited, but suggestions offered by the survey on structural reform were broad and general, and indeed calculated to produce confusing results. Presented with a list of statements which mixed fact, evaluation and proposals for change all together, the people responded with a thoroughly confused and contradictory set of answers.[98] On the face of it, it is hard to reconcile the 89 per cent who agreed that 'the federal government represents all people of the country so it should handle the important matters' with the 74 per cent who agreed that 'Each state in the country has different people with different needs, so it is mainly the states that should decide what government programs ought to be started and continued.' It seems plausible that there was a distinction in the minds of the respondents between general problems like inflation and specific programmes such as welfare, but this is not self-evident from the replies. This difficulty was well demonstrated by the report itself, when it tried to reconcile the substantial numbers supporting devolution of power with the 67 per cent agreeing that 'It's about time we had a strong federal government again to get this country moving again.' A footnote to the analysis suggested: 'It should be recognised that "strong" may well be interpreted to reflect trustworthiness and sense of purpose, rather than added legal and programmatic authority.'[99] This may be so, but there is no way of telling what were the respondents' intentions.

Whatever the aims, though, the methods for changing modes of government would be constitutional: a resounding 94 per cent of the whole sample would first try voting.[100] The next preferences were either to get together with neighbours, friends or civic groups or to write to elected officials; only a tiny minority (27 per cent, predominantly young and upper-income respondents) would either demonstrate or 'take aggressive action'. These figures, however, all refer to the whole of the sample; the published data tables do not include separate analysis for the distrustful; one can make only the loosest estimate of their propensity to act, based upon the fact that they are fairly evenly spread across all categories of the electorate. The few direct indicators of likely action show little variation from previous studies of participation in America. While 94 per cent declare they would vote, only 73 per cent claim that they had voted in the 1972 presidential election, and only 57 per cent in the 1970 Congressional elections – figures which are themselves higher than the actual turnout.[101] The highest figure for other forms of participation was the 69 per cent who had at some time signed a petition; only 33 per cent had ever written to their Congressman or contributed to a political party.[102] The only evidence on efficacy is that 40 per cent rated themselves positively on 'how up to date they are on what is going on in the federal government in Washington'.[103] The figures all suggest that there has been no change in the incidence in the electorate of those attributes ordinarily held to predict levels of action – thus if many of the distrustful are to take action on their grievances it will have to be generated by the unusual intensity of their feelings. The survey does suggest, in the few tables which present some trend data, that this intensity had increased over the last decade; at what point it becomes profound enough to generate action remains unknown.

The United States sample had been more active in the past and had higher scores on the various predictive variables of political action than the British. Despite the relatively similar expression of distrust, one might then guess that action would be more likely to occur in America.

One further suggestion of this possibility is found in the Senate report: the Americans have high optimism about the possibility of achieving a reformed and effective government, and, on the basis of recent experience, of the possibility of reaching this ideal through citizen action. 58 per cent of the sample believed that they could do something to change the present situation, and 86 per cent believed that the federal government could be run well.[104] 49 per cent thought that there had been a gain in the influence of citizen groups over the government in the last five years, against only 8 per cent who saw a loss.[105] This finding does not contradict the general complaint of the unresponsiveness of government: 'Yet those who feel real confidence in the impact of citizen groups do not credit government with responsiveness so much as they say the people themselves are demanding to be heard.'[106] Despite their reluctance to demonstrate, they saw the most shining example of this in the success of the civil rights movement; 67 per cent believed that marches headed by Dr Martin Luther King had been effective in obtaining legislation and obtaining it sooner.[107] There is no such optimism in the British findings, only a rather modest feeling among 40 per cent that some groups would benefit from devolution, though 68 per cent felt that they themselves would not.[108] And although one of the arguments made for devolution was that it would increase popular participation, this seems to have been a secondary consideration; only 10 per cent would want devolution if they were thus to be made worse off. As the Kilbrandon report concluded: 'These results suggest that devolution is seen by the majority of those in favour as a solution to *practical* problems rather than as something desired for its own sake.'[109] There may be a suggestion here of a more pragmatic approach to democratic government in Britain than in America – but perhaps this is stretching the data too far.

Stretching the data too far is the danger in using both of these surveys. The Senate survey particularly does not provide the kind of detailed analysis of the inter-relationships between attitudes which would allow deductions about intensity, consistency, activism and radicalism. Some basic facts have been established. The incidence of expressed distrust in both countries hovers around half the population and is not too different from that uncovered by Rosenbaum; there, on a general measure, 52 per cent in Britain, 40 per cent in America expressed dissatisfaction with government. In general confirmation of Rosenbaum's findings, critical attitudes were widely dispersed across the population, appeared to have been generated by policy discontent and to have escalated into a critique of the incumbents and structures of politics, and gave in the American case much greater attention to the incumbents than was found in Britain. In neither case was there any indication that the critique had been taken a step further, to the rejection of the norms of democratic government; the details of criticism and of proposals for reform seem consistent with each other and are made within a framework of democratic standards.

Neither survey offers direct evidence on whether the distrustful are likely to act on their complaints. They clearly do not possess in greater than average proportions any of the qualities which have generally been found to predispose people to political action. But there is one imponderable here, which cannot be answered from the surveys, namely to what extent the possession of distrustful attitudes may itself be an attribute capable of generating political action. If we deduce, for the moment simply from the fact that both governments have found it necessary for the first time to investigate its presence in their politics, that distrust has been on the increase, then it may well be that a new situation has been created in which intensifying discontent may override previous inhibitions and stimulate action.

Finally these surveys reveal in both countries a substantial gulf between the assessments of leaders and of the public. In Britain this was implicit in the differences between the raw figures of discontent and the rather complacent conclusions of the main report; in America it is made explicit through the parallel surveys of leaders and citizens. And the introductory comments of Senators Muskie and Gurney provide little hope of the feelings of the distrustful receiving more serious attention than they did from the Kilbrandon Commission. They respond ambiguously that the report is 'both encouraging, and, to professional public servants, depressing'.[110] Their only recommendation is that their committee continue its ten-year search for responsiveness and efficiency in government in the knowledge that 'the people also display a concern for community that can only be mobilized by leadership that welcomes citizen participation and trusts the people with the truth'.[111]

The limitations of survey evidence have become obvious during this analysis. It has proved possible to clarify, elaborate and frequently correct the description of political distrust provided by Dennis and his colleagues. It has not been possible to confirm or reject the contentious series of interpretative statements which formed their conclusion.

Whether 'in a brief span' a century of 'remarkable progress and steady evolution' has been shattered by 'forces of rapid transformation' remains unknown. That a 'homogeneous political culture' exists today appears doubtful; at least the reactions of public and leaders appear to differ enough to support a theory of political stratification. Whether it existed in the past either remains unknown. That Britain is still, if it was ever, characterised by 'a wide public regard for strong government', seems disproven by the widespread desire for more participation by ordinary people. But what the consequence of all this for 'the continuity of the system' may be remains uncertain.

Polls taken at a single time allow one only to describe the incidence and examine the meaning of distrust at that time. The evidence here suggests that as many as half the population of both Britain and the United States were critical of the way their governments operated in the early 1970s, and that they had matched the current situation against their notions of how good government should proceed, to identify specific inadequacies. It finds governments far more complacent than citizens, more prone to shrug off the complaints as the product of ignorance in Britain and to justify the situation by pointing to results in America. The evidence does allow comparison between the two nations. Disaffection seems more serious in Britain, in that it involves a questioning of institutions whose form is derived from the premises of traditional parliamentary sovereignty, in the name of principles of popular sovereignty. In the United States, the understanding of democracy which originally gave shape to the institutions also informs the criticisms of the distrustful; their specific complaints are mainly concerned with failures of administration and personnel within an accepted institutional context.

The evidence also provides some interesting lines of speculation about the consequences of this situation for the polities of Britain and America. Had we a verified theory of the relation between political attitudes and actions, and of the relative weight of attitudes against other causal factors of political action, some cautious prediction might even be in order. Lacking such a comprehensive framework, the indications for the future are slight and contradictory.

The skills which have usually been associated with political action (high educational levels, political self-confidence, past experience of organisational and political involvement for example) are not possessed by the distrustful to a greater degree than by the population in general. The record of populations in general for initiating effective political action is poor: on this basis one might expect political distrust to have little impact. But the distrustful do include a proportion of highly qualified potential participants, of the kind who, in recent years and in both countries, have broken out of conventional two-party politics without entirely rejecting the conventions of Anglo-American democracy. Such, for example, have been the growing number of independent and third party voters, the supporters of citizens' lobbies and idealistic pressure groups, demonstrators, direct action and community politics proponents.

Recent studies of the causes of political distrust in the United States have found it to be rooted in grievances over policies and outputs.[112] But the content of these grievances splits the distrustful into factional groups, with a tendency to polarise into 'cynics of the right' and 'cynics of the left'. Again, one might expect, and analysis of the 1972 presidential election is beginning to support the expectation, that political distrust may not provide the necessary unity for effective political action.[113] On the other hand, the 1972 election offered a clear choice on a range of issues which particularly polarised the distrustful; in the 1976 presidential election both candidates attempted to appeal across electoral divisions to the shared distrustfulness. There are necessarily two sides to the generation of effective political action by the populace – the attributes of that populace and the structuring of the situation by those with the power so to do. To the extent that the latter give public attention to the concerns of the distrustful the possibility of unified action from their side is enhanced, although the necessity for it and their sense of urgency may be weakened.

The conventional indicators of political participation give contrary signals about the probable consequences of political distrust. The point is that the presence of political distrust itself may change the expected patterns of cause and effect. The data reported in Table 16, for example, suggest the possibility of intense distrust providing an independent motivation to action; but none of these surveys throws any light on the conditions under which such an effect may be expected. It is too soon for the lessons of the current situation to have become apparent – but some understanding of the significance of political distrust may still be possible if there have been comparable situations in the past.

It has already become apparent that our knowledge of the past history of political distrust is scanty, but that the conventional wisdoms of a continuous presence in America contrasted with its absence in

Britain may be in need of correction. Survey research in the United States, for all its conceptual weaknesses, does indicate the presence of political distrust since at least the 1950s, but with significant changes in both the numbers of people expressing it and the social and political attributes of the distrustful.[114] Earlier empirical studies convey the same picture, though less comprehensively, from the 1920s, and both contemporary observers and historians provide scattered observations of distrust all the way back to the foundation of the republic.[115] In Britain, occasional opinion polls from the 1940s onwards indicate that distrustful feelings have been a long-term feature here too, with an incidence not too far below the levels found today.[116] Impressionistic studies, particularly of the working class, suggest that political distrust may have been a well-established cultural tradition:

> 'E's a real politician alright', they say, meaning that he is 'all talk and no do', and that 'such as 'im never really do owt for people like us'. Again, many of these are very old cries, and natural to working-people; but they are used very frequently today, and used with the flat assurance that it is the same all over, and in all parts of life.

These sentiments were recorded by Richard Hoggart in the 1950s, with the comment that they derived from the perception of 'a gulf between publicly professed morality and the reality'.[117]

The presence of political distrust is evidently not a new factor in either polity. The evidence may then be available with which to refine an estimate of likely consequences and to support the kind of general statements about historical trends, change and crisis which Dennis attempted on the basis of unverified assumptions. Statements of historical change are obviously nonsense without historical evidence; and, in addition, evaluations (as opposed to descriptions) of the present and predictions of the future are groundless unless they are rooted in an understanding of the historical context.

It would be unduly ambitious to attempt a complete history of political distrust in both polities here. My next two chapters will offer case studies of single episodes in nineteenth-century political culture: of Populism in Kansas in its formative months in 1890 and of Radical Liberalism in Birmingham in 1883 and 1884. Each was an episode in which the public rhetoric was uncannily similar to much that has been heard of late, sharing the features of a critique of government and a demand for changes in its operation that would enhance the popular role in the making of decisions. In both cases claims were made of the loss of political rights, indeed of the loss of democratic rights; the public noise in each period seems to offer clear signs of the presence of what I have defined as political distrust, and of an identifiable public following associated with its expression. Whether these superficial impressions are accurate will be a major part of my enquiry, which will attempt to discover to what extent there was authentic public discontent behind the headlines in these periods, what were the norms and criticisms of these citizens, and what, if anything, they did about them. No case study provides a conclusive basis for generalisation; they are too vulnerable to criticisms about their choice and to the production of alternative cases. This is particularly so here, where I have chosen them not for their typicality (given the present state of our knowledge what is typical is unknown) but for the sharpness with which they present the attitudes and behaviour which interest me. They are, then, not intended to indicate the whole history of political distrust in these two countries, but to examine with the completeness that is not possible for present day events what have been the meaning and consequences of political distrust and what significance historical cases might have for the understanding of the present.

3. Grass roots politics in Kansas

Interpretations of Populism

Modern survey data have reinforced the impressions of observers of the American political scene, that political distrust has been a recurrent and maybe a permanent feature of the history of the republic. Indeed, this might be expected, for by the late eighteenth century a cultural environment was fast developing which positively encouraged the expression of such political criticism. In political theory a distinctive American view diverged from the common path of Anglo-American radicalism. In everyday behaviour marks of deference to social distinctions and of automatic respect for position vanished from language and manners.

The new political theory developed in a cumulation of individually insignificant steps, fed from a variety of sources. Its intellectual sponsors included the radicalism of Commonwealth England and the rationalism of the Enlightenment. From direct observation came the intense determination to avoid such corruption of society and infringement of liberty as was perceived in contemporary England, and also the recognition that the social structure of the new world presented a political problem as well as an opportunity: that the exercise of power could not here be controlled in the way that British practice assumed, by the automatically countervailing powers of the estates of the realm, since such remnants of feudal social structure had been entirely left behind. By far the most important innovation was the expansion of the concept of popular sovereignty from the rather modest intention of predecessors such as Locke; this, together with the misgivings which followed about its likely consequences in practice, provides the root source of the endemic strain of political distrust in America.

The American theory of popular sovereignty had two central tenets. The first was that 'the people' should be continuously and directly involved in government, not simply a passive repository of sovereignty. The second was that the term 'the people' itself lost the ambiguity which had allowed an elitist interpretation before this time. It was now understood that it should embrace the whole (free, adult, male) population. Indeed it must in the American context, where no elite could claim either precedent or more than the most tenuous philosophical justification for self-perpetuation. To what extent and by what means these principles should be embodied in institutions was by no means a settled issue, and the new constitution for the United States reflected due caution in practice, but at least the premises of radical democracy were now placed firmly within the bounds of orthodox opinion.[1]

Popular sovereignty and the related abandonment of English 'virtual representation' in favour of mandated and closely controlled delegates have remained constants in American political culture. But so too have the misgivings of their early proponents. For the optimism of America's democratic ideals is underlain by the gravest doubts of the capacity of human nature to sustain democratic virtue: the triumph of reason over the passions of men, even given uniquely cooperative social conditions, has never been seen as assured. And this is of particular importance when no divine providence or self-correcting mechanism of social structure can be relied upon to intervene between human weakness and the polity. When the government is the people, who guards the guardians? The separation of power and an elaborate system of checks and balances against its usurpation may control the excesses of government, but, as Madison commented of the evil of faction, 'The inference to which we are brought is, that the *causes*. . .cannot be removed', since these lie in human nature.[2] Americans, it seems, have never wholeheartedly adopted the Enlightenment faith in the perfectibility of man; it is uneasily accompanied by a surviving Puritan perception of a permanent flaw in human nature which inevitably contaminates politics. Jimmy Carter is only the latest of many who have unthinkingly tried to absorb both positions in their observations upon American politics – with his optimism that a government returned to the people will reflect their essential decency, compassion and honesty, paradoxically coupled with a favourite quotation from Reinhold Niebuhr, that the 'sad duty of politics is to establish justice in a sinful world'.[3]

The first generation of independent Americans saw a possible solution in the removal, as far as possible, of the temptation to which men were so vulnerable. Their 'hostility to government' would be institutionalised as minimal government with narrowly circumscribed power; this should at least limit the potential scope of corruption, while a contrived system of checks and balances would deal with such lapses as would, no doubt, still occur. That solution, however, has become steadily less realistic as time has worn on and governmental functions have expanded, apparently inexorably. Neither greater familiarity through massive government involvement in the daily life of citizens nor major changes in the patterns of recruitment to politics and of political careers have effected any marked reversal of the initial suspicion of politics as a corrupting and degrading human experience.[4] Instead, two centuries of political experience have added a steady accumulation of evidence of human frailty to buttress public attitudes.

The problem is a deeper one than simply the control of corruption in the sense of criminal activity. What early theorists and the distrustful public have feared is the more profound temptation of power to override democratic norms and legislate with partiality or self-interest, or from any motive that makes the public interest a secondary consideration. Deprived of faith in a natural ruling class worthy of deference, deprived of hope of an automatic control in social structure, Americans have consistently criticised and suspected the operations of the political system which they claim simultaneously as their proudest national possession.

Nowhere in the history of American politics has the expression of this political distrust been more striking than in the Populist movement whose independent party, based in the agricultural regions of the west and south, and vehement demands disturbed the equilibrium of two-party politics between 1890 and 1896. If distrust has been endemic, its expression has not often risen above diffuse complaint about policy or clichés about politicians to the level of serious and widespread critical discussion of the norms of politics themselves. The Populists are an accessible and dramatic example of such fundamental questioning of politics and of the extension of discussion into action. However, this fact does not make them a special case, irrelevant to a more general understanding of American political culture. In my introduction I quoted evidence of political distrust in widely separated periods of American history: the Jacksonian era, the late nineteenth century, the New Deal. Each of these was a period of social upheaval and mounting dissent, with massive shifts eventually in political alignments and innovations in political behaviour. These periods have been linked by students of electoral history as similar moments of critical change in politics; it seems no accident, in the context of the dissent of the 1960s and the concurrent escalation of political distrust, that there has been speculation also of the imminence of another critical election.[5] At any rate, the Populists appear to be representatives of a regular pattern of politics in America, typical of those recurring moments when the permanent undercurrent of criticism surfaces and is articulated with some clarity and system.

On other grounds the Populists have been accused of more than being untypical in American politics: of standing altogether outside its tradition as radicals and extremists.[6] But, in fact, their rhetoric was notably unoriginal, borrowing its most striking slogans from the classic tradition of American democracy, their intellectual sources diverse (and often very inadequately absorbed) but not alien, and their solutions generally already in circulation in reformist circles. Despite the exaggerated figures that some individual Populists cut, they admirably illustrate the American pattern of distrustful attitudes towards democratic government. Democracy appeared as simultaneously their pride and hope and the focus of their scathing criticism. No more sincere theoretical adherents to its principles can be found (though their failings in the daily practice of the political arts do raise acutely the question of the relation of rhetoric to action). And they were profoundly aware of the old unresolved problem of human nature and its threat to political purity: their own daily experience of organisation and canvassing was a speedy road enough to disillusionment with the political virtues of the common man.

Similarly, it has been suggested from a sociological standpoint that the Populists stood outside the mainstream of the American community, as marginal men;[7] that they lived on the periphery of modern America in literal, geographic terms, but also economically in a newly urban and industrial society and culturally as the rearguard defendants of the values of a doomed agrarian world. Populism was indeed a sectional movement of the mid-west and south of the country, and many of its practical proposals were directed towards the restoration of the agrarian position in the economy. Neither of these facts invalidates their example as central exponents of the dominant political culture of the country. Indeed, one of the most frequent errors in the many attempts to find 'populism' in different historical periods, and even in different countries, has been the assumption that its essential nature comprises a whole complex of sociological and political characteristics; that along with a philosophy of popular government will inevitably be found (and here opinions differ) declining social status and conservative ideology.

The literature on the Populists at times descends to invective as bitter as that used by them. Passionate conceptual and historiographical controversies continue to rage, and any addition to the literature must be prefaced by a stand on crucial interpretations. Much of the emotion expended, as well as the variety of characteristics attributed to populism, may be explained by the fact that recent writing has often not been concerned with populism for its own sake, but has been using it as ally or as enemy in the analysis of current events. The political philosophy has survived; the objection to labelling this populism is simply that it may imply that the philosophy came into being only with the coining of the term in 1890. The political conditions which from time to time push people into both protest and reaffirmation of their political ideals have survived too. As C. Vann Woodward summarised it, in a comparison of recent years with 1890, they have been conditions arousing 'flashes of anger at injustice and neglect, disgust at private opulence and public squalor, indignation over fraud and bribery in government and corruption in high office, outrage over privilege of special interests and the arrogance of the rich'.[8] But the social base and the specific grievances and issues of the Populists of that period have no later parallels; nor is there any logical connection between the democratic philosophy and any particular programme. If such characteristics of the original Populists survive there is little evidence that they do so as a single complex of social attributes – as politicians who have tried to forge a new populist alliance have found to their cost.

Early accounts of the Populists were relatively neutral records of the movement; the interpretative conclusions of Hicks' classic account have not invalidated the main body of that work as the prime source of facts for all later schools of thought.[9] The first major interpretation of the movement came in the 1950s, from both social scientists and historians, much influenced by their experiences of McCarthyism. Although a specific link with political alienation was made only by Edward Shils, the intellectual background to both bodies of literature was the same. Thus in political science the identification of populism as a threat to American democracy was made from the same perspective of democratic elitism which found political alienation and anomie to be the products of illogic and ignorance.[10] Suspecting that the strength of contemporary McCarthyism lay in mass support, and noting some regional overlap between the two movements, Populism and McCarthyism were presented together as evidence of the inherent danger to democracy from mass involvement in politics. With the expectation that the ordinary citizen would be often authoritarian, incoherent in political principle and its application and apathetic about sustained and moderate participation, it is not surprising that the Populists were regarded with misgiving.

Given this estimate of the capacities of the ordinary citizen, the populist philosophy of participation was alarming. Furthermore, it was clearly incompatible with the institutional theory of democracy as a mechanism allowing intermittent opportunities for participation in elections only. The theorists of civic culture and institutional democracy thought that they had found the answer to the preservation of stable democracy, given the discovery that its greatest enemy was a large number of its own citizens. But by itself an academic redefinition of democracy is no answer at all – indeed it introduces a potentially explosive element into the situation unless and until it becomes the working consensus of the whole citizen body. For a somewhat incoherent understanding of the principles of democracy cannot, after all, be relied upon to result in apathy under all conditions. Where the norms of popular political culture still define democracy in a populist way there may be times when an elitist government is faced, not with a mass incursion of anti-democratic wreckers, but with an incursion of citizens claiming an extensive role by right. The norms of radical democracy have shown a powerful capacity to survive outside academic circles. To their proponents 'social mechanisms' and 'regular constitutional opportunities' may well seem indistinguishable from the system denounced by a rural Alliance chapter in Kansas, which declared 'against a government of politicians, by politicians and for politicians' and for 'a government of the people, by the people and for the people'.[11]

Meanwhile historians were reappraising the Populist movement, and here the work of Richard Hofstadter was the main influence. *The age of reform* was an important new account, but in it the Populists were accused of unprincipled pursuit of commercial advantage, and worse, of nativism, anti-semitism, jingoism and extreme susceptibility to conspiratorial theories of society.[12] Hofstadter effected a convergence with social science, not only by basing much of his argument upon concepts such as status deprivation but also by providing social scientists with the evidence, and himself claiming, that 'populist thinking has survived in our own time, partly as an undercurrent of provincial resentments, popular and "democratic" rebelliousness and suspiciousness, and nativism'.[13] Thence, in a two-way process of guilt by association, the Populists became early McCarthyites and the supporters of

McCarthy Populists. In cross-national comparisons both were even linked with the Nazis: 'In short', Victor Ferkiss concluded, 'Populist political thought is compatible in spirit with the plebiscitary democracy of a Huey Long or a Hitler.'[14]

The historians' reappraisal of Populism was promoted in part by the need for a fresh look at the origins of the movement. Classic accounts had used Turner's frontier thesis, arguing that the agrarian movements were channelling energy which earlier had been constructively released in the westward expansion of settlement. With the frontier thesis increasingly discredited, scholars seem to have avoided an obvious alternative explanation in the economic circumstances of agriculture in the late nineteenth century. In parallel to the transformation of the concepts of alienation and anomie from failings of social structure to psychological dysfunctions, explanations of Populism were offered in terms of status deprivation or of the cost in anxiety of modernisation or life in a peripheral social location.[15] By transferring the phenomenon to the minds of the Populists and the solution to psychological adjustment it was made easy to add irrationality to their sins. But the Populists themselves clearly recognised the primacy of economic problems among the causes of their woes. The trilogy of targets they attacked, of land, transportation and money, was close to the mark and the solutions they suggested not such obvious evidence of crankiness as some critics would have it.

Accepting that the prime cause of the Populist outburst, the motivation which pushed them into a fresh consideration and criticism of the functioning of politics, was a steady cumulation of the perception and experience of economic injustice does not devalue the importance and independence of culture. Economic and idealist explanations of social events need not be mutually exclusive or contradictory; in this case, as comparative analyses have shown, ideals and cultural expectations were crucial in shaping the way that the economic facts were understood, the forms which protest took and the solutions which were proposed.[16]

The question of whether the Populists looked forward or backward in their solutions was canvassed by the 'Hofstadter' school of the 1950s and taken up again by the revisionists of the 1960s. The Populists were first presented as backward looking agrarians, clinging to 'a sentimental attachment to rural living' – the agrarian myth whose political implications derived from the fact that 'its hero was the yeoman farmer, its central conception the notion that he is the ideal man and the ideal citizen'.[17] The alternative saw them as consistently radical, as Pollack's extreme counter-argument asserts. For Pollack, unequivocally, 'Populism was a progressive social force. It accepted industrial society, posed solutions not seeking to turn back the clock, and was strongly pro-labor.'[18]

But in seeking to define the Populists as consistent radicals or consistent reactionaries, an inappropriate standard is being imposed on them. Politically, the Populists were neither – as reformers they sought change, yet adhered to traditional social assumptions: 'for them there was innovation aplenty in the implementation of the nation's unfulfilled democratic ideals'.[19] But in the case of their substantive policy proposals, their ideas were clearly radical, though they were hardly the coherent if unintentional Marxists Pollack describes. A clear example of such radicalism is a point on which the Populists were among the first of the moderns. They did understand that they had to deal with a newly complex situation and they did not simply attempt the hopeless task of reinstating local community as a countervailing power. They recognised the need for big government to confront big organisation and their faith in it was almost utopian, at least until the disastrous experiences of the state administrations elected in 1892 doused their optimism. 'Hostility to government' was replaced by demands for a major broadening of its scope; minimal government was recognised to be no longer available as a way of protecting the purity of the democratic process. The Populists early faced the modern dilemma of the reconciliation of popular control with a complex government fulfilling many technical functions; they failed to solve the problem – even to consider it adequately – but they are of interest not just as last-ditch preservationists but as exemplars of the continuing attempt in American politics to mix old values and new functions.

The mixture of radical and reformist ideas propounded by the Populists no more justifies labelling them as confused or inconsistent than did the failure of ordinary citizens in the 1950s to match the academic definition of liberalism or conservativism justify the accusation of ideological incoherence. Indeed the same mixture of a conservative morality and a liberal economic programme seems to have been a persistent pattern among large numbers of the American electorate. A study identifying about a quarter of Americans in 1960 as simultaneously ideological conservatives and operational liberals questioned whether this cross-cutting of classic liberal and conservative positions might not have been a normal pattern historically. The authors quoted in support of this speculation Commager's conclusion of Americans in general: 'They clung to the vocabulary of laissez-faire, yet faithfully supplied the money and the personnel for vastly expanded governmental activities.'[20] Yet it still came as a surprise to some analysts of the support for George Wallace in the 1968 Presidential election to find the same pattern: 'The peculiarity of the Wallace voter is that there does not seem to be a convenient traditional pigeonhole in which to place him.'[21]

Rather than brand any of these groups as inconsistent or confused, a redefinition of consistency should be considered which will give them credit for a distinctive political outlook with its own coherence and considerable resilience in the face of changing circumstances. Such a move would do much to restore the tarnished image of the Populists; further, it would support the recent undermining of the 'scientific' argument for democratic elitism on the basis of evidence of political stratification into an intellectually coherent elite and a muddle-headed lower stratum.

Studies of Populism in the 1950s were primarily interested in finding historical support for their theories of the political potential of the masses, or rather of the threat to democratic politics from the masses. The weakness of these studies was not only in their insensitive attempts to categorise the Populists; they also paid small attention to the evidence, making biased selections from what little was already available, with no attempt to find new sources.

But the numerous studies of the last decade have made both methodological and substantive contributions.[22] The pendulum may sometimes have swung too far into uncritical adulation of the Populists in these studies, but in general the tone of the debate has been notably raised by their advances in methodology. In the absence of archives of the movement itself, scholars have made increasing use of those records which do allow a reconstruction of the historical experience of ordinary people: newspapers, census tabulations, land ownership records, occasional collections of correspondence.

Our knowledge of the Populist movement is now far more detailed; and with masses of new facts unearthed some earlier judgements have been overturned. The various prejudices of some Populists were not a feature which particularly distinguished them from the general population of the time. Their political opponents seem to have been as conspiracy-minded as they themselves, and to have attempted enthusiastically to smear the Populists as anarchists, communists, revolutionaries and agents of foreign governments. And the connection with McCarthyism has been shown to be unfounded, both in terms of social bases of support and of ideology. As a result, the Populists can now be treated as serious and rational participants in the American political process, whose ideas may not have been always coherent, consistent or practical but who were certainly not merely ignorant hayseeds motivated by prejudice, resentment or even psychological disorder. This does not require the equally extreme assumption that the Populists were all simple, selfless democrats or living models of the principles they preached. In fact, as a rejection of the earlier allegations against them remarked: 'The great majority of Populists were provincial, ill-educated and rural, but so were the great majority of Americans in the nineties, Republicans and Democrats as well.'[23] Then as now, it is not just patronising, but simply wrong to assume without further investigation that beliefs ill-expressed somehow betoken the absence of any sincere and motivating philosophy.

The political culture of Kansas

While scholars debate endlessly whether there is any single sociological phenomenon of 'populism' it is equally arguable whether there was even a single American movement of Populism, despite the national organisation which nominally brought the regions of south and west together. But although no state party was typical of the whole in every way, Kansas has claims as an example from which more general statements about the political principles of the movement can be made.

Kansas was always a leader in the Populist movement. It had a foot in both southern and northern camps through the affiliation of its Alliance with the Southern Alliance and its stance with the northern states on independent political action. It contributed a number of leaders to national Populism, but the state movement was never overshadowed by one man, as Nebraska came to be in the prolonged and ambivalent courtship with Bryan, or as Minnesota was by Donnelly. Kansas was the first to establish a People's Party. A convention assembled in Topeka on June 12, 1890, 'from the Farmers' Alliance and Industrial Union, the Patrons of Husbandry, the Farmers' Mutual Benefit Association, the Knights of Labor and single tax clubs', and: 'A resolution to place a full State, Congressional and county ticket in the field was carried by unanimous vote...The name "People's Party" is adopted as the title under which we will base our political action.'[24]

The Kansas People's Party was among the most successful – in 1890 it sent 91 representatives to the lower house of the State Legislature, five Congressmen to Washington and was able to force the election (by the State legislature) of Populist William A. Peffer, editor of the *Kansas Farmer*, as United States Senator. In 1892, in fusion with the Democrats, 48.44 per cent of the popular vote went to Weaver for President, and a Populist governor and state Senate were sworn in, amid much rejoicing of the faithful at the 'first People's Party administration on earth'.[25] The state was also regarded by contemporary Americans as a forward example of Populism. William Allen White's famous editorial, 'What's the Matter With Kansas', was widely reprinted and national disapproval well summed up by the comment that no new states were wanted till Kansas was civilised. Although there was an excited national interchange of ideas and there were many parallel developments in different states, the activities in Kansas cannot simply be explained away by the diffusion of examples from elsewhere, but must be credited with a good deal of spontaneity and originality.

While the sources available for Kansas are particularly good, they well demonstrate the difficulty of reaching to the grass roots of nineteenth-century political opinion. The Populists have left no national organisational records and few local ones; the predecessor organisation, the Farmers' Alliance, is little better.[26] The best records of both Alliance and Populism are in independent newspapers, where meetings were reported and policies publicly debated; here, fortunately, the sources available for Kansas are unparalleled. A local historian and booster extolled Kansas as the centre of inspiration and innovation for American journalism.[27] Certainly it had a prolific and lively local press and a number of serious papers with statewide circulations. Every small community in the 1890s seems to have had access to publications of diverse political affiliations, and in this largely agricultural state the press did much to weld together communities and break down the physical and social isolation which has sometimes been taken to account for the political eccentricity of Kansans, and which certainly inhibits anywhere the growth of group consciousness and effective political organisation.

Yet, for all this social importance, there are still problems in inferring grass roots opinion from the press. It is always a second best to direct statements from the people themselves. There is the question of the relation of editorial to readers' opinion. There are no independent data available to check this; even the correspondence columns seem largely to have been used by the leaders of political action, and the published letters no doubt were selected in line with any bias of the editorial staff. However, the gradual swing of opinion, from support of political action through the old parties or non-partisan Alliance tickets to support for a third party, as reflected in the reports of the resolutions sent in to the *Kansas Farmer* by local sub-alliances, seems to be roughly parallel with the swing of editorial opinion.[28] Who, if anyone, led and who followed is impossible to say, but there is confirmation of the congruence in the actions of the general public. They joined the Alliance in greater numbers in the midst of the political ferment – membership in Kansas rose from 100,000 in January 1890 to 140,000 in July – and they broke dramatically from the voting habits of thirty years in the November election.[29] Further, one may assume that the editors were well-known local personalities and opinion leaders in political matters, and also that the people, at a time of political excitement, were attentive to the press and tended to subscribe to papers whose views they endorsed.

Then there is the question of how far public utterances diverged from private feelings and practices. A certain amount of guesswork is involved here, too, since so little remains of personal communications. Most Populists, unfortunately, did not keep their correspondence; none but the official correspondence of Populist Governor Lewelling survives in Kansas. But the private correspondence of Ignatius Donnelly, the Minnesota Populist leader, opens up a veritable can of worms, with revelations of personal feuds, corruption, deception and cynicism among the activists of that state which must call into question the fine, idealistic rhetoric of the Kansas press.[30] There is no way of clearing the Kansas leaders of suspicion on this score, except to note that the *Great West*, the Minnesota paper of comparable statewide importance to the *Advocate* and the *Kansas Farmer* in Kansas, was also more of a battleground, where cults of personality, abuse and accusation were more conspicuous than was idealistic political debate; a difference which suggests that the tone of Kansas Populism was somewhat more elevated at the very least.

I have concentrated upon one short period, the six months from January to June, 1890, in looking for expressions of the Populists' beliefs about right government. The six months before the establishment of their own political party formed a crucial period in which public opinion was shaped, leadership opinion changed, and both crystallised into a consensus upon the necessity of third party action. It was also a period in which many new newspapers were founded specifically to transmit Populist ideas, while some older papers changed their affiliation and declared for independence or Populism. My account of these ideas is taken from a systematic sample of Populist papers from across the state, and from the *Advocate*, whose circulation was statewide, and Peffer's *Kansas Farmer* and the *Ottawa Journal and Triumph*, both of which had influence outside their local areas.[31]

It was only briefly that widespread grumbling about politics rose to the level of principle. Political ideals were usually taken for granted, simply submerged by the urgent problems of daily existence and suppressed by the mindless 'military' style of political appeals by way of 'brass-band parades' and 'sloganized battle-cries'.[32] Intense examination of the implications of criticisms of the political system and of the means to achieve the practical demands of the Farmers' Alliance developed very suddenly. The immediate catalyst was the blatant double-dealing of state politicians, who had come to power in Topeka in 1888 by promising the farmers relief and then shamelessly rejected every single reform proposal put before the next session of the legislature.[33] The philosophical debate was short lived. Once the party was formed in June, 1890, the columns of the press were suddenly full of tactical considerations, policy and programmes and the practical details of electoral competition.

Not that the People's Party sprang out of air. It sprang out of the Farmers' Alliance, which had a long history of battle and failure as a political pressure group, and of rather more success as an educational and social force. This long history, and the continuity of leadership with reform and third party movements before it, goes some way towards explaining why neither the policy nor the political solutions put forward by the Populists were strikingly original. As many as 60 per cent of the Kansas leaders 'were active in the third party reform movement before 1890. The usual route traveled had carried them from the Republican Party to the Greenback Party, then to the Prohibition Party or the Union-Labor Party, and then into the Populist Party.' They were not simply 'Rattle-brained fanatics' or a 'ragged elite': in fact 'more than half had graduated from one or more colleges ...almost two out of three had had some contact with the college environment', and these generally capable men and women were 'unsurpassed in their ability to give dramatic expression to the sentiments or interests of a significant segment of the Kansas populace'.[34]

Nor was it true that a reluctant Alliance was dragged kicking and screaming into third party action by 'a type of professional third-party politician who would not let the idea die'.[35] Hofstadter's assessment carries somewhat of the same implication when he suggests that the farm interest only found an effective political role when it abandoned third party ambitions and settled for conventional pressure group activity, as in the successful career of the American Farm Bureau Federation in the 1920s.[36] But in the nineteenth-century agricultural world the necessary prerequisite for successful pressure group activity simply did not exist. Organisation tends to match organisation, and the bureaucratic, technically-oriented government department deals most effectively and in non-partisan ways with the specialist professional interest group. The Alliance had no major counterpart in government – the Department of Agriculture was only granted Cabinet status in 1889 and government activity in agriculture was still limited, with virtually no legislation passed in the last third of the century. The point of access for nineteenth-century agriculturalists to the political decision making process was through their legislators and the parties whose influence was so great in their selection and election. Small wonder, then, that the years of non-partisan lobbying by the Alliance had yielded so little result, for it was used by political machines and legislators for partisan ends but had no way of holding them to account. The only possible weapon the Alliance could use was the withdrawal of its members' votes from the offending party. As the two parties equally let them down and looked to their eyes increasingly like 'two sausages made from the same dog'[37] the strategy of independent voting and thence third party action was bound to follow. There were regrets and misgivings about the abandonment of the non-partisan Alliance, perhaps in part because it was a tacit admission of thirty years of ineffectiveness, and because the deep, habitual loyalties to the old parties were not easily broken. But opinion did change in the early months of 1890, and when the People's Party was formed it was more from conviction than from manipulation.

Kansans had long criticised the government for ineffectiveness, but with fluctuating intensity related to the advances and reverses in their economic conditions. In the boom years of the 1880s optimism ran high, but disastrous years from 1887 on brought a torrent of criticism. The hard times came both from such natural disasters as drought and grasshopper invasions and from the distant workings of the international finance and commodity markets, which seemed to conspire to make good crops and bad equally catastrophic for the prairie farmers. The persistent failure of government to do anything to relieve increasingly desperate conditions in many parts of the state then inevitably encouraged the conclusion that they were a particularly neglected group in an allegedly egalitarian society; perhaps even that 'the American bison is suffering less at the present time'.[38] Increasingly, people felt not just hardship but rank injustice, and from here the crucial step in the argument was easy and criticisms in terms of norms and of political responsibility speedily followed.

Just this line of reasoning was followed by Mrs I. E. Hart in her essay 'What Are You Going To Do About It?', which she 'read before sub-alliance No. 321, Summit township, Cloud county', in June, 1890.[39] I quote extensively from this piece because it draws together the whole analysis whose parts repeatedly appear in separate editorials and letters. Final responsibility for 'the present condition of things' she laid with an apathetic electorate who had neglected their political responsibilities, leaving the way clear for unscrupulous opportunists to make their millions at the expense of the workers: 'The toilers are paying the penalty of sleeping at their post.' Hope of improvement lay in the fact that 'the people are waking up to realize that the bread they have cast upon the waters is returning unto them, not void, but as bitter herbs in the form of larger debts, mortgaged farms and ring rule'. Furthermore, the people increasingly perceived the direct connection between economic exploitation and political corruption:

> The peculations of the money lord, the speculations of the grabber of natural opportunities, compel untold numbers of willing workers to beg for the privilege to labor, and when given that, must pay one-half they earn for their chance, and the worker, man or woman, must as one of the 'inconvenient multitude' give one-fourth the remainder to aristocratic law makers, who seem to believe in the survival of the fittest, and to be fittest must be, regardless of common sense, a millionaire, and these last pave their way to legislative halls with the proceeds of the labor of those that send them there; paradoxical as this may seem it is true, for they can and do purchase votes enough to counteract the will of the just.

The people's redress would come through the elimination of political corruption, thus freeing legislative decisions from control by the plutocrats. First the people must be 'aroused to *think*'; then it would be clear that they 'have no right to stand as beggars at their legislative halls; the occupants of those halls are there on the suffrance of the people, and should be made to adjust their deliberations to the will and wishes of those who place them there'. Recognition of the problem made the means to a solution obvious and Mrs Hart concluded as she

had begun: 'The only hope of the country lies in progression obtain-
able by the masses of the people by the ballot. So long as that weapon
is held by the people it is their own fault if they are at the mercy of a
plutocratic power.'

Mrs Hart's critique was couched in general terms against the whole
political system, with only Congress singled out for special scorn. This
was the tone of most of the political criticism in the Kansas press, with
the simple diatribe against politics and politicians in general most
common and a ratio of about four to one of specific references to federal
as compared with state or local institutions. This might seem a paradoxical concern for rural Kansans, living in isolated communities;
Washington must have seemed remote and the most obvious corruption
that in their own community, or perhaps in Topeka. Though he sees
the Populists as the leaders of a period of political transition, Robert
Wiebe describes the political perspective of the 1890s as still highly
parochial – 'as the process moved beyond their community, interest
dwindled rapidly'.[40] But if such precision is ever possible, the transition
from the local perspective of the early nineteenth century to the
primacy of national institutions suggested by both attitudes and patterns of participation in the latter half of the twentieth century will be
found to have occurred before the Populist agitation.

Wiebe does rightly point out that political parties were vital as
channels of direct attachment to the outside world; parties were one of
the most salient political institutions and their national role was well
understood. But there are also good reasons why the Federal government, among formal institutions, seemed so important to Kansas
farmers. For one thing, it was clear that most of their policies required
action at federal level; currency reform was clearly a federal matter,
for example, and similarly regulation of railroads and marketing could
hardly be effective within a single state when routes and outlets were
located all across the continent. And when it came to political ideals,
the whole body of precedent, myth and philosophy on which they
drew ensured that their perspective would be national. For their political heroes were presidents, their texts were national possessions and
the events in which they found inspiration were national too. So they
presage the modern system, which Wiebe ironically saw foreshadowed
at the same time in an abuse the Populists suspected, a new role for
Congressmen detached by industrial magnates 'from their localities to
serve as representatives for national business interests. . .the beginnings
of a new political system, grafted upon the old, that operated from the

top down rather than from the bottom up'.[41] For the Populists, with a partial understanding of new circumstances, sovereignty was to work from the bottom up, but government was to be national and not local.

Any likelihood that the Federal government might still have seemed an abstract and impersonal villain to the simpler Populist supporters was conveniently disposed of when one of the United States Senators from Kansas offered himself as a symbol of all they saw wrong with democratic government. Senator Ingalls' contemptuous comments, in an interview by a New York reporter, could hardly have been a more inflammatory rejection of the ideals which his constituents were even then discussing in unprecedented public debate. The *Advocate* immediately reprinted a long extract, and other local papers followed suit. Ingalls was quoted as saying:

> The purification of politics is an iridescent dream. Government is force. Politics is a battle for supremacy. Parties are the armies. *The decalogue and the golden rule have no place in a political campaign. . .In war it is lawful to deceive the adversary,* TO HIRE HESSIANS, TO PURCHASE MERCEN-ARIES, *to mutilate, to destroy.* THE COMMANDER WHO LOST A BATTLE THROUGH THE ACTIVITY OF HIS MORAL NATURE WOULD BE THE DERISION AND JEST OF HISTORY. *This modern cant about the corruption of politics is fatiguing in the extreme. It proceeds from the tea-custard and syllabub dilettantism, of the frivolous and desultory sentimentalism of epicenes.*[42]

Ingalls' interview was an important contribution to the founding of the Populist Party in Kansas and to his own ouster later that year after eighteen years in the Senate; he had been criticised before, but now radical editors used his remarks as an effective weapon in a major campaign against him – a campaign which forced Republicans to over-look his sentiments or come out against their party. And Republican support was crucial to the new party; it has been calculated that ex-Republicans provided some 36 per cent of the Populist vote in 1890 in Kansas, against 31 per cent from ex-Democrats and almost 30 per cent from the former Union-Labor ranks.[43]

In their criticisms of politics the Populists were not simply firing random shots in the air. There were good reasons for their specific targets as well as their general inclination to concentrate on federal government. It is true that the most visible parts of government received the full force of their wrath, but, when the other side of the distrust equation is examined – their ideals and plans for their implementation – it becomes clear that critical attention was focused on just those aspects of politics whose reform would achieve their aims. They had no quarrel with the fundamental principles of American politics, nor with the structures consequently established by the Constitution. Their quarrel was with the way these principles and institutions had been degraded and distorted in practice and thus particularly with the men who held power and the parties who appeared to control both elections and the legislative branch of government. Their criticisms of both were direct and unabashed.

Politicians called forth some of that particularly picturesque rhetoric which has misled some observers into believing the Populists only simple countrymen with no method in their madness. 'Politician' had anyway long been a term of abuse in America, so the declaration against 'a government of politicians, by politicians and for politicians' was heavily weighted with implication.[44] Their greatest fear for their own organisation was its infiltration by political 'wolves in sheeps' clothing'; 'True Blue' wrote ominously of having seen one or two 'old politicians' at the Ellsworth County Alliance meeting, and a few weeks later the *Kansas Farmer* editorialised against the 'professional politician', 'the man who sings while he steals' and would enter the Alliance only to betray it.[45] Party men were 'strutting bosses' and vermin to be rooted out of their entrenched positions in the political system:

> Now, farmers, when hawks bother your chickens, you not only try to kill the hawks but you destroy their nests. So on rats and chinch bugs. You tear out and destroy their nests and breeding places...As long as the politicians hold the county and township offices, they will hold the legislature also.[46]

The motives of men who became professional politicians were highly suspect. The theme of sucking the people dry, as 'leeches on the body politic' or 'pap-suckers', was constantly repeated; and 'They are paid for the work of betrayal like Judas. Don't let them kiss you.' They were 'office-seekers' and 'loaf-hunters' not just for the official rewards of office: 'The Congressmen count their salaries as only a drop in the bucket compared with the boodle they expect to get for helping to lobby through bills that are to work for the ruination of their constituents.' Since money, not principle, was their guiding light, they were generally available to the highest bidder and thus 'today the *few* control legislation through professional and corrupt politicians'.[47]

Politicians would do their best to disguise these facts from the people, and their best was usually enough, for they did possess a certain Machiavellian ability which kept them in office through betrayal after betrayal. 'Demagogues' was a favourite label for these 'butter-tongued ones'.[48] One local Republican believed to be in the Alliance for no good reason, was attacked forcefully: 'Here in Washington County there are a few men like H.M. (red ink) Reed, afflicted with a "diarrhoea of words and a constipation of ideas".'[49] And an inexperienced farmer trying to organise a sub-alliance in Cottonwood County, Minnesota, evidently felt helplessly outflanked, as he wrote to Donnelly that 'the worst of all is, there is a few old Republicans here who preach that the aliance is a sham & caution People to stear cleare of it'.[50]

The deception was about achievements as well as intentions; a *Hiawatha Journal* editorial commented that Congressmen had introduced that session a vast host of reform bills and no doubt would point to that fact with pride, even though none were likely to be enacted:

> But this thing has been practiced too long. We doubt not the people will refuse to be humbugged by such pretences any longer...If there is not something done during this session we predict some unexpected business. The people will not do this business for politicans any longer.[51]

In Congress either nothing was done or the wrong things. So the *Galva Times* complained that 'nothing at all has been done except for one side to rail at the other and vice versa', and suggested that the members might usefully be retired to private life, while an *Advocate* editorial asked why had Congressmen been devoting their time to discussing first the erection and then the removal of statuary in Washington – 'giant marble allegorical representations of the U.S. Navy'.[52]

The nub of all these criticisms of politicians was that they had forgotten their role as representatives and, more strongly, as mandated delegates of the people: 'It has come to pass that the *willing servant* of the people *on the stump, is the tyranical master* of the people in *the hall of legislation*', while Congress had become 'an autocratic body that sneers at the petitioner and flings him a stone when he asks for justice'.[53] Even though news of political unrest in Kansas had filtered through to their delegates, there seemed little hope of a new relationship:

> Yes, congressmen who have misrepresented the people for years, without a thought of responsibility, are now writing home to ask what they should do. This is not from any lack of knowledge as to what is just and desirable in the case, but for an ostentatious display of willingness to serve the people – next time. Beware of representatives who are willing to confess ignorance as an excuse for failure in the duties of representation.[54]

Indeed, the general opinion was that Senator Ingalls was typical of them all when he said cynically in his famous interview: 'Occasional surrender of individual judgement to public opinion is prudent, and

respectable deference to wide-spread error is now and then expedient.
It is always well to keep the pole-star in view, but when the wind is
dead ahead, the skilful navigator will either tack or drop anchor.'[55]
The net result of the domination of political activity by men of low
calibre, impure motives and weak principles was seen to be the dissipa-
tion of the people's resources, the flouting of their will and the denial
of the principles upon which the American political system had been
founded.

The same conclusions were drawn when the Populists looked beyond
personalities and stereotyped figures and criticised the institutions of
government. Again, the most visible targets gained the greatest attention, and so political parties bore the brunt of the attack. One might
expect the Republicans to be singled out for special attention in a
solidly Republican state (Republican candidates had carried 90 per
cent or more of the counties in every gubernatorial election since 1862).
But in fact the blame was rather equally distributed, no doubt with a
view to recruiting from both the old parties. In any case, a Democratic
administration in Washington promised no better than a Republican,
controlled as it would be by gold-bugs and easterners. In place of partisan criticism, then, the Populists turned to the institutions themselves
and examined the role they played in government.

In a parallel to their economic complaints, the Populists found
monopoly at the root of their political problems. The parties seemed
like 'two bureaus, outside of all law, two huge political trusts'.[56] Their
hold on the political system was so complete that they had been able to
connive successfully for years on behalf of a single master (the monied
interest). Thus they presented an illusion of open competition while
actually controlling every aspect of politics, from the perceptions of the
voters to the choice offered them at elections and right on through the
discussion and enactment of legislation.

Distortion of the relationship of the people to their legislators through
the ballot was achieved in many ways. The most constant complaint
of the Populists was that there was no difference between the parties
and thus no choice in an election. A satirical journal in Topeka advertised: 'Wanted in this office at once, a pup with three legs, one eye, and
two teeth, whose olfactory glands are in good condition so he can tell,
by the smell, the difference between a republican and a democrat on
political questions', and the *Washington Post* summed it up, 'the labor
is between the devil and the deep sea when asked to choose between
the two old parties'.[57]

Elections offered no choice and there was no greater opportunity for the prior exercise of influence within the party machinery:

> A few arrogant and dictatorial, self-constituted political bosses in the parties, assume the right to control, with iron hand, the policy and action of the parties. They deny the people the right to do their own thinking. They are emboldened in this high handed and audacious assumption of power by the lordly masters whom they serve. They assume the right to make nominations, to dictate candidates and the policy of their party, and should any man or men dare to question their right or wisdom they are roundly denounced as 'traitors'.[58]

Furthermore, no principle seemed to limit the activities of the parties – an *Advocate* editorial concluded that 'Satan has a mortgage on them and their masters', and 'An Alliance Woman' that 'all the old parties can legally claim now is their name. They left their principles long ago.'[59] They would buy voters and legislative votes shamelessly, and laugh it off as good politics; as to policy, recent experience in Kansas proved that they would promise anything in order to win power, but forget their promises after polling day. With long experience of reform movements which had mostly been lost causes, journalists had no shortage of examples of repeated perfidy. Geo. C. Ward, a Union-Labor activist who wrote regularly to the *Advocate* from Kansas City, Missouri, spoke to optimistic readers – 'Let me remind them of a little history', and outlined a series of specific pledges given to Greenbackers by both Republicans and Democrats, whose candidates were duly 'sent to Congress, to forget their pledges and betray the people'.[60]

Monopoly, corruption, deception and the insincere theft of reformers' programmes were not, however, the end of the anti-democratic activities of the parties. To analysts of macro-voting patterns the Populists are of passing interest because they provided a way station for voters transferring their loyalties from one party to the other in the great realignment of voting blocs in the 1890s. But down there among the grass roots this involved an education on the meaning of the ballot, and a serious critique of the parties for their debauchery of the pride of American citizens. For, as their critics acknowledged, the old parties had been enormously successful in basing their prime electoral appeal on blind loyalty and habits: 'What has thus placed the people in such a disadvantageous position? There is but one answer to the question – It is Party Allegiance and Partizan Zeal.'[61] There was repeated exhortation in the press not to vote, as Mrs Hart put it, 'merely because the candidate is of "our party," "father voted that way," or "don't like to be called a mugwump," or some other just as intelligent reason'.[62] The incentive to do otherwise was derived from the same ideals of political action by which this thoughtless voting was condemned, described in a verse written for the *Ottawa Journal*:

> Indeed, the PEOPLE are supreme –
>   Where they maintain their right to be;
> Nor idly sleep, nor fondly dream,
>   Nor compromise their dignity
> By serving men they would not name,
>   And measures which they ne'er approve –
> Thus prostituting, to their shame,
>   Their better sense to party love![63]

The strength and persistence of these emotive attachments to the old parties is clear from the obsession of writers with the question:

> The worst, the dirtiest collar a man ever wore, is the party collar. He wears it after it has become so covered with filth that the stench of it would drive a hungry horse from his supper...he wears it after its usefulness has gone, simply because he has got it on and has not independence and manhood enough to tear it off.[64]

It is clear, too, from the repeated offers of last chances to the old parties, for example in the *Kansas Farmer* editorials right up to the establishment of the People's Party, and in the very slow gathering of momentum for a break, shown in the resolutions coming into the papers in the six months preceding this decision. The well-known 'Song For the Toiler' was precisely right when it opened:

> It was no more than a year ago,
>   Good-bye, my party, good-bye.
> That I was in love with my party so,
>   Good-bye, my party, good-bye;
> To hear aught else I never would go;
>   Good-bye, my party, good-bye.[65]

It was the electoral process that concerned the critics most; after all, what chance was there that men nominated and elected by such means could rise above these sordid origins when they arrived in Congress? The Populists gave less direct attention to the institutions of the Federal government themselves; when they were discussed it was usually Congress and rarely the Presidency which they attacked. They muttered, sometimes, of monarchical tendencies, but the lack of serious discussion of the Presidency must reflect their understanding of the balance of power in Washington at that time. As Woodrow Wilson had written only five years earlier, 'the predominant and controlling force, the centre and source of all motive and all regulative power, is Congress'.[66]

In Congress, the party system was the root of the trouble again: 'What matters it whether the tyrant that robs us wears a British crown or sits upon the throne of party caucus?'[67] The caucus demeaned Congressional dignity by the contrivances of regimented voting on legislation, filibustering and wheeling and dealing, all with more concern for the spoils of office than memory for election promises. Congress was 'beyond the reach of the people' also because of the secrecy in which its decisions were taken;[68] an example was a House Ways and Means Committee decision on the tariff, taken with no counsel for the people present and so 'the people were sold out'.[69]

Turning to the Senate, the concern became a general attack on elitism, though one writer compared the two houses and found the House distinguished only by its skilled filibustering for party supremacy and the Senate by its prime concern for 'useless sectional controversy'.[70] The usual discussion of the Senate was through a comparison with the British House of Lords. From time to time the columns of local papers contained articles on the Lords, and on reform agitation in Britain; even when not made explicit the analogy with the Senate seems intended. The Senate was seen as pledged to the same interests as the House but yet further divorced from the people and decidedly and distastefully aristocratic in its tendencies:

> The Senate of the United States has for many years, been an exponent of wealth – a kind of 'English House of Lords' in an American Republic; representing money, rather than men, and has proven itself a kind of 'Genteel stumbling block' to all legislation in the interests of the industrial classes.[71]

The common thread in Populist criticisms was the pervasive role of party in American politics. Yet they were confused as to the proper grounds of criticism. They were, of course, only grappling with a problem which has perturbed American political theory from the Founding Fathers to the present day. But the confusion carried through into their proposals and action and remained an inhibition on decisive activity throughout the life of the movement. The position of the parties outside the constitution led some to criticise them as entirely illegitimate organisations with no right of intervention in the political process; thus 'there shall be direct responsibility to the people of all their business agents...And never another great stuffed idol must be allowed to frighten the people as has the party fetich for the last twenty years'.[72] But these were a minority, and the greater number of critics came to uneasy terms with their inevitability. With the existence of parties grudgingly accepted, their criticisms were on the grounds either of inevitable stagnation and decay – a sort of organisational life-cycle theory – or, with less theoretical elegance still, simply on the grounds of multiple abuse of political norms, presumably from original sin rather than for any inherent structural reason. Out of long political experience, John Davis, the editor of the *Junction City Tribune* and a successful candidate for Congress in 1890, set down a life-cycle theory of parties:

> Political parties never advance. All progress in America is made by and through new parties. Each new party is born from the grievances of the people in some particular line. Under its patriotic leaders it abolishes the special grievances which gave it birth. It performs its special mission. It then stops, passes into new hands, forgets to die and becomes corrupt. It feeds on the memories of the past. It becomes a party of spoils. It is an organized appetite only, with its face turned steadfastly towards the rear.[73]

More graphically, others made the point repeatedly that there was no hope of reforming the old organisations. New wine in old bottles and new patches on old breeches were appealing analogies, as was the advice 'We had as well set out our old corn-stalks in the Spring and expect them to yield a bountiful supply of ears because they had done so the year before.'[74] But when it came to the question of alternatives to the party system, there was little more constructive offered than the hope that the mistakes of their predecessors might be avoidable. If there is any irony in the Populists' profound faith that politics could save them, it is in their optimistic launching of a new party with virtually no serious consideration of how the recognised dangers of organisation might be avoided.

The inadequacy of their preparation for action went much further than just their theory of party organisation. Distrust of politics is a two-part set of attitudes – criticisms made within the context of ideals. The criticisms of the Populists were trenchant and their choice of targets and identification of corruption show an accurate perception of the processes of power at that time. These criticisms were also entirely consistent with the ideals which they declared as their source of hope for politics. Here there were two components: rather general ideas about the proper nature of government and of the role and rights of the citizen therein, and more specific points about the scope of government, the structure of its institutions and the qualities and duties required of its personnel. The first, the general ideals, were both ennobling and an inspiration to action for the ordinary American citizen. The latter, which provided the specific direction for their action, also laid a trap for them. For they contained no new proposals; the Populists were reformers, not radicals, and therefore could only pin their hope of a future avoidance of past errors on an optimistic view of human nature, that citizens could, and would next time, control the situation and enforce virtue. Together, the two sides of their political ideals do much to explain both the whirlwind start of the People's Party and its pathetic and swift crumbling in the face of political realities.

The political beliefs of the Kansas Alliancemen first explain why they did not seriously consider any alternative to political action for redress of their grievances: 'It is politics that has placed the people in the condition they are today, and through politics alone can they hope to get out.'[75] From time to time, indeed, there was talk of revolution, but never literally as a solution for the present. 'Revolution is a last resort', Mrs Hart declared in her Alliance lecture.[76] Thad Spencer, writing from Reading, Kansas, asked 'Did George III listen to the petition of the colonists? Not much, but when he saw them in arms he was willing to treat with them';[77] but he was not actually calling for armed insurrection in Kansas – merely for the strongest form of political action, a third party. Leonidas Polk's toast, at the national convention of the Farmers' Alliance in St Louis in December, 1889, to 'The New Revolution' was widely reported, but he had in mind nothing more than a restoration; the revolution would last only until 'the sovereignty of the people shall be re-established in the glory of its majesty and power'.[78] Revolution became part of Populist rhetoric for no more dangerous reason than the power of the political symbol of the origins of the republic: 'Republics are born of despotisms by *bullets*, or armed revolution. They are kept in existence by *ballots* or peaceful and continual evolution.'[79] They envisaged no radical, and certainly no violent change, but only the overthrow of tyranny by people armed with the weapon inherited from the first revolutionaries – the ballot.

They had no doubt, either, of the potential power of their weapon. 'In a country like ours where the people rule by the casting of their ballots, expressive of their will, there is not the slightest excuse in resorting to force to right wrongs.'[80] The equally optimistic 'Alliance Woman' wrote that 'The battle of the polls is as harmless as the dewdrop or summer sunshine, but as effective as a cyclone.'[81]

Furthermore, from reform of the political system the desired substantive consequences would undoubtedly and happily flow. 'Remove such leeches from the body politic and replace them with free men good and true who fairly represent the people, and the present depression and financial suffering will disappear as if by the magician's wand, and busy towns and happy homes will be seen in their stead.'[82] The Populists saw no intrinsic quality of politics that might undermine its capacity to solve social problems whose magnitude they fully understood. Instead they had unqualified confidence in reformed politics:

> Give the people justice, and you will not see the people looking around for work to do, neither will you hear the voice of discontent any more, which now reaches from ocean to ocean. But on the other hand you will see prosperity in this fair land of ours. Then we shall see the times spoken of in the Bible, in which every man shall sit under his own fig tree, and one shall not plant and another eat the fruit thereof.[83]

Why this simple faith in politics as the universal panacea? That there was an element of naivety in Populist confidence became clear in the shattering disappointments of the various reform administrations, which were outwitted at every turn by political opponents and lobbyists, so that only scraps of minor legislation from their programmes were enacted. But the source of their optimism in their theory of democratic government is clear in their speeches and letters as they moved into political action, and the frequency of its appearance leaves no doubt that it was not just an emotional appeal by manipulative would-be party leaders, but a genuine and deep sentiment of the membership at large.

The supporters of the new movement were inspired by the sense of being part of a long and noble tradition of American citizenship. Their view of the right nature of American government was derived from a rich and accessible corpus of example and mythology, upon which they drew constantly to legitimate both their complaints and their solutions. Naive it may have been, but they did stand up and cheer to calls such as this:

> Laboring men of America! The voice of Patrick Henry and the fathers of American Independence rings down through the corridors of time and tells you to strike. Not with glittering musket, flaming sword and deadly cannon; but with the silent, potent and all-powerful ballot, the only vestige of liberty left.[84]

The particular dignity of the American citizen was his right and duty to 'exercise an honest, legal and judicious ballot'.[85] This was the distinctive possession of the American: 'The principle upon which the republic is founded is free and virtuous suffrage.'[86] The revolutionaries had been prepared to fight to win this weapon for the defence of freedom; 'the ballot given to us by our patriotic fathers' (coupled hopefully with 'that manhood given to us by the God of Nature') was weapon enough to fight all wrongs.[87] It is easy to see the appeal of this kind of argument to the man in the street, for it flatters him and cannily suggests that both might and right will be on his side when he goes into battle. That, of course, is important in generating action, but it is also important that this was no trumped-up appeal but took its authority from the major texts, the epic heroes and the highest dramas of American history. It is far easier for the Davids to stand up against the Goliaths of political power when armed with a tradition and philosophy which incite them to do so and imbue them with moral conviction.

The distinction of the antecedents the Populists discovered is well summed-up in the preamble to the 'Declaration of Principles adopted by the Cowley Alliance' in April 1890 – headlined by the *Advocate* as 'A New Declaration of Independence':

> We believe that a return to the principles enunciated by the fathers of our republic, and recited by Washington in his farewell address, and by Jefferson when he said 'that in the homes of our people lie the safety of our institutions,' and the utterances and inspired words of the immortal Lincoln, that 'a government of the people, for the people, and by the people was the best and only safety for human liberty;'[88]

Lincoln's famous phrase was the most quoted slogan in the Populists' discussions; it appeared in the press items more than twice as often as any other reference to persons, places or incidents. Jefferson, various aspects of the revolution, and the Declaration of Independence followed as prominent symbols of their political theory.

Lincoln was a hero whom many of the Populists could actually remember, but they used his memory in very limited ways. There was no direct talk of his role in the Civil War and no doubt the susceptibilities of southerners were in their minds here. They did remember his declaration of the traditional toast 'United we stand, divided we fall', and added this authority to their call for non-partisan action.[89] Generally they simply called on his name, or repeated and paraphrased his words, leaving the listener to draw the appropriate conclusions. Once or twice he is slyly drawn into the argument on their side, as in the parenthetical reference to ' "the great common people," (that Abraham Lincoln loved so well).'[90] Another writer, looking back with regret to the noble aspirations of the early days of the Republican

Party and with envy to its rapid ascent to power, acclaimed Lincoln's leadership in the last great upheaval:

> Sundry old party issues are mostly settled, and in the new revolution of political thought and action, which is upon us even at the door; new men, new leaders may arise, who would do for this generation of people, what was so bravely, gloriously and patriotically attempted, and pretty well performed by Abraham Lincoln.[91]

The Populists were not and did not intend to be particularly original in their use of Lincoln's words, or indeed with any of their slogans. The Greenback Party platform of 1880, for example, had included the claim for 'government of the people'. They were simply restating what they took to be the fundamental inspiration of American democracy.

The guarantee of freedom through the exercise of the ballot and the precedent for decisive action against tyranny were the main contributions of the revolution, but it gave much more besides. The Populists found there villains analogous to those they faced: they matched George III with King Caucus and pointed to his repeated deafness to public opinion,[92] and warned of vigilance against Benedict Arnolds and Red Coats in their midst.[93] And it gave them heroes, not least those unnamed men like themselves: 'A century ago a few farmers "Fired a shot that echoed round the world." That shot was from the rifle's mouth; it declared that the struggle for political freedom had begun. . .We believe that Kansas has stepped to the front and uttered a new declaration of freedom.'[94] A feeling of direct continuity with the founding fathers, their 'patriot sires', was clearly important to them. In Minnesota, where ethnic groups were more diverse and more antagonistic than in Kansas, lauding patriot sires might well have seemed ironic. But the foreign-born found their own symbols: a Scotsman remembered 'The Bruce', 'the Massacre of Glencoe', and the Covenanters, while 'The Poles of Silver Lake' found inspiration in the anniversary of the free Polish constitution of 1791.[95] The revolution gave them, too, Lexington and Bunker Hill and Patrick Henry and other evocative catchwords; and it gave them George Washington.[96] Washington became a political myth in his own lifetime; a century later it was still enough to let his name work for itself. When they did more than call upon his memory, the Populists remembered him both for his revolutionary leadership and, most frequently, for the sentiments of his Farewell Address on national unity and on the 'baneful effects of the Spirit of Party generally'.

Their main source of abstract ideas about government was Thomas Jefferson. Much emphasis has been placed, particularly by their critics, on their Jeffersonian view of society – the dream of a rural idyll of individualistic agricultural entrepreneurs sustaining a virtuous republic under the beneficent influence of honest toil and communion with nature. The agrarian myth has had a much wider currency in American society than this implies; the Populists were hardly unique in their nostalgia and were certainly not romantic about life close to the soil.

In matters of political theory they rightly claimed Jeffersonian ancestry. The *Galva Times* published an article extolling Jefferson:

> Always and ever he looked and listened for the concert of the people... He believed that all men are politically equal. He believed in letting every man rear his own place through his own genius and his own opportunity... He is the glorious gold, the shining metal in the glittering quartz.[97]

A Democrat moving towards a Populist position claimed Jefferson as father of his party, but rightly recognised that he, along with Jackson, had become 'endeared by tradition to the hearts of a majority of American citizens'.[98] Jefferson was remembered for taking a firm stand against the elitism of the Federalists,[99] but primarily for his earlier authorship of the Declaration of Independence. The Populists' acquaintance with and use of Jefferson's ideas was no more detailed than with Lincoln, and the relevance they found for their own situation was well enough summarised in the second paragraph of the Declaration. The assertion there of equality, the right of 'Life, Liberty and the Pursuit of Happiness', and especially the thesis that 'Governments are instituted among Men, deriving their just Powers from the Consent of the Governed', required no further exegesis for them. The same text provided justification for their determined intervention in the affairs of state, for it seemed to them that their real aim was nothing more than 'to provide new Guards for their future Security' against tyranny.

The Declaration of Independence contributed moral conviction to their action, and principles to direct their plans for reform. A Jeffersonian phrase also contributed to the explanation of their plight. As the banner above the platform at an Alliance picnic at Roys Creek, Kansas, declared: 'Eternal vigilance, the price of liberty'.[100] Conveniently this favourite slogan both pointed a moral and provided a maxim for the future. For the Populists recognised that their enemies in the past had not been only British and Jews, capitalists and politicians, but had included their own negligence and apathy: 'They [the workingmen] have sown the seed, and their would-be masters have reaped the benefit thereof. . .by aspiring political power which the trusting people placed in their hands, forgetting that "eternal vigilance is the price of liberty".[101] But if the lesson was well learnt things would be different in the future – hence an argument in support of education in political economy the better to sustain 'eternal vigilance' in the face of the increasing complexity of government.[102]

This need for education, and the concomitant faith in human potential, was another important point for which they acknowledged direct inspiration from Jefferson, and this I return to below. Their views coincided with his on other matters: they could have found authority in his words, though they did not do so explicitly, for their general rhetoric of republicanism, their definition and justification of political revolution, their emphasis on the direct election of officers of the state, and their confidence that this would be effective through the capacity of the people to judge other men and elect them wisely to positions beyond their own practical capacity. On the other hand, the passage of a century of economic development made their views on the scope of government very different from those of Jefferson. And on the crucial matter of party, they either did not know, or did not bother with, Jefferson's resigned acceptance of the 'natural' contest between parties of whig and tory persuasions. Washington's Farewell Address was a much more appealing condemnation of party than anything Jefferson offered. To credit the Populists with Jeffersonian principles then is not to imply an exact or accurate resemblance with his thought; it is to recognise the source of some of their most basic ideas as well as the pride of place in their pantheon which they themselves awarded him. And to the extent that they were unacknowledged Jeffersonians, it was simply a reflection of the way in which many of his ideas had become the commonplaces of American culture. Jefferson's heritage 'was not, after all, a system of economics or politics. . .but an imperishable faith expressed in an imperishable rhetoric'.[103]

The Populists' other supposed patron saint, Andrew Jackson, was of far less direct significance to them, for all his importance in political history in advancing just the principles of radical democracy which they also advocated. I found just three references to Jackson and the longest of these was mainly concerned with his anti-bank policy.[104] It is doubtful whether this conspicuous absence was simply due to the hostility of a strongly Republican state to a Democrat hero – Minnesota was much more of a swing state and he was not invoked there either. Certainly they did not make anything of the responsibility of the

Jacksonian movement for introducing the abhorred professional party machine. The Jacksonians were neglected rather than rejected explicitly. The explanation may lie in the fact that the Jacksonians were no more innovators in democratic theory than were the Populists. Their contribution was the embodiment of accepted (Jeffersonian) principles in working institutions. 'Indeed the most consequential political changes entered silently, without formal consideration or enactment', and changes of this kind bequeathed little memorable rhetoric to later reformers.[105] What was borrowed from the Jacksonians was the language of their economic analysis, but superficially similar anti-monopoly slogans carried very different meanings in these two periods, a point which perhaps escaped the notice of distinguished historians who have alternatively presented the Populists as the heirs of or the rejectors of Jacksonian democracy.[106]

These, then, were the major sources of inspiration to the Populists as they discussed general principles. There were lesser heroes and authorities too, from the Fall of Quebec and the French Revolution to divine approval of the new party: 'All hail the young giant of Freedom and Love. Its source of reform is sent from above.'[107] But did these diverse fragments add up to a coherent philosophy of government?

The crux of the political philosophy of the Populists was the principle that sovereignty resided in the people. In theory, this was not a matter of debate in the United States – it was the official constitutional doctrine. In practice the concept has always been fraught with difficulties of definition and implementation. The Populists, too, were unclear on basic matters, notably who were 'the people' and how might their will, supposing a single will existed at all, be identified and fulfilled.

Interpretations of Populist thought often credit it with the intention of somehow dragooning a single uniform outlook within society: 'Moral consensus rules, or, in different language, society is and should be a self-righteous moral tyranny';[108] or of demanding a simple majoritarianism, under which minorities might theoretically exist but would inevitably be railroaded out of any effective say in political decision by the power of the majority. It is easy to attribute to the Populists one's own particular bogeyman or to imply coherence and intention, usually sinister, where none really existed. The American Populists were not sitting down to write a philosophy of politics, but reacting to specific abuses of power in a way suggested by the symbolic values of their political tradition. The result is that what they really meant by 'the sovereignty of the people' is nowhere authoritatively defined; it can only be pieced together from the evidence of their political thought – which may clarify their intention – and the specific references and practical proposals which may both suggest intention and give grounds for deciding what kind of polity, regardless of their intentions, they would actually have produced.

The Cowley County Alliance Declaration of Principles appears to put the extreme position of popular sovereignty baldly – 'Whereas, we believe, as was stated in a recent interview in the New York *World*, "that the rights of the people are paramount and superior to constitutions"'; but their itemised proposals made clear that they were not calling for a political system of unregulated government by the people. They wanted constitutional safeguards against the usurpation of power by any group, brought in by constitutional means: 'We demand that the necessary steps be taken by Congress to amend the national constitution so as to be in harmony with the best interests of the whole people.'[109] The necessary steps were no more radical than the reforms being generally bandied about at the time: the direct election of senators at least and perhaps of the president also, the Australian ballot and the Crawford system of primaries. Members of the Cloud County Alliance clearly envisaged no radical change when they resolved 'That men in office are the servants of the people, and not their masters, and their only duty is obedience to the will of the people; that is what this government meant when it was formed, and we will try to start things from that foundation again.'[110] An article reprinted from Polk's *Progressive Farmer* also implied no problem in reconciling the idea of popular sovereignty with present structures:

> [The farmers of North Carolina and of these United States] believe that the people are sovereign. They believe that a 'public office is a public trust.' They believe that a public officer is a public servant. They believe they have some rights besides 'paying their taxes and voting, as they are told.' They believe that under our system of government, parties are a necessity, but that they should be parties 'of the people, by the people, and for the people.'[111]

Nobody dealt seriously with the problem of how, or whether, minority rights should be safeguarded or whether there was any such thing as a unified will of the people. It is, of course, an easy thing for those who believe themselves the majority to argue, as the Populists did, 'What will benefit a great majority will benefit all',[112] but, on the other hand, they did not think of the political process as simply a mechanism for ramming through the majority will. On the contrary, Senator Ingalls was roundly castigated for his attitude, described thus:

> His highest ideal of the exercise of the franchise, that most sacred of the rights of freemen, is by his own definition, '*to defeat the antagonist.*'
> The merits of the issues involved and the character of the candidates are not factors in the contest. The one sole and only purpose of politics is 'to battle for supremacy' of parties.[113]

The will of the people was to be expressed through the ballot – 'the people rule by the casting of their ballots, expressive of their will',[114] and through a ballot on a genuine choice. In fact their majoritarianism was simply a straight preference to the perception of existing 'minoritarianism'. Trying to locate this demand in a coherent philosophy is as problematic as the attempts to make the Populists out as authentic proponents of class warfare in the socialist mould. They did use the rhetoric of class from time to time, but only to 'deprecate class legislation' or, as one report argued, only because politics is already organised that way.[115] The point which they made in both cases, and intended as more than a pious hope, was that the triumph of one group over another was not their aim, but that they intended to place concern for the general interest above any particular interest, whether a class or a minority of any sort: 'The alliance wants such legislation as will equalize burdens and benefits of government, affording equal protection to all the citizens.'[116]

If their theory of popular sovereignty is vague and almost non-existent, not to mention naive about the realities of political power, perhaps more can be deduced from the practical proposals they offered for ensuring more satisfactory participation by the people in their government. Here, too, there was a good deal of spur-of-the moment improvisation, but also some more solid evidence of the kind of polity they envisaged. Only one idealist came out for virtual direct democracy:

> The American people are at heart loyal to the republic. They mean to rescue the ship of state from its dreadful perils. They will insist that there shall be direct responsibility to the people of all their business agents, i.e. their officials. There must be no legislature, no electoral college, no appointive power to stand athwart the people and their servants. And then king caucus must be dethroned.[117]

Less sweeping, though still on the radical side, was the argument that:

> To correct these evils and prevent their occurrence and ensure such laws as will be good for the people they themselves must see, read or hear discussed

all enactments. And before these enactments become laws the people affected by them should have opportunity by their own voice of saying whether or not they were what they wanted.[118]

The specific proposals for reform endorsed in the resolutions of alliance after alliance are, however, nearer in effect to the moderate analyst who argued:

> Under our form of government the people cannot go to Topeka or Washington in a body and enact their laws, because it would be impracticable. But the people select by vote people to represent them and act for them in making laws. Thus the persons thus selected are the servants of the people.[119]

The main source of the resolutions of local alliances in 1890 was the St Louis Platform, drawn up at the national Alliance convention in 1889. Its central demands were on the great issues of land, transportation and money, to which many alliances added their own pet grievances – right down to Chase County's declaration, making reference to the precedent of the Boston Tea Party, 'That this Alliance will not buy any of Arbuckle's or package coffee'.[120]

The St Louis Platform had only one clause dealing with reform of the political system itself: '12. We favor the Australian system, or some similar system of voting, and ask the enactment of laws regulating the nomination of candidates for public office.'[121] There were educational articles explaining the operation and advantages of both the Australian ballot and the Crawford system of primaries in several papers.[122] Local sub-alliances and contributors to the press, however, had more measures in mind with the same aims of maximising the opportunities for participation by citizens and minimising the possibilities for the exertion of undue influence by minority groups. There was a steady trickle of resolutions demanding the direct election of senators and there was frequent support for votes for women, both of which became national Populist policy in the Cincinnati Platform of 1891. Kansas women already had the municipal vote and could point to evidence of their competence there, and there were some notable women in the state party leadership. Meantime, one farmer's wife found some consolation in the thought that 'our sons are all members of the alliance and will vote their mothers' principles'.[123] Another suggestion was the conversion of more offices from appointive to elective posts, right down to the election of postmasters, and they began to toy with the idea of the initiative and referendum, both of which also became national policy later.[124]

All these reforms were directed at those institutions which had received the brunt of their criticism, and especially at the electoral process. Their occasional critical references to the procedures and practices within Congress are matched by only occasional and minor references to possible reforms. The main problem they had seen was the corruption of Congressional votes by money. One hopeful letter from a Johnson County farmer thought simply that 'the laws should be framed so that it would help men to be honest'.[125] The *Farmer's Friend* published an extract from a radical author suggesting that the solution was to pay representatives adequately, and thus remove the temptation and the need to augment their incomes; contrariwise, in Minnesota a certain amount of support developed for the reduction of official salaries: 'I think that county and state salaries for servants are to high. that there is nothing that will purify polatics as much as a reduction of salaries.'[126] Another of Donnelly's correspondents argued similarly that this would 'wipe out a good deal of Corruption. most County officers and Aspirants spend ten to fifteen hundred dollars to Buy the Election, and hence, "no poor man need Apply".'[127]

This last comment is at the heart of another of the Populists' political concerns. The strategies discussed thus far were for placing legal constraint on political abuse, but equal weight was given to solutions beyond the scope of law. There were three main points of concern here: the type of man needed in reform politics – set against their preoccupation with the corruption of the 'professional politician'; the type of intermediary organisation which could effectively and honestly link the people and those institutions formally established by the constitution – set against their concern with the massive corruption of parties; and, of major relevance to both these, the active and continual involvement of the people themselves – which raised, of course, the question of their capacity for wise choice and sustained control.

The fact that 'no poor man need Apply' suggested a problem in the qualities of their present representatives beyond that of motives of ambition or greed: they were also men who neither understood nor shared their constituents' problems. The elimination of ambition as a motive was to be the most easily solved: 'Let us make a call – first in townships, then counties, then by congressional districts; let the office seek the man.'[128] For Protestant Kansas the notion of the call to office, with its implications of unsought duty, was a logical solution, and one whose theological flavour fitted nicely with the notion that the call was to be servants of the people. This was the way to find men who would 'truly, faithfully and impartially represent the best interests of all the people', and men whose loyalties would not be for sale – 'men who we know care more for home, wife and children than for the successes of the grand old party', wrote one Republican from Americus, Kansas.[129]

The principle of the office seeking the man might also contribute to finding representatives who understood and were sympathetic to the particular interests of their constituents. This was an area on which the Populists were vulnerable to accusations of purely sectional interest and of misunderstanding the nature of democratic politics, for what they often said was that only a man of farming interests himself could represent farming interests: 'Minnesota is an agricultural state – therefore it ought to be ruled by agriculturalists.'[130] The implication could be that representatives would carry a mandate to observe only a sectional interest and not to deliberate upon the public good. In Britain this would have been heresy, but in America it did not look so far from the orthodoxy of strictly mandated delegates. But, again, this may put too elevated a construction on the Populists' intention. Certainly part of their concern came from years of sad experience of representatives who were lawyers or business men by profession – hence their specific motions excluding such men from Alliance tickets and even from Alliance membership: the Coldwater Alliance in Comanche County, for example, resolved to support no banker or lawyer candidates, but only 'farmers or farmers' friends'.[131] Partly their solution was based on the cynical conclusion, again drawn from experience, that representatives were most likely always to put their own interests first; to elect farmer representatives would thus simply ensure that their own self-interest would happily match that of their constituents:

> A man will legislate for the interests of his class, and if we send millionaires there they will enact laws for themselves. We must nominate and elect men whose interest is identical with our own if we ever get justice. . .the same policy must be adopted in politics as in our individual finances, that is if a man wants to be a success in Kansas, or elsewhere he must see to his own affairs, not leave them to his neighbours, for they have enough of their own to see to. Now apply this to the record of congress for twenty-five years past and we shall see that the lawyers and capitalists that we have sent there. . . have been too busy seeing to their own affairs; therefore it becomes necessary for a laboring man to go to Washington.[132]

As to the attribution to the Populists of a naive faith in the myth of the virtuous yeoman farmer – there is nothing to suggest that it had occurred to them that there would be any inherent virtue in men whose roots were close to the soil; common sense, reason and self interest were their justifications.

The distrustful have, by definition, both a critique of the present polity and an ideal of right government. The emotional charge from putting the two together and finding a great gulf between ideal and reality may spur them to action, particularly when their theory impresses upon them the right, and indeed duty, to participate. The most stringent test of ideals is to implement them and to cope with all the pressures of responsibility and organisation without compromise. So the distrustful must actually do better, or resign themselves to permanent discontent. If distrust is only skin deep – popular frustration at exclusion from power rather than genuine belief in the viability of some normative standard for political activity – then the truth will out once high-minded rhetoric is converted into action. The Populists were bitterly critical of the old parties and uncertain of the place of party organisation in a reformed political system. How far did they attempt to avoid the traps into which the old parties had fallen?

Henry Demarest Lloyd's bitter denunciation, in the aftermath of the fusion debate of 1896, has often been taken to prove that they were no better than the organisations and men that they sought to replace: 'Curious that the new party, the Reform party, the People's party, should be more boss-ridden, ring-ruled, gang-gangrened than the two old parties of monopoly. . .Our Initiative and Referendum had better begin, like charity, at home.'[133] But few saw any alternative to forming another party. The losing battle fought by proponents of independent action called on the constitution of the Alliance: 'Have we not resolved "to labor for the education of the agricultural classes in the science of economical government in a strictly non-partisan spirit?" ';[134] but this argument seemed based more on estimates of the relative practical advantages than on serious principle. In reply the slogan was regularly trotted out of 'principles before party' with the implication that a high minded, issue oriented movement was possible, but with no real effort to translate this into working plans: 'Principles first, then party: but party never, unless its triumph means the triumph of principles.'[135] There were some misgivings of manipulation by the professionals, and one writer foresaw a different source of vulnerability: 'Without a political organisation we have both the other parties by the nape of the neck. If we organize a party either of the old parties will have us by the seat of the breeches. . .we will, from their point of view, all be shystering office seekers.'[136] More seriously, one writer wondered: 'If the reform party should succeed today, is it sufficiently informed so to legislate as to place it beyond the power of any party to foster another system of laws equally bad with the present?'[137] It was left to a Democrat to contribute an article considering the possibility that inherent organisational requirements would make the People's Party in the long run as bad as any other. He argued that its policies made this unavoidable, for the practical requirements of, for example, administering nationalised railroads were beyond popular control – 'only a monarchy can run such things'.[138] His article was printed without comment or response; it was as near as anyone came to recognising this central dilemma of modern politics.

The most common opinion was that, although the establishment of their own organisation was a last resort, it had been forced upon them by events: 'again, the farmer is being driven into organization to perpetuate government for and by the people'.[139] And there was a great deal of optimism, simply that things would be different this time: 'Then why cannot we, who have common interests at stake, lay aside all party differences, bury all side issues, join our forces, organize an independent movement and triumphantly elect our own men to fill the offices, thus allaying all political prejudices with the sunlight of human love.'[140]

On the other hand, there are several points to be made in defence of the Populists before they are dismissed as either hypocrites or innocents. They had, in their proposals, already dealt with two of their major criticisms. By offering a party ticket of their own they were injecting a genuine choice into the electoral arena (and one which was highly successful in 1890). If their plans for letting the office seek the man came to pass, they would also have eliminated one source of power for party organisations. It is clear, too, that many of them did not envisage a permanent organisation. It would wither away with the speedy solution of their problems – an Ostrogorski-like solution of 'discarding the use of permanent parties with power as their end. . . restoring and reserving to party its essential character of a combination of citizens formed specially for a particular political issue'.[141] Or it would wither away according to a natural history of parties, as John Davis predicted. This latter theory did not really imply a cynical acceptance of the corruption of party in their own case; the corruption was something for the future – theirs to be the glorious parallel with Lincoln and the noble ideals and achievements of the early days of the Republican party.

On the face of it, the early decisions in the formation of the party seem to have been taken fairly democratically, though an eye witness account suggests a good deal of manoeuvring behind the scenes.[142] It is clear that public opinion was at least in step with the Kansas leaders, perhaps even ahead of them. The two crucial conventions, in April and June, seem to have been models of amicable discussion, the more so when compared with the stormy events of the same period in Minnesota, which included the blatant rigging of a state convention and the dismissal of the state treasurer for embezzlement.

There was some question of the wisdom of building the new party on the Alliance organisation, since the Kansas Alliance subscribed to the southern, secret order. A *Hiawatha Journal* editorial complained that 'We do not understand the workings of the Alliance or what will be its peculiar undertakings in the future. No outsiders can have an opinion of a secret order that is worth considering.'[143] A Kansan wrote to Donnelly in Minnesota for advice, because 'the Alliances in Kansas are secret we want a free open thing a public free speech with open dore and free speach'.[144] Some local chapters evidently carried on business as before – the report from Harper County commented on the nomination of an Alliance ticket, 'really the meeting put us in mind of a good old-fashioned Republican convention in this county'.[145] But the *Junction City Tribune*'s report of the establishment of the party remarked on the general feeling that the nomination process should be an open one, and the report of the proposal that the Saline County Alliance adopt the Crawford primary system suggests attempts to practise what they preached.[146]

This is scarcely much evidence of serious forethought on the Populists' part about the problems that would confront them, either from the internal pressures of organisation or the external pressures of the political world. Were they still only hypocritical, power-hungry politicians? The later years of party activity certainly offer many examples of unprincipled action, and the origins of the party are not without blemish. But one can hardly blame the Populists for not solving these problems; fortified with the analysis of Michels on the pressures of organisation, later reform parties have done little better, and much the same solutions – 'responsible' or issue oriented parties for example – are still being proposed. But the Populists didn't really try, and so to some extent are culpable of failing to meet their own standards.

Yet there is another side to the picture. The Kansas Alliancemen had little choice in 1890. They were not theoreticians, settling at a drawing board to construct the optimal model for upright and effective action, with the full battery of facts at their disposal. They were ordinary men, with pressing practical problems, making *ad hoc* responses to an urgent political situation, without the benefit of full facts and without the benefit of a full and coherent theory. Their political philosophy gave a powerful spur to action, but little practical guidance. When it came to organising and governing, their slogans were of little help. The discrepancy between democratic beliefs and the application of democratic principles may really exist in the masses of the population, as surveys have suggested, but it has not yet been proved that anti-democratic behaviour arises deliberately rather than from ignorance. The average citizen may never have thought beyond the ringing slogans of popular political culture.

— But the leaders of the Populists were educated men and it is harder to clear them of the charge of hypocrisy. Certainly it is true that the movement would never have taken off and achieved its notable successes in Kansas without their leadership. In Minnesota the membership yearned openly for leadership and for another Lincoln or Washington at their head, without perceiving any threat to popular sovereignty in this hope.[147] One can say of the elite that they were opportunists in the sense that they saw that the surge of concern with politics must be converted into action quickly, while it lasted, and they did so. Their own debates in the columns of the press do convey sincerity, and not so much a deliberate flouting of principle as a preoccupation with responses to the pressure of events. There is, though, one more test of their sincerity and realism, namely their attitude to 'the people' and to their capacity to exercise sovereignty. Cynicism here would surely condemn the leaders by their own declared standards.

One ground upon which the Saline County Alliance was urged to adopt the Crawford primary system was that 'a very important advantage. . .is that it tends to bring the candidates and voters into a closer acquaintance'.[148] The *Ottawa Journal* printed an interview with Terence V. Powderley, leader of the Knights of Labor, in which he endorsed political action, but commented that 'The work of organizing a new party, if such a thing seems necessary, lies not with the leaders but the people themselves, and it is upon the heads of the people that I would place the whole responsibility in forming such an organization.'[149] Here were two people properly concerned with the place of the ordinary members of the movement in political action. Behind the specifics of legislative reform, upright candidates, new organisations, lies the pervasive presence of the people – who must have the capacity to judge whether legislation will be in their interest, the wisdom to select men of ability and the competence to organise for permanent oversight of the polity.

The importance of the ordinary voter to political processes was accepted, and his plight in the face of the growing scale of government recognised: 'The voters' motives and purposes determine the character and quality of the government...The machinery of politics is becoming more complex every year and as a result the prostitution of public offices to base and selfish purposes is growing to alarming proportions.'[150] But the citizen was not to be excused from responsibility because of this new complexity; he was sternly reminded that the degradation of politics had been permitted by his lethargy, gullibility and abdication of powers: 'The American people have not stopped to think for years, and never would have stopped if the money had not been taken away from them', was an unusually cynical indictment from a member of the Lone Elm Alliance in Kansas.[151] But even he did not intend to imply an inevitable incapacity. In fact his plea was for time to think and to coordinate the current flood of ideas about politics. The general line of criticism was rather gentler: that the people had been easily deceived, that they had been preoccupied, like pack-horses, with their burdens, or in the words of an Ottawa leader in a moment of discouragement, that they had been apathetic, ignorant and blindly supportive of the old parties.[152]

What none of these comments suggested was that this was an inescapable state of affairs. The record of the citizens had been deplorable, but commentators did not judge their potential political efficacy from past performance. The more optimistic saw a change occurring spontaneously: for example, the reporter of a farmers' picnic on the banks of the Chikaskia River in May 1890: 'The political delusions are passing off their eyes like a dark cloud from off the sun, and they are beginning to realize the position of Adam and Eve in the garden of Eden, and are looking about for thread and "fig leaves."'[153]

Many thought that the only problem was to catch people's interest, and there must have been ample grounds for optimism in events in Kansas at this point. Alliance lecturer Mrs Hart, for example, encouraged her audience with the assurance that 'the people of this fair land, are, when once aroused to thought, intelligent enough to know what they want'.[154]

This was, no doubt, a necessary exhortation, flattering the audience and boosting their self-confidence. There is, unfortunately, no evidence of the self-assessment of the ordinary members of the Alliance, but there is some evidence of the activists' opinion of the general membership, exhortations aside. Only very occasionally was the simplest view expressed (the one that hostile critics of Populism tend to attribute to the movement) 'the mass of the people are always right on any question of vital importance'.[155] A more measured discussion argued that: 'If the legislatures of all the states and the entire congress were to resign at once, there would be brain enough in the country to fill every vacancy a hundred times, and that with talent fully equal to the present standard.'[156] But, this leader writer adds, 'we shall be glad to see the day' when there will be a greater and more intelligent interest in politics, and this is the most common line on this theme. The leaders of Populism were under no illusion as to the ignorance and apathy of many in their potential reservoir of support – but they were also confident of the possibility of change. One of the most consistent themes was of the present low level of political ability and the importance of education, general and political, to enable citizens fully to exercise their sovereignty. There was no contempt for the electorate, and the most conspiracy-minded observer would be hard put to find evidence of an intention to manipulate a simple-minded populace. The success of their movement was recognised to depend upon elevating the intellect and interest of the electorate and they were concerned with ways to do this. The trilogy of aims 'Agitate! Educate! Organize!' was the same as that of nineteenth-century radicals struggling with an equally discouraging situation in Britain, but the optimism was much greater. 'Something must be done to change men, before any ballot law will get them to vote right', acknowledged an editorial.[157] But they found plenty of encouragement:

> Doctors always first disagnose the disease before they apply a remedy.
> 'Educate the people,' was the last legacy of George Washington.
> 'Educate the people,' was the unceasing exortation of Thomas Jefferson.
> 'The education of the masses is the bulwark of our political institutions,' said Daniel Webster.
> 'The intelligence of the American people is the safe guard of our liberty,' said the immortal Henry Clay.[158]

Furthermore, even in private correspondence the Minnesota leaders, otherwise notable for vindictiveness and political scheming, took the same attitude towards their people – that the ability was there, if only it could be mobilised and educated. One writer said of the Alliance, for example: 'It is a great school for the study of human nature. I have great faith to believe that it is destined to revolutionize public sentiments and arouse the people from their lethargy in a way, and to an extent unprecedented in the history of this nation.'[159] And the Kansas Populists did embark upon a scheme for the education of the people, beyond the work already being done by the itinerant lecturers and organisers of the movement. In May, 1890, President Clover of the Kansas Alliance announced that 'Believing in the education of the common people in the principles of good government and economic questions', he was establishing a commission to consider the best means of educating the younger generation 'to profit by our failures as well as by our success, and be taught their duties as citizens and as free men and women'. His announcement concluded: 'I have heard many old men say that they had no idea...what robberies could be committed in the name of Liberty, and we don't want our children as ignorant and easily misled as we have been. "Eternal vigilance is the price of liberty".'[160]

The political creed of the Populists was not founded on simple-minded faith in the people, nor merely a front for cynical manipulation by politicians; they made a frank assessment of the problem and then pinned their faith on a reconstructed man: 'The work before us is to educate the people along the right lines, and the people will attend to the rest. It is better to be right than to belong to a party.'[161] And, in good Jeffersonian style, A. W. McCormick wrote in from Great Bend, likening the moment to the opening of the French Revolution and declaring: 'Education is the demand of this hour. Whatever develops and educates the best sentiment in the heart of the people at the firesides is a benefit and a blessing to the nation, for it is through these homes that the commonwealth breathes.'[162]

The Populists came down, with Jefferson, for the Enlightenment theory of the perfectible nature of man. Yet there have been contradictory hints in their statements that their hopes for the future were not of unqualified optimism. Certainly, if education was to be the solution, it was for the long term; furthermore, it was to make eternal vigilance effective, not unnecessary. And they could not think only in terms of the distant future, but had to confront immediate needs and prospects – a time scale on which they were all too conscious of the continuing vulnerability of those in power to corruption and of the citizen body to be gulled into apathy. The tension between long term and vague optimism and immediate and specific realism appears repeatedly in the political thought of the Populists. This latest example is only another dimension of the problem created by the gap between an inspirational philosophy and its implementation in practice, seen already in the strong push to action which that philosophy provided without any constructive guidance on the avoidance of old organisational failures. By technical measures of ideological coherence and constraint the Populist political philosophy would rightly be found wanting. But it would be as much of a mistake therefore to dismiss it and them, as to attempt to present them as effective political actors with a viable reconciliation of the contradictory requirements of modern government and democratic theory. More sophisticated and detached theorists have failed to solve the problems which the Populists confronted, sometimes without really recognising them, and many of their dilemmas are still current today. It is worth concluding by reviewing briefly some of their contributions to understanding these dilemmas, along with the ways in which their example demonstrates the role of political culture in shaping political events.

The Populists fit the pattern of the politically distrustful precisely. The definition of distrust as a perception of discrepancy usefully directs attention to their preoccupation, the gulf between those principles ostensibly accepted by every participant in politics yet flagrantly abused by the substitution of quite opposite guidelines in practice. They identified real offences by individuals and within institutions, in judgements much more profound than the usual complaints of promises broken by politicians. Their solutions, both through their own intervention and in proposals for structural reform, were directed at precisely those practices which they condemned, and in theory were entirely consistent with the principles they upheld. The inadequacies of their position emerged at a later stage, when in practice there were many questionable features of Populist political activity, from which the defence of pressure of events, inexperience or even good intentions cannot altogether excuse them. Thus the irony of the history of Populism is that the movement itself developed just such a discrepancy between principle and performance as it had intended to eliminate from politics. This could be seen as evidence of that inherent flaw in political man which Americans have always suspected, but it also points to two more immediate problems, which have persistently undermined democratic reformers in American politics: the nature of their philosophy

of government and the typical capacities and experience of the distrustful.

The political culture of the Populists both helped and hindered
them. Straightforward desperation was undoubtedly part of the reason
for the outburst of independent political activity in Kansas in 1890.
But it was largely because of their political beliefs that action rather
than fatalism resulted from their desperation, and that action took the
form of a political movement aimed at changing political institutions,
as comparison with the British will underline in my next chapter.

The positive contribution of Populist political culture came first
from its general vitality. At the start of the new party those involved
were inspired and excited by the prospect, as if this really was to be the
assertion of their dignity as democratic citizens; a contemporary
observer described the early days as 'a religious revival, a crusade, a
pentecost of politics in which a tongue of flame set upon every man,
and each spake as the spirit gave him utterance'.[163] More specifically,
the political culture gave positive encouragement through several related items concerning the role and potential of politics and the place
of the ordinary citizen in relation to political institutions. First, there
was the certainty that politics was not only the proper place for their
grievances to be resolved, but that, once purified, it guaranteed success.
Yet more important was the fact that these citizens did not feel helpless
against their government. The alleged link between political alienation
and feelings of inefficacy and powerlessness did not exist for the Populists. They did appreciate that their resources and experience were
woefully inadequate by comparison with the powerful. But they were
reassured that nonetheless they had a duty to take political action and
that when they did so might and right would surely be on their side.
The clue to this paradoxical mixture of realism and optimism was that
for political purposes they did not see themselves as detached individuals, separately confronting a distant polity. They shared a very
real collective identity, not a class consciousness derived from distinctions of economic or social structure, but a political identity as 'the
People'. This perhaps is the answer to that theory which holds that the
act of voting must always be irrational, since a single vote will never
make any difference to the result. The Populists thought in terms of
the collective vote of 'the People', before which obstructive minorities
or electoral manipulation must inevitably give way. For them, 'We
the People' was not merely a rhetorical flourish to the preamble to the
Constitution; whatever the framers of that document had intended, it

was an entity of which they knew themselves to be a part and in which they understood that sovereignty rightly resided.

Thus, on the one hand, political culture overrode a potential incapacity which has often been expected to inhibit action by the distrustful. Individual feelings of powerlessness may be irrelevant when it is collective action that is envisaged. But on the other hand there were features of their political culture which combined with the objective facts of their political capacities to reduce severely the probability of effective action.

Their political beliefs were inspirational but not programmatic. The notion of 'government of the people, by the people and for the people' is a fine one, but offers no clue as to how it might be translated into effective structures. Further, the new or reformed structures have to be effective in two different and possibly incompatible ways. Distrust in Kansas became intense at the point where the failure of political institutions to deliver expected material and social benefits became intolerable. Practical failure was then explained by the normative failure of the institutions. But the Populists barely touched upon the dilemma of choice between the equally desirable but possibly irreconcilable values of democracy and efficiency (a particularly crucial choice in complex industrial societies where, as they did understand, government must play a large role). Few have confronted this as directly as the reluctant Progressive who declared that 'We would, if we had to choose, rather have bad government with democracy than good government without it. . .Democracy is a soul satisfying thing.'[164] For the democratic elitists the choice went the other way, with the implications somewhat obscured by the simultaneous effort to dissociate the ideas of democracy and participation. More commonly the problem is simply passed by, nowhere more clearly than in the Presidential campaign of Jimmy Carter, who combined to great rhetorical effect the Populist language of aspiring to involve all the people more closely and continuously in government with denunciations and proposals in the name of the managerial criterion of efficiency. Perhaps President Carter, with the intellectual and practical resources of the country at his command, will begin to resolve the difficulties of creating a government which can be effective on both counts. Ironically, it would seem that the ordinary distrustful, disproportionately drawn from the lower educated and the politically inexperienced, must depend on leadership, from experienced politicians or the educated minority of their own number, to provide a core of analytical and executive skill if either of their aims are to be implemented. The case of the Populists underlines the problems, but provides no evidence on either the practicality or compatibility of their aims.

The experience of Populism does offer a lesson to those with political power, about the nature and threat of distrust. Cynically it might be said that the lesson is that swift action to co-opt or undermine may save, for a while at least, much of the existing power structure – divide and rule remains a handy maxim. But the more serious lesson should be that the distrustful critique may be justified and should be taken seriously, but does not immediately threaten democratic politics itself. The rhetoric in which the Populists expressed their distrust would not sound archaic in political debate today. Indeed they might feel very much at home. Public dissatisfaction may once more have reached a point where it cannot be defused simply by offering new policies. The national parties in 1888 had begun to respond to discontent; the beginnings of change can be identified in their underlying philosophies and new campaign methods in that year, and their platforms did offer clear alternatives, for example on the crucial tariff question.[165] Similarly, in the 1972 Presidential election or the 1974 British election voters had as real a choice of policy directions as has been seen of late, and yet the air was full of the cry that there was no difference between the parties. This makes sense only with the recognition that discontent has escalated above policy matters to a more fundamental point. Policy choices come too late once the belief has grown that both parties will equally betray any promises and all their supporters when they gain office.

This withdrawal of diffuse support – general loyalty or legitimacy – may result in the political system being shaken by massive realignments, the appearance of new political forces, and by responsive structural adaptations. But the evidence of the Populists suggests that to see the presence of widespread distrust as the makings of a deeper crisis of democracy is at least premature. If their criticism is taken even further the potential threat will be much greater, for the commitment to norms and values is a deeper one and the consequences if that falters inevitably far more radical. The Populists wanted a restoration of democracy, not its overthrow, and they believed that new men and modified structures would be enough to achieve this. But the presence of distrust is a warning that, left unresolved or treated with contempt, a deeper disillusion with norms and values themselves may grow, and then democracy indeed will be threatened.

The open expression of distrust and solutions to it came easily to the

Populists. They were confident that they were acting only as distinguished Americans had advised and acted before them. Their political culture was highly supportive and easy of access to the simplest citizen. Their historical knowledge and intellectual background were not profound, but they did not need to be. The commonplaces of American political culture gave all that was necessary to legitimate their criticism and encourage their action. Indeed, this supportive frame of reference not only structured consequences, it legitimated distrust itself. 'Eternal vigilance is the price of liberty' was Jefferson's precis of the ambivalence that had been present even in the first optimism of the independent states, where: 'Faith ran high that a better world than any that had ever been known could be built where authority was distrusted and held in constant scrutiny.'[166] The Populists believed that the abuse of power had reached an abnormal level in their own time, but their discussions and measures against abuse confirmed their belief that authority must not temporarily but always be 'distrusted and held in constant scrutiny'. Their hope was to restore a lost balance, not to inaugurate an immediate Utopia; this balance would be gained, but not easily, through the recovery of effective popular sovereignty. It was not naivety but traditionalism which gave them their faith that trust would be restored through the use of the ballot, so far as it would be restored at all, and led them to couple the means and the end so hopefully in their rousing antiphonal chorus:

> voting on/voting on/
> Let us work/And watch/let us vote/and trust/
> And labor till the vict'ry comes.[167]

4. Rank and file Liberalism

Class and political culture in Victorian Britain

In February, 1891, John Abercrombie, a Scot settled in Douglas County, Minnesota, wrote reminiscently to the State Populist leader, Ignatius Donnelly:

> Come down nearer to our own times, to what I witnessed with my own eyes, when the British Workingman wanted an extension of the 'Franchise', when wealth, nobility and all the strength of an erudite sophistry as personified in a Salisbury; and all the strength of the cunning of a politician as personified in a D'Israeli, when all combined said no, even we shall shut up the public parks so you can meet there, never, to discuss your rights; could *we* then in a brief few months gained our ends had we not been imbued with a spirit of humble unison; the lathe, the forge, the loom, the mine, the quarry, the railroad employee, combined, cried, onward, we are one, 'out' with D'Israeli, 'in' with Gladstone and it was so. There is no difference between the motives that impelled the British Workman then, and the American Laborers, who are Farmers, now, and there ought to be no difference in the principles of mode of action which are absolute union based on humility and single-ness of heart.[1]

There cannot have been many working men who participated in both the British political reform movement of the 1860s and the American Populist Party. Which makes it doubly disconcerting that a rare eye-witness comparison should make precisely the opposite point to mine. Perhaps the passage of time had given a romantic glow to Abercrombie's memories of the franchise reformers' successful assault on the Hyde Park railings, or perhaps the internecine ethnic and personal rivalries of Minnesota Populism lent some justification to his comparison. But a review of the politics of the British working class towards the end of the nineteenth century finds, rather than unity and singleness of heart, a largely negative situation, characterised by passivity, fragmentation and a cautious pragmatism.

In America, the Populists showed how profoundly loyal citizenship could generate both a biting criticism of the political system and a logical programme of reform, and they seemed but an exaggerated example of an endemic American trait of disaffection with politics. In Britain there were only intermittent outbursts of constitutional criticism and, while it does not automatically follow that critical attitudes were absent from the minds of the populace, there is an obvious practical problem in proving their existence. Most assumptions about the political culture of the Victorian man in the street are inferences from the behaviour and public reasoning of statesmen or borrowings from the classic contemporary observers. There is remarkably little first hand evidence, even of the acquiescent, if ignorant, cast of mind so often assumed to have been the norm.

In searching for more than speculation about the existence of distrust in British political history the object is not to find a case typical of some mythical, homogeneous political culture. The political culture of a nation is rarely a consensual matter and where there is common ground it may well reflect compromising acceptance rather than enthusiastic endorsement of institutions and procedures. The Kansas Populists were not typical of all their American contemporaries in their political culture any more than in their social characteristics. Valid comparisons from their case are with individuals or movements who share their critique and philosophy – a syndrome which has not been the exclusive possession of any single social group in America (although some may have articulated it with more sincerity than others, since for the underprivileged its fulfilment involves no altruism or sacrifice). The structural location of the distrustful will be important to the meaning of distrust, where this is couched in terms of a particular class or group interest rather than in the inclusive interest of the people; it will always be of significance for the consequences of distrust, because of the systematic variation across societies in the incidence of political expertise and sophistication. Thus, the first requirement for a historical case study of political distrust in Britain must be the clarity of the critical political attitudes themselves, regardless of their relationship to 'normal' political expression. Whether these attitudes were, or are inevitably, the expression of a single group or class, or are potentially available to all, is a subsequent but important question.

Several accounts of the working class in Britain suggest that political distrust may have been endemic there.[2] Indeed, this may have been a clear point of difference between the workers and middle class, since the propensity of the latter to deferential attitudes and behaviour is well supported by evidence.[3] But these intimations of distrust are based upon memory or local folklore as often as on hard evidence; clearly it was rarely articulated in forms which survive as public records. However, political reform movements sprang up from time to time, from the nature of their proposals apparently critical of the *status quo*. Therefore, in a reversal of the procedure of the previous chapter, where the political criticism of the Populists offered a starting point, and the philosophy and the movement were found to underpin and follow from this, in Britain it is necessary to start with an implicitly critical political programme and to work back to its environment in search of its source and rationale.

The radical Liberalism of Birmingham in the late nineteenth century implied a position critical of contemporary national government, through both its rhetoric and local practice. Conveniently also, in aspects of political and social context there are enough points of similarity to simplify comparison with the Kansas Populists. Political distrust is a perception of people who are members of the polity they criticise; the high point of Birmingham Liberalism followed the admission of a considerable portion of the working class to the political community as active participants. Both Liberals and Populists had some political experience, similar political rights, access to political information and communications, and both were peripheral to the exercise of real power. Despite the vast differences in social circumstances between the Kansas farmer and the British worker, both were situated in rapidly modernising societies where economic position and social relationships were a rich and ambiguous mixture of the characteristics of pre-industrial communities and industrial society.

The merits of the Birmingham Liberals as a case where distrust might be expected to appear are several. In the first place, their rhetoric has much in common with that of the Populists, with Joseph Chamberlain leading them with the inspiration of Lincoln's ideal of 'government of the people, by the people and for the people'. The duty which the Populists felt that this ideal laid upon them, of sustained vigilance and criticism, seemed a deliberate and logical legitimation of distrust. If the logic holds good in the British case too, the radical democracy of the Liberal demands should be one component of political distrust.

A second and connected aspect of their political programme reinforces this expectation: earlier reform groups had tended to demand an extension of existing political rights, while, in its policies and by the fact of its innovative organisation, the Birmingham Liberal caucus made a significant challenge to the survival of existing patterns of power. Earlier in the century, reform movements of all classes had concentrated upon gaining extensions of the franchise. After the 1867 Reform Act there was a certain air of satisfaction prevalent, that the working class had now been given their full and fair political weight, even though in practice the overt intention of the Act was outrageously undermined by the injustices of the registration system and the anomalies of the distribution of Parliamentary seats.[4] But the Reform League withered away and the occasional attempt at organisation outside existing partisan bodies had such slight public impact as to confirm the standard accounts of passivity among the lower orders. Chamberlain's Liberals supported demands for the further extension of suffrage, now to the agricultural workers, but they also insisted that the vote should acquire new power and meaning.

Their local party structure was an elaborate hierarchy, from ward associations up through a Central Committee, formally responsible for policy making and candidate selection, to a smaller Executive Committee and finally the Management Committee of elected officials of the citywide Association. It was violently criticised because it seemed to establish a new relationship between the Member of Parliament and his constituents, one in which the representative would be instructed and closely controlled rather than dispatched to Westminster to make decisions according to his best judgement.[5] Alarmed opponents felt that the caucus would 'Americanise' British politics, by which dire threat was meant principally the introduction of the patronage and corruption then rampant in the urban machines of America, if not more widely.[6] Joseph Chamberlain rightly treated the general point as more serious than the subsequent specifics, but in the defence of the new structure he drew these together and turned them to his advantage. The corruption charges he rejected as unwarranted pessimism, but he did cheerfully acknowledge American influence on the philosophy of the caucus. Its aim, he declared, was simply 'to make more real, more direct, and more constant the influence of the people in the management of their own affairs', and their emulation of America was solely because 'Americans have acted on the opinion that government, whether of the nation or of a party within it, rightly belongs to the majority'.[7] But if this was so, what the radical Liberals were really calling for was no less than a fundamental rearrangement of the sources of political power in Britain, and they were doing so in the name of principles of democracy which were quite incompatible with the traditional norms of parliamentary government.

The caucus, the citywide organisation of the Liberal Party for the three-member Birmingham constituency, had developed by 1867, to cope with the mobilisation of an electorate vastly expanded by the Reform Act of that year. If voting was a new experience for the city's workers, political activity was certainly not – their reputation was already national and based on fifty years or more of campaigning for the fair representation of the city nationally and the extension of the franchise. Their most notable organisation had been Attwood's Political Union, formed in 1831 and significantly subtitled 'of the Lower and Middle Classes of the People'.[8] After 1867, within the framework of permanent organisation there were fluctuating levels of involvement and debate, usually centred around national or local elections. But a period from mid 1883 to the end of 1884 promises to offer the same rise in concern with political institutions and procedures, without the immediate pressures of electoral strategy to distract the attention, which occurred in Kansas in the early months of 1890.

Political reform was again prominent in public debate. By this time, too, workers enfranchised in 1867 had had time to see for themselves how far their admission to the electorate had been a genuine grant of power. Demands for further reform had been heard sporadically for years. But by the summer of 1883 factions were taking up positions for and against legislation, and anticipating the introduction of a bill before the next election. Gladstone had said in 1880, as he formed a Liberal government, that reform was an issue that 'entailing as it would a new dissolution, ought to be deferred till towards the close of the Parliament just elected'.[9] He proposed legislation at an autumn Cabinet in 1883 and may well not have been influenced at all by the public agitation which had been gathering strength through the summer. But the attention of the people of Birmingham had been sharply focused on the question earlier in the year, certainly by the beginning of July when a public speech by Chamberlain calling for reform was reported and discussed at some length in the local press.[10] From then until the Franchise Bill received the royal assent in December 1884 the progress of reform was closely followed. Editorials and reports in the press, and rallies and discussions in the streets, were regular events. It was a concentration as temporary as the philosophical period of the Populists; once the Franchise Bill was passed it was assumed that the other bone of contention, redistribution, would also be dealt with, and attention turned away to other issues.

But during those eighteen months people were continually and controversially exposed to challenges to the existing patterns of political behaviour. Two Birmingham Members of Parliament, Chamberlain and Bright, were among the most prominent national reformers, and they were constantly in contention with each other and with their parliamentary colleagues. With the Lords' rejection of the Franchise Bill in July, 1884, the constitutional position of the upper house became a burning issue. Chamberlain's involvement in the controversies over the Irish question, as well as the discovery of the vulnerability of Parliamentary procedures to obstruction by the Irish minority, again focused attention on the basis of representation of a diverse electorate. In April, 1884, Lord Randolph Churchill, 'with an effrontery that almost reaches the sublime',[11] announced his intention of contesting Birmingham at the next election, and thereby generated not only angry partisan reaction but also some debate on the desirability of aristocratic representation of a predominantly working class constituency. At this time also, the caucus pressured one of the city's members, Mr Muntz, to resign, both for health and doctrinal reasons, and a new candidate had to be chosen. In local elections the hold of the caucus seemed to be weakening and the Conservatives to be presenting serious opposition. And in October of 1884 the local tradition of disciplined political demonstrations turned into destructive partisan rioting at Aston Hall, when Liberals swamped a Conservative fund-raising fete. Political rights and political duties could hardly fail to be much in people's minds.

At first glance the caucus seems to have been massively supported by the ordinary people of the city. Under Chamberlain's leadership, the Birmingham Liberal Association more or less swept the board in parliamentary, municipal and School Board elections from 1868 through the early 1880s. The Birmingham electorate tripled after 1867 to an estimated 45,000,[12] and Liberal support came not only in voting but in meetings, parades and canvassing activities – and apparently came willingly from the vast majority of the local political community. But why did they support so steadily an organisation based on such radical and contentious ideas? Was it from conviction and a coherent analysis of the wrongs which this radical creed was to right? Or were the rank and file, as some critics have suggested, seduced by brass bands and demagoguery into mindless acquiescence, or driven there for want of a convincing alternative or from docile deference to their local 'commercial aristocracy'? And did this apparent unanimity of behaviour anyway rest upon a common social situation and shared political beliefs which can be simply defined as 'working class'?

Whether the caucus was simply a tool of ambitious politicians, manipulating the public for its own advantage, or alternatively a thoroughly democratic organisation genuinely involving the new mass electorate in political decision making must remain an open question for the moment. Certainly the protagonists' own claims must be taken with a pinch of salt – Chamberlain's declaration that 'It cannot be too strongly insisted on that *the caucus does not make opinion, it only expresses it*',[13] for example, must be read in the context of the hierarchical committee structure. Major resolutions were formulated and powerful speakers chosen to present them to the membership by a Management Committee with an average attendance of five or six, and the editor of the major local mass circulation daily paper was reproved when his editorials stepped out of line with caucus policy.[14] On the other hand, the local wit who commented:

> Of the Six Hundred, only three,
> Suffice to rule our destiny.[15]

clearly underestimated the extent of popular consensus, and indeed enthusiasm. Rallies would regularly bring out anything from a few hundred to one hundred thousand in support of the party line, numbers which cannot simply be accounted for by manipulation or bribery.

Part of the explanation for the genuine support for the caucus may perhaps be found in the crusading nonconformist sense of duty, which transcended class lines, of this city 'where politics were conceived of by so many leaders and followers as the extension of a gospel'.[16] And part of the explanation may lie in the standard account of the political behaviour of the Victorian working classes: that their political actions were governed by their willingness to defer to their social – or political – betters. The standard account of the political behaviour of the Victorian working classes, however, is itself a matter on which preconceptions and controversies have been as rife as in the case of the Populists. The evidence is mostly indirect and often from biased contemporaries and, furthermore, much of this evidence suggests that, as late as the 1880s, the working classes were indeed still plural and their attitudes towards politics equally diverse. Yet this is not to say that the concept of class can be ignored. Its objective and subjective identification may be complex, but it was by the middle of the nineteenth century a crucial factor in British politics.

British radicals in the eighteenth century had shared a political philosophy with their American contemporaries. Its rhetoric reappeared in reform movements throughout the succeeding century, but, whereas in America it had remained dominant and intellectually alive, here it was increasingly stagnant.[17] Economic radicalism, based upon a conception of an hierarchical society of social classes, gradually supplanted political radicalism, based upon a belief in the primacy of the political rights of individual citizens in a society of equality (in civil rights, but not necessarily in social or economic position). By the mid nineteenth century class had been institutionalised, with the acknowledgement of class-based social and economic organisations, and the potential for class conflict contained by allowing for a modest degree of social mobility.[18]

Yet the recognition by all sides of class as a legitimate concept in political debate did not rest on a tidy transition from traditional social divisions to a society which, by objective criteria of economic attributes or types of social relationships, or in the consciousness of its members or indeed in their political behaviour, could be described in terms of mutually exclusive groups. The process of social change was long, erratic and incomplete and each of these aspects had its own timing and significance for politics.

It seems likely that, while there was an overall rise in living standards during the nineteenth century, in terms of relative income the rich grew richer and the poor poorer. But this did not mean that some straightforward criterion, such as the division between wage earners and those with other sources of income, demarcated a homogeneous working class. There was a similar process of polarisation between wage earners over the middle years of the century, so that by the 1870s a minority of perhaps ten per cent formed a labour aristocracy, whose skills were reflected in both income and status.[19] But there was a considerable time lag in the development of similar distinctions in social relationships, both between and within classes. Reference to even the unskilled workers as a depersonalised mass is probably not appropriate for most of the century, since neither the factory system nor urban life necessarily or immediately resulted in the isolation of a proletariat from personal relations outside their own stratum. Not only did the wide diffusion of small property ownership and hence employment in relatively small units remain more characteristic of the economy than the massive accumulation of wealth by a new class of capitalists, but even within many factories the relationships between employers and employees remained traditional, personal ones – patron–client relations of mutuality rather than the impersonal linkage of the wage packet.[20]

This mixture of traditional and industrial relations not only blurred the impact of economic differences but had an effect on the subjective sense of class of the workers themselves. As late as 1886, a Dr Ogle, writing on the census, reported:

> It was suggested, as had been suggested many times before, that the employers should be distinguished from the employed...nobody was more anxious than those concerned in the census that, if it were posible, such a distinction should be made, and special directions were given on the schedule that every worker should state whether he was master or man; but it was all in vain: workmen would not do anything of the kind. He believed that out of the 26 millions of people in England and Wales, there were not 1,000 who had returned themselves as journeymen anything.[21]

The development of a consciousness of class, both as a source of personal identity and for the expression of a group interest in society, is the crucial link if the objective facts of class are to be translated into political culture and action; here it was itself incomplete and there was a further lag and complexity in its reflection in politics.

For all the differences of income and status between workers, they had a shared sense of identification with a working class in general. The dividing line was drawn, as in the twentieth century, between blue collar and white collar worker, and below this great divide the labour aristocracy were, paradoxically, as sure of their shared membership of the working class as they were of their social superiority to their fellow workers.[22] But social consciousness and political consciousness were not necessarily integrated. Ostrogorski observed the effect of this distinction, and its cause, in his observations upon the Birmingham caucus: 'Shopkeepers, clerks, and superior artisans, this is the sphere from which most of the active members of the Caucus are taken. Their great eagerness to join it has a good deal to do with their moral position in English society.'[23] Two factors thus mediated between class consciousness and politics: the survival of traditional relationships and the question of moral position.

Traditional political relationships outlasted traditional social relationships, just as these last showed a lag behind economic facts. Poll books for elections before 1872 show time and again the same pattern of working class electoral participation:

> The influence of employers over their own workmen was of such an all-pervading nature that there was rarely any question of bringing direct pressure to bear on them to force them to vote for their masters. The workman would normally vote for his employer because he knew him, because he respected him (or at least regarded him as a symbol of authority), because it was universally expected of him, because the livelihood of so

many men depended on the employer that his interests seemed akin to
theirs, and not infrequently because employer and employee shared the
same political views.[24]

There is no reason to suppose that such ingrained patterns changed
radically with the introduction of the secret ballot. Certainly in
Birmingham they appear to have survived until after the political
reforms of 1884–5.[25] Chamberlain had enlarged and rationalised his
family firm and the whole screw manufacturing industry before he
embarked on a political career. His biographer recounts how he took
over Nettlefold and Chamberlain and 'relentlessly but honestly'
eliminated all competition, in a process with later political parallels:
'Nothing is more important for an understanding of Chamberlain than
to remember that in Britain he had been a pioneer of large-scale production by consolidated enterprise.'[26] When he stood for political office,
he had a guaranteed body of support, despite these modernising
activities, from the employees of his own enterprise: 'His whole
sympathy was with the working classes. Intimate with his own working
people in the factory and in their homes, he knew how to win their
allegiance. . .there never was a strike amongst those in his service.'[27]

Since Attwood's Political Union had brought together the 'Lower
and Middle Classes of the People', Birmingham had been known for
political cooperation between the classes. Its economic structure was
notable for the proliferation of small workshop industries, and so there
were inevitably close relations between masters and men. Many of the
city's artisans were self-employed or wielded considerable delegated
authority as foremen and on the spot decision makers in small concerns. Far from this making it, as is sometimes alleged, atypical of
Victorian industrial milieux, in the context of the very slow change
towards the class politics expected of an impersonal industrial society
it is clear that, as late as the 1880s, it was still typical of a tenacious
political traditionalism.

The connection of moral position to politics was through a cultural
value which cut across class lines and divided workers from each other.
This was a factor distinctive to the time – 'the great Victorian shib-
boleth' – respectability:

> Here was the sharpest of all lines of social division, between those who were
> and those who were not respectable: a sharper line by far than that
> between rich and poor, employer and employee, or capitalist and pro-
> letarian. To be respectable in mid-Victorian Britain had the same cachet as
> being a good party man in a communist state. The respectable man was a
> good man, and also a pillar of society.[28]

Though respectability was primarily a state of mind, the poor and destitute could not afford those minimal social standards necessary to qualify and so, in this case, the upper parts of the working class were marked off from the lower – and they well appreciated the distinction: 'And they were right: for their lot does just offer them the opportunity of being gentlemen in spirit and in truth.'[29]

The greatest political impact of this factor may well have been on the reactions of those in power. The perception that there were two different kinds of workers was widespread and entered significantly into calculations of the wisdom of political reform. There was some confusion about the political propensities of the unrespectable lowest orders, on the one hand labelled the 'dangerous classes' while on the other reassuringly found to be virtually irrelevant to politics: 'as un-political as footmen, and instead of entertaining violent democratic opinions, they appear to have no political opinions whatever; or if they do possess any, they rather tend towards the maintenance of "things as they are" than towards the ascendancy of the working people'.[30] Or, as Bagehot put it, with evident relief, 'the most miserable of these classes do not impute their misery to politics'.[31] But the 1867 Reform Act had anyway not been concerned with this group, but with the respectable and self-respecting upper reaches of the workers; here too confusion appears in contemporary debates. Few shared Disraeli's public confidence that respectability would triumph over class and provide a new body of responsible and Conservative voters. Bagehot's fear was pervasive: 'As a theoretical writer I can venture to say, what no elected member of Parliament, Conservative or Liberal, can venture to say, that I am exceedingly afraid of the ignorant multitude of the new constituencies. I wish to have as great and compact a power as possible to resist it.'[32] Bagehot and his near-contemporary, the social observer Charles Booth, both made it uneasily clear that even ignorance might seem a blessing by comparison with another tendency which they identified in the better educated levels of the working class. It was in Booth's category of 'Working class, comfortable' that 'we find the springs of Socialism and Revolution'.[33] The labour aristocracy in constituencies like Birmingham offered a greater threat than that of 'primitive barbarism' in Bagehot's view: 'A great many ideas, a great many feelings have gathered about the town artisans – peculiar intel-lectual life has sprung up among them. They believe that they have interests which are misconceived or neglected.'[34]

Bagehot believed that moderate and responsible government could only survive the admission of the lower classes to politics through the inculcation of deference in the new electorate. In a deferential nation 'certain persons are by common consent agreed to be wiser than others'.[35] But this had thus far been achieved less from any instinctive inclination in the national character to trust a wiser class than because of a massive confidence trick, somewhat unwittingly perpetrated by the ruling class:

> As yet the few rule by their hold, not over the reason of the multitude, but over their imaginations, and their habits; over their fancies as to distant things they do not know at all, over their customs as to near things which they know very well. A deferential community in which the bulk of the people are ignorant, is therefore in a state of what is called in mechanics unstable equilibrium. If the equilibrium is disturbed there is no tendency to return to it. . .if you once permit the ignorant class to rule you may bid farewell to deference for ever.[36]

To Bagehot's anxious eyes it appeared that this equilibrium was immediately threatened by that stratum of the working classes which, while in fact as ignorant as ever, misguidedly no longer saw itself as ignorant. For the reason that Bagehot's deference worked was that it comprised two beliefs – a view (fortunately mistaken) of where power lay in politics, and a view (Bagehot believed accurate) of the incapacity of all but the few to engage effectively in politics. Thus deference was the loyalty given to the pomp and circumstances of ceremonial and the 'theatrical show of society',[37] but equally essential was the self-denigration of the deferential. In the contemplation of the 'wonderful scene of wealth and enjoyment' ordinary men felt humbled – 'their imagination is bowed down; they feel that they are not equal to the life that is revealed to them'; they believe that 'a common man may as well try to rival the actors on the stage in their acting, as the aristocracy in *their* acting'.[38] In modern terminology, Bagehot was claiming that the deferential were so because their observation of society engendered strong feelings of political inefficacy. The combination seemed as productive to Bagehot as apathy did to the democratic elitists of the 1950s, for it provided consent without interference from the immoderate masses.

The high levels of participation by the enlarged electorate of Birmingham might, on the face of it, seem just the kind of threat to stability which Bagehot envisaged. Yet, as a test of his analysis, Birmingham politics reveal the problems of his concept of deference. He believed its effect to be that, dazzled by the bright lights of power, the people were content to let the real work of governing proceed in the shadows:

> If you look at the mass of the constituencies, you will see that they are not very interesting people; and perhaps if you look behind the scenes and see the people who manipulate and work the constituencies, you will find that these are yet more uninteresting. The English constitution in its palpable form is this – the mass of the people yield obedience to a select few; and when you see this select few, you perceive that though not of the lowest class, nor of an unrespectable class, they are yet of a heavy sensible class.[39]

This would appear to be just the case in Birmingham, with its 'heavy sensible' political elite of Christian businessmen. But there is no evidence that the Birmingham citizenry were thus dazzled. Their support went to men who stood openly in opposition to the traditional ruling elite, and who, though not Republicans, had been openly suspected of Republicanism by the Queen. The most prominent local leader, Joseph Chamberlain, was himself ready to fight the Parliamentary leadership, to resign office on grounds of conscience, and finally to leave his party and take much of the local rank and file over to the opposition with him. Such constant controversy, regularly and thoroughly aired in the local press, must surely have presented a severe challenge to any blind loyalty to distant symbols of power. If the Birmingham electorate was deferential, it cannot have been in the sense of dazzlement by symbols or respect for the suitable breeding of a natural ruling class; it can only have been to the superior qualifications or proven ability of their political leaders in political matters. Such deference is a recognition of the advantages of a division of labour in politics – a rational rather than emotional willingness to let the best qualified men govern. This is a deference without Bagehot's connotations of inefficacy, for it allows the political self-respect of the citizen to remain intact. The citizens' estimate of their own political role is crucial for understanding the political behaviour of the mass electorate of Birmingham. For on the face of it, much of this behaviour appeared to be automatic responses to initiatives and commands from the caucus leadership. But if they were indeed giving their support unthinkingly, then they were more inadequate even than Bagehot's political type. For they espoused, in the constitution and structures of the caucus, ideals which were entirely incompatible with the notion of deference, calling for the channelling of communication, and indeed of sovereignty, upwards from the bottom of the organisation. Could those at the bottom genuinely believe this and yet willingly behave in a contrary fashion? Or were they, like the Populists, largely unaware of the contradictions between the inevitabilities of mass organisation and their own political philosophy?

Class and deference loom large in both contemporary and academic discussions of Victorian politics. If they meant much to the rank and file Liberal membership in Birmingham, the political culture there will inevitably have been very different from that of the Kansas Populists, despite the slogans of radical democracy which both groups appeared to endorse. The social and cultural context in which the Liberals existed was full of confusion and contradictions, and these must surely have impinged on their consciousness of their own social identity and political potential.

The political culture of Birmingham

In October 1883 the Management Committee of the Birmingham Liberal Association prepared a resolution to be presented to the forthcoming meeting of the General Committee, the Eight Hundred, and thereby inaugurated the official campaign in the city for the speedy passage of reform legislation. They demanded the 'extension of the Franchise to Householders in the Counties', and that this be ' "immediately followed by a measure intended to correct the anomalous condition of our representative system" ' – i.e. redistribution. The motion concluded:

> That while this Association is prepared to accept these measures as instalments of the necessary reform of the House of Commons, it looks forward to the ultimate extension of the Franchise to all Englishmen of adult age, not disqualified by crime; equal electoral districts; shorter Parliaments; and the payment of members.[40]

These seem modest demands by comparison with those of the Populists, and even in Britain they were hardly novel to those who remembered the Chartist days. When the Liberals spoke of their aim of achieving government of, for and by the people, were these the only practical reforms they proposed to that end? Occasionally the rank and file seemed to want to go further, once provoking an anxious newspaper editorial warning that 'persons concerned in promoting popular demonstrations will do well to reduce their demands as far as possible to practicability, and to be temperate in them'.[41] But such demands were rare, and grass roots leadership in any independent action was entirely absent throughout this period.

In the case of the Populists it was clear that the pace of events was

forced by the pace at which public opinion developed, and that the
state leadership needed to do little but coordinate the spontaneous outburst of strong feeling. Birmingham sources give the clear impression
that the popular mood was a response to leadership. There were few
channels for the spontaneous expression of public opinion even though
that public was probably literate and thoughtful above the national
average.[42] Birmingham did support a flourishing local press, but this
consisted of a small number of large-circulation papers, in sharp contrast to the multiplicity of small publications in Kansas. Though no
records of its circulation have survived, it is clear that the halfpenny
Liberal daily paper, the *Birmingham Daily Mail,* prospered and was
successfully directed at the working class from its establishment in
1870.[43] For the twenty years or so till the rise of the cheap national
dailies around 1890, this, together with such mass-circulation national
weeklies as *Reynold's,* must have been the main source of political news
and comment for the local working class; the *Mail* provides the main
source for this study of rank and file politics in Birmingham, since for
all its limitations it is virtually all that survives.

The *Mail* was regarded by the upper reaches of Birmingham society
as representing well both the opinions and the vices of the lower orders
– its editor recalled that 'respectable citizens' were known to refer to it
as the *Daily Liar* and that one city alderman would remove copies
found in his home 'with a pair of tongs'.[44] By the time that he wrote
his memoirs, the editor, H. J. Jennings, had become an embittered
convert to Conservatism, but there is probably not too much bias in
his allusion to the caucus as a case of the tail wagging the dog – 'and
what a remarkably docile dog it was'.[45] But he certainly gave the dog
no outlet for its own thoughts in his columns. The *Mail* was definitely
a one way channel of communication. There was none of the correspondence from readers, nor the articles by political outsiders that
appeared in the Kansas press; the *Mail* offered extensive news coverage
and long editorials but no genuine discussion.

There was also no outbreak of small independent radical newspapers
as there was in Kansas. The hegemonic rule of the caucus over radical
politics seemed to extend to the press also. The only 'independent'
crusading publication, the monthly *Town Crier,* was in fact secretly
sponsored by a group of Liberal notables. The difference in style between this satirical journal and its nearest Kansas counterpart, Judge
Ballard's *Hury Kain,* is summed up by their mastheads, which
symbolise much of the difference between the two movements from

which they sprang: the *Hury Kain* guyed the Farmers' Alliance motto and the stereotype of the illiterate hayseed with its 'Ekel Meanness to All, Speshul Wickedness to Nun'; the *Town Crier*'s title page bore (untranslated) quotations from Virgil and Horace and a couple of lines from Shakespeare.[46]

The direct evidence in the Birmingham case is then of the views of the local political elite; the facts of the large loyal readership of the *Mail* and the large loyal following of the elite in political activity imply that there was substantial congruence between the views of elite and mass membership. It seems likely that the dominant direction of influence was from elite to mass, but that the support of the mass was genuine and not coerced. Still, this is a poor substitute for the first-hand views of the Victorian working class, but perhaps the closest that one can now come to their thoughts.

Demands for extensive reforms of the political institutions of the country must surely grow out of some dissatisfaction with the existing rulers or institutions. In Birmingham, as in Kansas, I looked first for criticism of the British political system. But criticism was conspicuous by its absence in the *Mail*. The reform movement was not aroused by any particular gross abuses of power, nor did its sense of grievance escalate from any economic or social discontent. The genesis of the 1883 reform movement was more from the parliamentary and intra-party machinations of men whose eyes were upon the timing and content of the next electoral appeal to the country or the emergence of an heir to the ageing Gladstone.[47]

The absence of criticism can certainly not be attributed to an ignorance of events, for the readers of the *Mail* were exceedingly well informed on national affairs and indeed on Parliamentary procedure, which had been made topical in the last few years through the wrecking tactics of the Irish 'obstructives'. More plausible is the explanation that their own party was in power nationally and locally, with its performance giving reasonable satisfaction. At any rate, occasional specific points of criticism never coalesced into a comprehensive indictment and were most usually partisan attacks on Conservative opponents.

'Politician' was a term rarely used, and never pejoratively. Party leaders were labelled 'public men' and defended against 'the systematic imputations of dishonourable motives which are directed against our leading public men by their political opponents. This sort of thing is getting so serious indeed that it has become one of the greatest drawbacks of public life.'[48] As an editorial said forgivingly a few days later, 'we are all liable to make mistakes at times'.[49] Criticism was perhaps implied in the long editorial on 'Lazarus at Dives' Table', but the idea that perhaps poor men should be sitting beside the rich in Parliament was not strengthened by the presentation of any evidence of negligence or bias by the rich as legislators.[50] Even the point of this editorial was somewhat undermined only a week later in the complacent comment on municipal nominations, that 'the number of actual working men in the Council is not of so much consequence as knowing that the interests of the working classes are well looked after'.[51]

The Populists' main criticisms were against parties and abuse of elections, but the Ballot Act and the recent Corrupt Practices Act had eliminated in Britain many of the specific abuses which offended Americans. So long as they were able to sustain their loyalty to a party within the system the Liberals were unlikely to make any serious criticism of party politics in general; it also made it harder for them to rise above the petty detail of partisan sniping to a serious consideration of democratic procedures and standards. Registration requirements, which actually arbitrarily excluded from participation many workers who formally had the vote, were never mentioned in the *Mail*, though they did crop up in a lecture delivered to the Junior Liberal Association in 1882; there H. F. Nash criticised the many anomalies even in the existing definition of the electorate:

> We have franchises enough to bother a Philadelphia lawyer...And how many disfranchisements are there? – you must not live over seven miles away, you must not have a dose of medicine from the parish, you must not remove from one district to another, you must not have short leases, nor must your washing be included in what you pay for lodgings.[52]

Nash used the word 'anomalies'. For all their ostensibly radical philosophy of popular sovereignty this is the word which best sums up the immediate complaints of the Birmingham Liberals about their own position and treatment within the political system. They used the stronger complaint of injustice for the plight of the disenfranchised agricultural labourers, describing the reform proposals as 'a measure to execute an act of justice, which it is a scandal on our history has not been executed years ago'.[53] Only on the question of redistribution did they perceive themselves too as the victims of injustice, for the under-representation of cities such as Birmingham meant that national elections could be won 'by a minority of the votes cast', as by the Tories in 1874.[54] Yet they were perfectly willing to go along with the official party policy of legislating the extension of the franchise first and leaving the matter of redistribution for later consideration. The resolution which set out caucus policy in 1883 demanded only that a Franchise Bill be 'immediately followed' by a redistribution measure and this was evidently accepted without demur.[55] Justification was only offered to the readers of the *Mail* when Conservative pressure to take the two questions together became intense, and then an editorial suggested placidly that the separation of the two was entirely logical, because 'until you have voters you cannot have constituencies'.[56]

The one constitutional matter on which feeling in Birmingham became as passionate as that of the aggrieved Populists of Kansas, was the iniquity of the House of Lords. It was not merely aroused by the veto of reform by the Lords in July, 1884. Their uselessness in general was remarked upon caustically in a report, in July, 1883, of a nine hour sitting in which not a single matter of importance had been discussed.[57] In August of the same year the Lords threw out two government bills, and the *Mail* commented: 'Such tactics cannot be misinterpreted by the bulk of the people. They only go to place the House of Lords in a still more contemptible light than it has hitherto appeared in, and bring out in stronger contrast its power as an instrument for thwarting the wishes of the people.'[58] In 1884, at a meeting of the Eight Hundred, Crosskey proposed a motion:

> Affirming that the time has arrived when the House of Lords should be deprived of the power it now exercised in a manner insulting to the people and detrimental to the best interests of the nation. He remarked that no less a struggle, although it would not be fought out by the fearful arbitrament of civil war, has arisen as to whether the English people were to govern the English nation, or whether an entirely irresponsible and unrepresentative body was to thwart the will of the people (Applause).[59]

And after the Lords' veto, an unusually angry editorial declared 'representative government ceases to have any force when such a result is possible', and went on to accuse the Lords of being unrepresentative, irresponsible, probably even incompetent and certainly prejudiced.[60] In a warning to the Lords later in the same month the *Mail* made it clear that what deference there was in the country certainly did not extend to the ermine and coronets of the Lords: 'They have afforded – nay, forced – an opportunity for their enemies to stir up all the anti-aristocratic feeling that is latent among the people of this country as of most others. The people are asking themselves, "Who are these men who dare to arrogate a right to oppose our wishes?"'

It reported that the previous evening 20,000 at a local rally had 'joined in singing the doggrel verses of which "Crush the House of Lords" was the motive and the refrain'.[61] This editorial is one of the few indications that the general readership might take a more radical view than the official line; the warning to the Lords was followed by advice to political organisers to be temperate and practical in their demands.

The Liberals were optimistic about the pace of political progress: 'But if the nation governs itself, and this country is to be ruled by its own voice as it now is greatly and before long will be absolutely', was their complacent assessment.[62] The desirability of reform was taken for granted, and there was little justification given for it, either in the form of complaints or of philosophy. Presumably the argument in an editorial on labour representation can be extended to the whole question of political reforms: 'It is altogether unnecessary that a newspaper read by the people should waste space proving that the people's wants are better known and likely to be better served by one of themselves than by any wearer of purple and fine linen.'[63] The Birmingham demands for government of the people did not arise from any sense of the abuse or expropriation of power, as did those of the Populists. Perhaps then they did not even mean the same thing when they used the American slogan. The other side of the coin, in the distrustful model, is the evidence of what ideals and examples motivated them, what they understood to be the proper exercise of power and their rightful place within the political system.

There was little talk of democracy as an ideal. To the opponents of reform, democracy was the dreaded end product of gradual extensions of citizenship – a fear well expressed in the Parliamentary debates of 1866 by Mr Lowe's speech on 'the fatal injuries which democracy would inflict upon the British Constitution'.[64] But at the height of the Liberal reform campaign in 1884 a curious report appeared in the *Mail*. The Hon. J. Russell Lowell, President of the Birmingham and Midland Institute, which was much involved in adult education, was the speaker at its prize-giving ceremony. He declared that he thought it wise for the occasion to keep off subjects of 'immediate political interest'. And so his chosen subject was 'a topic of comparatively abstract interest' – he spoke on Democracy.[65] The American ideas now circulating in this country were nothing new, Lowell said, since they had, after all, originally caught the germ from the British Constitution:

He believed it to be a fact that the British Constitution, under whatever disguises of prudence or decorum, was essentially democratic. Fairy tales were made out of the dreams of the poor. The sentiment which lay at the root of democracy was nothing new. It was merely the natural wish of the people to have a hand, if need be a controlling hand, in the management of their own affairs.

Lowell quoted Lincoln's famous phrase, but stripped it of all its emotive force by describing it simply as 'a sufficiently compact statement of it [democracy] as a political arrangement'. Democracy for Lowell was primarily an institutional arrangement, not a spiritual experience or a human right.

H. F. Nash managed a slightly more elevated view of man's political rights in his lecture on that subject to the Junior Liberal Association, though he did not even mention democracy. His philosophy of government was a curious *pastiche* of Locke, Paine and commercial analogies, but it boiled down to representative government with an extended – presumably adult male – suffrage; government was created to perform for society those functions which could not be effectively executed by individuals; it was 'called into existence by the *general choice* – that is the people must vote, and the majority of men forming a society of human beings choose those who are to rule them'; and the agricultural labourers had been wrongly deprived of the vote for 'they never give up their right of voting as to who shall constitute the Government – that is their inalienable right by which all others are protected, and is a *Perfect* right of man'.[66]

When Nash spoke of the labourers as having been deprived of the vote, he meant not only that they were now prevented from exercising their natural right, but also that there had been a time when their ancestors had enjoyed the full rights of citizenship: 'However long it may be before household suffrage, equal electoral districts, and annual parliaments are again practiced in England, the fact remains that they have existed.'[67] Here he was invoking the once potent myth of Saxon democracy, which had inspired the Levellers and Diggers in their political demands and had cropped up regularly in eighteenth-century political thought. Paine was probably the last to use it seriously and effectively, but the memory persisted, both in 'bourgeois radical tradition' – well illustrated by Nash's lecture – and in the minds of the working class as a vague dream of a golden, rural past, 'Alfred's England'. The Socialists abandoned it, for various doctrinal reasons, perhaps unwisely, for 'even a scientific programme can be sterile if it is not infused with an imaginative spirit'.[68] In the long run a myth may by itself be inadequate as a guide to political action, but, as the case of the Populists showed, political myths may be powerful movers of men into action.

Nash made the most of any historical precedents which might rouse the imagination of his audience, but even in his account they look pathetically thin on the ground. From the Saxons he moved on to the abuses perpetrated by the monarchy – 'each succeeding sovereign played just what pranks he liked with the representation of the people'.[69] He asserted the continuity since the seventeenth century of 'radicals, whose estimate of Royal or irresponsible rulers is summed up in the sentence, "There's small choice in rotten apples".'[70] Paine and the Chartists were called upon as examples that 'prove conclusively that the working classes have been frequently the very *best judges* of the nation's needs and the methods of supplying them'.[71] But Magna Carta, which occasionally even appeared as a Populist watchword, was rejected, as class legislation against the workers.

Nash's lecture was given to a packed audience of Junior Liberals, reported, and published as a pamphlet, but can hardly be said to have had a mass circulation. Nor was its delivery particularly designed to fire the emotions of his listeners – rather it leaned towards the academic and the long-winded. But the columns of the *Mail*, explicitly addressed to the working class, offer even less in the way of inspiration or imagination. Bradlaugh was once likened to Wilkes, 'One of the champions of liberty against bigotry', in an editorial supporting his fight to take his Commons seat.[72] But the reasons for raising the occasional historical precedent were rarely to inspire with the sense of a distinguished radical tradition. With allusions to the Commonwealth period and the French Revolution the Lords were advised to 'remember they have been disbanded in the past' but this was a warning to them that they might be unleashing an uncontrollable popular agitation, an event which the editorialist was anxious to avert by compromise.[73]

Chamberlain managed more of a fighting tone in a speech at a reform demonstration in the Potteries in October, 1884, when he raised the memory of the first Protestant martyrs and declared that, like them, 'the Tories have lighted a flame throughout the length and breadth of the land which will not be quenched'.[74] But he used this example to lead up to the advice that 'effervescence or ebullition will do little unless there is organised power and directed effort'.

Previous reform movements were occasionally remembered, particularly in the weeks before the big August Bank Holiday demonstration in Birmingham, the high spot of the reform campaign: 'the surviving veterans of 1832 stand shoulder to shoulder with the Reformers of 1884'.[75] But these were passing references, and nothing suggests anything like the glorious memories or present sense of mission which John Abercrombie had carried with him all the way from Hyde Park to Douglas County, Minnesota.

Proud memories of local leadership for reform seemed as important as anything in the national past to the Birmingham Liberals. The *Mail* reported Dr Dale's speech at a 'great and enthusiastic meeting in the Town Hall last night'; Dale, a prominent civic leader, Liberal, and Congregational minister, remarked that 'the spirit of this meeting shows that the old fires are still unquenched, and that the passion for freedom still beats in the hearts of this constituency'.[76] An article on the day of the Bank Holiday demonstration plodded informatively through a history of past demonstrations in Birmingham.[77] Yet these memories seemed more calculated to imbue the reformers with a thoroughly Victorian sense of respectability than with any fiery political passion. Perhaps one should make some allowance for the fact that the British are not known for becoming passionately and publicly emotional about their politics, or indeed about anything else. But the difference from the tone and content of the Populist press cannot simply be a function of national character. The Populists' sense of history and symbol was vivid and very much at the front of their minds; in eighteen months of daily editions of the *Mail* in Birmingham the scattered and drab references I have given are all that are there.

It has been argued elsewhere that the apparent placidity of the working class, in the face of the grant of symbolic political equality accompanied by effective political subordination, can be explained without recourse to the problematic subjective content of their ideals and understanding of politics. By this argument, the accessible 'hard' facts of 'objective structural constraints' imposed upon the first workers admitted to politics, through restrictive registration, the high cost of politics, elite control of the media and of political organisations, explain adequately enough their actual helplessness; the initial and inevitable capitulation was then transmitted to later generations as the norm: 'The normative bond which *was* forged and *is* relevant to the mass of the British people was pragmatic acceptance, not moral commitment.'[78] But this presupposes that the workers who were first admitted to the electorate in 1867 were new to political activity, whereas in fact they had a long tradition of political involvement and

were new only to voting. It presupposes also that it is only the availability of resources and institutional channels of access which deter-
mines the political behaviour of the ordinary citizen. But political
behaviour depends both 'upon what is legitimized and what is made to
appear possible'.[79] The case of the Populists clearly showed that the
appearance of possibility may not be entirely within the control of
political elites. Immediate practicality may enter into the estimation of
'the possible', but subjective factors exerted a strong enough influence
for the Populists to override the blockages to political action in existing
structures through the creation of a new and initially effective structure
of their own. By giving sole attention to what was possible to British
workers through existing structures attention is diverted from the
complementary fact, that these workers were predisposed to accept
what was presented to them as possible. It was not that they had no
political philosophy at all, from which they might have derived either
moral commitment or moral opposition, but that their loose collection
of political ideals and their tradition of political experience explicitly
limited their vision of alternatives and suggested to them a relatively
passive role. Thus, Populists and Liberals had in common a situation
of political and economic inequalities, and a political structure which
allowed the ordinary citizen only the most limited access to political
activity. Objective factors alone do not explain the vastly different
political reactions of the two. The modest criticisms of Parliamentary
government by the Liberals become comprehensible in the context of a
political culture vastly different from that of their Kansas contemporaries.

The public rhetoric of the caucus was not, of course, pragmatic
acceptance of the political system. Indeed, the very fact that its philosophy was so much more radical in the British context than were the
same ideas in the United States may have been an important inhibition
against acting forcefully on its propositions. To make public declaration
of opposition to the established norms of society is not an easy act.
And the average Birmingham worker was not a 'marginal man' with
nothing to lose; he was an industrious and self-respecting artisan, with
a social status that was respectable, even if it was lowly. His support
for radical democracy was possibly a local rather than national perspective, made easy by the prevailing Liberal atmosphere of the city:
'If you go to the sea, anywhere you like, and take up a spoonful of
water, it will be salt, and if you will return any member from any
district in Birmingham you like, he will be a Liberal.'[80] The columns

of the *Mail* do yield a few clues as to what was really believed about politics and political action.

When the Populists talked of revolution they meant a swift and sudden reversion to traditional values. The Liberals certainly did not envisage anything so abrupt. When Henry George hailed a huge Town Hall audience as 'the leaders of the band of Radical England', Liberal leaders were alarmed.[81] A fortnight of controversy had preceded George's visit, and an editorial had already warned of the dangerous potential of massive reform, in an ancient and slow-growing polity, for 'destroying all public confidence'.[82] An editorial on 'revolution' did credit such socialists as William Morris with humanitarian intentions – but 'advocates of reform. . .must be content to go by steps, circumspectly'.[83]

'Working with power and the total structure of society as terms of reference, the Liberals were much more drastic revolutionaries than Labour', one authority on their history has declared.[84] To predict who might have made a revolution is an exercise in futility; this conclusion depends on asserting the pre-eminence of political authority over economic factors. But the Birmingham evidence does not in any case suggest that the radical Liberals had a coherent social policy. The *Mail* editorialist was able to dissociate political and social change; the former was evidently safe, the latter, exemplified by socialists and single-taxers, involved dangerous men striking directly at the principles of private property. The Liberal rank and file clearly received George's social radicalism with enthusiasm. The *Mail* reported that the lecture hall was packed for George's lecture, and that the 'Ayes' – for Henry George – had it, when the vote was counted at the end of the meeting – 'not a pleasant or a healthy sign' as the editorialist commented.[85] The meeting was chaired by Mr Crosskey, a Liberal dignitary and member of the Management Committee of the Liberal Association, who had been at pains to dissociate himself from support for George's views when his intention of presiding was attacked. Official Liberal Association policy, expressed through the columns of the *Mail* for weeks before the meeting, was to discourage attendance. Yet there is no evidence of whether the audience found any connection between it and their political affiliation or demands for political change. There must have been considerable cross-pressures at work on many of them, given this dual loyalty to Liberal political ideals and radical social ideals, but they continued to support the Liberals in politics for another decade or more. Despite the attraction of George's ideas, perhaps the existing social structure did offer them adequate opportunities to rise. Or when it came to *political* action, possibly the symbolic meaning of voting Liberal still had a stronger pull than the attractive but incompatible social radicalism: 'For the nineteenth century man, the mark or note of being fully human was that he should provide for his own family, have his own religion and politics, and call no man master ...emancipation from traditional bondages and restraints found its political expression in being a rank-and-file Liberal.'[86] But the controversy over social questions does foreshadow the future problems of Liberalism in competition with Socialism.

It is indeed hard to think of these nominal radical democrats as presenting any severe threat, even in the limited terms of political radicalism, when they greeted Gladstone's Reform Bill with this plaudit: 'The Government have brought in a splendid measure – bold, yet not too bold; Liberal, yet with a conservative leaning to old constitutional lines.'[87] The Liberals presented themselves as moderate reformers, not as dangerous radicals; they believed that they were demanding 'nothing that is unjust or unfair, or outside the spirit of the Constitution'.[88] They were certainly prepared to accept the most modest immediate progress – the overdue grant of the vote to agricultural labourers and the promise of a redistribution measure to follow; upon its introduction in 1884 the *Mail* hailed the latter as not theoretically perfect, but the essence of compromise – 'it revolutionises the representation of the people without being in itself revolutionary'.[89] On two points only the *Mail* was more radical than the official party line, perhaps reflecting its readership's opinion, for it sustained its position after the party and parliamentary battle was lost. It supported equal treatment for the Irish: 'if we can trust Englishmen and Scotchmen with the franchise, we can trust Irishmen'.[90] And it supported women's suffrage, although 'it is not sought to make politics a cause of fireside dissensions by giving married women a right to vote on equal terms with their husbands'.[91]

Nothing here would have overthrown the British Constitution. And these immediate demands were justified only on the briefest grounds of justice or rightness. Only the occasional hint suggests that the Liberals may have perceived the meaning of the vote in the idealistic terms of a radical theory of popular sovereignty: 'But beyond the comparatively low ground of self-interest, there is the higher one involved in the full recognition of the principles of self-government. The rationale of that principle rests on the assumption that the people do give expression to their actual voice.'[92] There was little here to inspire, especially by comparison with the Populists' presentation of the vote both as an act of self-fulfilment and as a more than adequate substitute for a bayonet in changing the course of their country and righting social wrongs.

Potentially radical preoccupations at this time were the related questions of the control of Members of Parliament and the qualifications which should be required of these representatives of the people. The rank and file were generally interested in the latter, the leaders in the former as manifested in the philosophical concepts of mandates and the nature of representation. The *Mail* reflected its orientation towards the rank and file by giving more attention to the latter, but it did give publicity to the caucus view by reporting a speech which linked both questions; this was the statement made by Mr Jaffray when the Eight Hundred met to nominate a new parliamentary candidate:

> His qualifications must be, first, that he would consolidate the Liberal vote, and that he would sink every consideration but that which would subserve the interests of the Liberal Party. He should be a man without crotchets – (hear, hear) – a tried man, a man without blemish and without spot. (Applause). The qualifications of that man must also consist in this, that if perchance his candidature should in any way imperil the return of three Liberal members for Birmingham that he would give way in favour of someone who would be more likely to bind together the Liberal vote.[93]

The Management Committee's nominee was accepted with acclaim.[94] This argument in itself had radical implications for the theory of British parliamentary government, in its substitution of total subservience to party for the older conception of the independent member deliberating and voting in the general interest. In the context of the general political philosophy of the caucus what was meant, of course, was subservience to the people, for whom the party organisation was only a mouthpiece. Chamberlain justified this relationship not out of strong philosophical conviction but on pragmatic grounds. A great many people had now been admitted to a share of the political process and must therefore be given the means to participate; sheer numbers required the establishment of systematic channels of contact. He continued:

> Now, the special merit and characteristic of the new machinery is the principle which must henceforth govern the action of the Liberals as a political party – namely, the direct participation of all its members in the direction of its policy and in the selection of those particular measures of reform to which priority shall be given. A fear had been expressed in some quarters that such proceedings may interfere with the proper independence of members of Parliament, and may be used in the coercion of the House of Commons. This theory is surely not complimentary to Liberal members,

and it may be asserted in contradiction that, while all of them would resent a French *mandat imperatif*, none are unwilling to interchange opinion with their constituents, or to have the advantage of a thorough knowledge of their wishes.[95]

The *Mail* gave almost no attention to the question of mandated representatives, and whether this was because it was a matter of consensus or simply not of concern to its readers, there is no way of telling. Nash dealt with it firmly in his lecture to the Junior Liberals; he supported close control of delegates – 'the very first principle of representation is delegation', he said, and quoted Paine in support – 'government is a trust in right of those by whom that trust is delegated'.[96] He suggested, also, that it was not after all such a radical innovation: 'When Governments are overwhelmed with difficulties from which the genius and experience of all the skilled statesmen are unable to extricate them, what do they? They *appeal to the people* to settle for them their policy, and *their* decision is considered final.'[97] If this was a point beyond need of discussion in Birmingham, it suggests a general satisfaction with their own relationship with the Birmingham members and indeed with the general functioning of the House of Commons. It was not the Commons that blocked the people's will, but the Lords. As the *Mail* commented on the Lords' veto of the Franchise Bill: 'Representative government ceases to have any force when such a result is possible. Practically it comes to this, that the people are not in any sense masters of the legislative situation.'[98]

The aspect of representation which was not beyond need of discussion, to which the *Mail* regularly returned, and on which perhaps it was more in tune with its readers' opinions than with the notable apathy of the Liberal Association leadership, was the question of labour representation. The fieriest moment came when feeling in support of the election of working men to Parliament coalesced with partisanship. When Lord Randolph Churchill and Colonel Burnaby announced their intention of contesting Birmingham, the *Mail* advised them to recognise 'the stern condition of their natural unsuitability for the parts they are anxious to play', and explained:

> It would be out of accord with the natural fitness of things if either the scion of a ducal house or a colonel of Horse Guards was elected to look after the industrial interests of Birmingham, with its teeming population of working men and women, whose wants, whose wishes, whose political aspirations are an unknown and unknowable language to those aristocratic personages who, to gratify a spirit of adventure, find amusement in contesting Radical Birmingham in the Conservative interest.[99]

This attack by no means excluded the current Liberal leadership from suitability as representatives, for Garvin's assessment of Chamberlain was probably true of most of them, that each was 'intimate with his own working people'. But there had long been a minority, but persistent, view in the city that working men would best represent working men, which took the theory of representation a step further than the official line – from mandated delegates to mandated delegates whose social characteristics matched those of the majority of their constituents. The Birmingham Trades Council floated the idea of an independent working class candidacy in 1868 and Holyoake, who was to stand, later justified it in stronger terms than ever did the *Mail*:

> The master class no more feels as the workmen feel than the old aristocratic class before 1830 felt, or as the middle class proved they did, when afterwards they came into power. . .at that time there was no strong feeling on the part of the working class in favour of representation of their order . . .and it had never occurred to the middle class that the industrious majority were entitled to any personal representation. Certainly they never offered or facilitated it.[100]

The Trades Council persevered with its perennial lost cause, but failed regularly either to raise the £1,000 estimated as necessary to support a campaign and a member, or to gain a promise of non-opposition from the Liberals.[101] In municipal affairs there was marginally more official encouragement for this innovation, perhaps because Chamberlain was influenced by his reading of Mill to believe, somewhat patronisingly, that the benefits to lesser men of mixing with and learning from the example of disinterested civic leaders would be considerable.[102] It may also have been partly a recognition of public opinion, for Schnadhorst, the Secretary of the Liberal Association, acknowledged that 'there had always been a minority of Liberals in favour of separate labour representation, "but now that minority is a majority" '.[103]

But these few concessions did not satisfy public opinion, and the *Mail* reflected this feeling:

> Labour, which is another name for the people, is at length beginning to perceive that at the Parliamentary table Lazarus the poor man ought to sit side by side with Dives the rich, gently but firmly insisting on his right to select what kind of food is best suited to his digestion and health, rather than humbly waiting beneath the great man's mahogany for crumbs and kicks, and licks from the dog. . .A whole nation is prepared to assert the right of Lazarus to sit at the table. Why, then, should Lazarus be deprived of his right because he cannot afford a serviette?[104]

Still the rank and file did not rise up forcefully and demand working class representatives. They elected them only where the Liberal organisation cooperated. They quite obviously did not share the analysis of self-interest that led the Populists to doubt any man and his motives for political office. Nonetheless, the very demand is the antithesis of deference, whether this be to social status or to proven skill. Nash argued his case too, and asserted that 'education cannot give capacity. The power to think is a gift existing as fully in the lower as in the upper classes, and the past history of our own country proves conclusively that the working classes have been frequently the very best judges of the nation's needs and the methods of supplying them.'[105] The persistence of this idea suggests at least a flicker of independence in the working class of Birmingham.

When they turned from the character and control of representatives to the institutions of politics, the complaints and proposals of these radicals were again limited in scope and modest in intent. The Commons came in for almost no comment; the delaying tactics and 'Billingsgate language' of the Irish members were condemned, but no general conclusions of failure in the system were drawn from their observations.[106] They were probably far better informed about procedure and events in the House than were the Populists about Congress, but familiarity did not breed contempt. Only when the Commons seemed threatened were they roused to both strong complaint and action against 'this monstrous obstruction to the will of the people by which the House of Commons is blotted out of the Constitution'.[107]

When it came to the Lords, the Liberals lacked all sympathy, and here they were convinced that bias and privilege operated against the general interest. A Lords' veto was feared from the start of the reform campaign in 1883, and editorials developed from general criticism to some discussion of the Lords' place in the Constitution:

> We live in an age which, while it does not care wilfully or unreasonably to destroy existing institutions, requires that those institutions should adapt themselves to the principles of parliamentary government in its popular sense...But the House of Lords can only escape the dreaded fate of reconstitution by going with the stream. Popular forces in this country are too strong to be dammed by the privileged few.[108]

Thus the Liberals' only deeply felt complaints were against hereditary aristocratic privilege – an analysis which suggests far less perception of the new realities of power in a great industrial society than lay behind the 'conspiratorial' view of the Populists about the role of eastern financiers and great industrialists in politics, for their rhetoric masked a shrewd perception of new sources of political power. The Birmingham workers had indeed a good case against the obstruction of the Lords; the curious dissociation of social and political analysis in their minds may have helped to divert them from other threatening inequalities of power in society.

Just as their analysis failed to penetrate to the social roots of political abuses, so their proposals for change were duly modest. The official line never suggested the abolition of the Lords, and warned against it when popular forces seemed to be moving in that direction; the *Mail* defended the Liberals specifically against charges that this was what they hoped for: 'But the Liberal Party. . .is strongly in favour of maintaining the monarchical institution; it does not want to abolish, but only to reform the Second Chamber, giving it more of the representative and less of the hereditary character.'[109] Bright's Bank Holiday speech was criticised for its moderation in proposing only some limitation of the Lords' veto power; the *Mail* favoured dealing with the hereditary principle, and another editorial had spelt this out in greater detail:

> We could tolerate a Second Chamber revising, modifying, and to some extent even checking the action of the first, if it were in some way responsible to public opinion, and if it exercised its rights, to quote Mr GLADSTONE, by 'the rule of wisdom and moral fitness'...An ideal Chamber should consist of the best and wisest of the national intellect.[110]

And this was to be achieved by the creation of Life Peers.

Nothing resembling a coherent philosophy of government emerges from the fragmentary proposals and justifications for reform of the Liberals. Chamberlain spoke powerfully of the rights of the people and was cheered enthusiastically for his somewhat enigmatic declaration that 'government by the people means government for the people'.[111] Whether this was a Freudian slip or an intentional modification of Lincoln cannot be deduced from the context. Yet when critics were not arguing that he was intending to give the people a thoroughly unconstitutional power of direct government, they were attacking on the grounds that he was in effect governing for the people and manipulating the appearance of consent. Certainly there was a good deal of opinion management in Birmingham, and the measures of reform which the caucus supported would not have made any notable contribution to the achievement of American-style popular sovereignty.

The mass Liberal electorate, on the other hand, heard only this occasional slogan of popular government through their daily press.

The powerful symbol of 'the people' was never seriously offered as inspiration. Yet the reforms which they were prepared to support – universal suffrage, working men in Parliament, abolition of the Lords – would have gone further than the official policies in the direction of popular sovereignty. Paradoxically, it seems from this evidence that the leaders were exceedingly radical in their philosophy, yet moderate in their actual proposals, while their followers had little conception of philosophy, were more radical than their leaders in specific proposals, and were not just moderate but deferential to leadership in their actual behaviour.

In his speech on reform at Greenwich, Chamberlain declared that 'full confidence in the people...is the only sure foundation upon which any Liberalism can be based'.[112] He made this point of trust in the people his own, so much so that Lord Randolph Churchill was seen as adding particular insult to injury when he appropriated Chamberlain's slogan for his own Birmingham campaign: coming 'with a borrowed cry about utilitarian principles and "trust in the people"... rattling Mr. Chamberlain's thunder'.[113] The question of trust for the Populists was of the willingness of the people to trust political leaders. In Britain the direction of doubt was reversed. The Liberal rank and file, of course, showed a partisan unwillingness to trust the Tories, along with an apparent confidence in their own leaders. If this seems obvious for members of the party in power, then it must be remembered that the greatest defection to the Populists in Kansas was from lifelong members of the Republican Party, which then held both state and national power.

Trust in the people is clearly an essential prerequisite if a political elite is to acknowledge the viability and desirability of the full exercise of popular sovereignty, but it was a new line to take. Until very recently the question of the extension of the franchise had been dominated by the barely disguised fear of admitting the people to politics. Though trust had become the official line by 1884, Gladstone's Queen's Speech suggested no eagerness to turn over sovereignty to the new voters. Chamberlain's trust, however, does appear to have been genuine and may indeed have been an important factor in the willingness of the masses to follow his leadership; as the *Mail* remarked of the Irish, 'to trust them is the way to make them trust us'.[114] It was, after all, Chamberlain's shock at the general ignorance of the populace and his passion against sectarian education which brought him into political activity, only after 1867, and he saw education neither as a panacea nor simply as a method of providing a skilled work force: 'One thing is certain, that if education becomes general we shall no longer find Dorsetshire labourers contented – I will not say contented but compelled – to work for nine shillings a week.'[115]

The Birmingham Liberals nominally espoused the same political philosophy, but there is here only the palest echo of the sense of injustice and the conviction which were so strong in Kansas. Certainly part of the difference in tone and content is derived from differences in the sources themselves, rather than from the real feelings of the people. The Birmingham popular press was a very different kind of animal from that of Kansas. The *Mail* was certainly read daily and widely by the Liberal working class and one can safely assume that it was their staple political diet. But it was not set up in opposition to any existing political press or institutions. Kansans acted politically as though they believed what they read in the press; just so did the men of Birmingham, for their press was not notably radical. But though the outstanding impression from the *Mail* is of how little coherent thought there really was behind political action, there were hints of occasional independence among the rank and file, whose public expression may have been stifled because of elite control of the press. One direct source of the political views of the artisans of Birmingham has survived and in a limited way provides a check on the representativeness of the columns of the *Mail*.

Every Sunday evening from 1850 to 1886 an audience of up to 150 gathered in a room at the Hope and Anchor public house in Navigation Street, in the centre of Birmingham, to listen and vote on debates staged by a group of their colleagues.[116] These covered an impressive range of subjects – literature and history as well as their major interest in current affairs and general political questions. Minutes of these meetings were religiously kept. In the early days these were normally only formal records of speakers for and against the motion of the day and details of the final vote. Later they were expanded to give the arguments of the major speakers; thus they are a mine of direct information about what some members of the working class were actually saying about politics.

How representative the members of the Hope and Anchor Sunday Evening Debating Society were of the whole working class is hard to say, since the standing and occupations of few can be identified with any certainty. But it seems probable that they were typical of the 'better' type of working man so prevalent in Birmingham. In 1862, in a protest letter to a Whitehall department, they described themselves as 'a meeting of Gentlemen, Tradesmen and Artizens'.[117] Of the list of forty-three debaters named in 1883 and 1884, three appear in the Court Directory section of the city directory, which presumably qualified them as gentlemen, in local society at least.[118] One of the three was Jeremiah Thomas, the chairman and minute-writer for many years. Another was one of the two Liberal councillors among the members, Joseph Lampard, a boot and shoemaker. The second councillor was George Hemming, whose family ran a successful local brewery. Neither took a very prominent role, though Lampard had been a regular speaker in earlier years; nor was either in the top caucus leadership. Only six more debaters can be reliably identified: a rose engine turner, a carpet pin manufacturer, an iron fender manufacturer, a cooper, a washing blue manufacturer and the registration agent for the Birmingham and North Warwickshire Liberal Associations.[119]

The two stalwarts for thirty years were Mr George Bill, rose engine turner, and Mr Allen Dalzell, a carpet pin manufacturer.[120] From the directory, it appears that both had small workshop businesses in mixed residential and commercial working class streets near the city centre. The 'worthy host', Mr Robert Edmonds, was re-elected Vice Chairman at every annual meeting, but never recorded as joining in the debates; but at Christmas he did make a contribution of 'several bowls of good whiskey punch which were done ample justice to'.[121] Clearly the debaters were not representative of one very important segment of political opinion in the city, that of temperance groups.

The debates were spirited and usually friendly. Members paid careful attention to rules of procedure, with occasional resort to rulings from the chair on the right to speak. Some subjects, like the 'Events of the Year' debate in January and the debate on the Queen's Speech, were annual fixtures; others were highly topical – the verdict on Bradlaugh's contested parliamentary seat, the visit of Henry George to Birmingham and the Aston Riots were among the subjects in 1884.

Most impressive was the level of information and detail the speakers contributed. For example, they did not just debate the Queen's Speech in general terms – in 1884 Mr Dalzell reviewed it paragraph by paragraph critically, while Mr Bill thought it very poor 'untill we came to the 20th paragraph' on reform. In his analysis 'he described the constitution of the present House of Commons', giving a statistical breakdown of its membership by class and occupation.[122] In 1885, on the subject of redistribution, Mr Sketchley discussed inequities in the social distribution of wealth, and quoted official returns, Giffen and Leone Levi to back his point; this set off a considerable barrage, over the next few weeks, of statistical research from all sides of the argument.[123]

When the society was wound up in 1886, Mr Bill commented that it had been 'the best Sunday School for politics that had ever been established in our town'.[124] Four years earlier Mr Dalzell had applauded the incentive it gave speakers to gain instruction; to this Mr Bill added that 'not only was it instructive but also effected in a marked manner influences outside as many political and social movements had originated from this room'.[125] Councillor Lampard 'also responded & said that from his experience of the Room, it had removed bigotry, it had proved that it was a School for improvement, & had shewn to the ignorant that we were desirous of improving all who attend'.[126] There spoke the satisfied voice of Victorian self-help, though the debaters were not all rampant individualists – they generally supported trades unions, and wanted, for example, the extension of state intervention in education, welfare and housing.

In a glow of optimism after the 1867 reforms, Mr Charles Hibbs (listed in the Court Directory in 1884) addressed the meeting on 'What will be the probable course of future legislation consequent upon the admission of the people in power?' He painted 'a vivid picture of the advantages that would accrue in the future from the spread of education, the removal of unjust laws, the equalisation of taxation and the removal of legislation for ever from the hands of a class and bestowing it on the sovereign will of the people'.[127] Here is a more radical programme and vision than ever was found in the columns of the *Mail*. Nearly twenty years later, disillusion and distrust might well have been expected to set in. To augment and check the picture derived from the columns of the *Mail*, the account which follows is taken from the Minutes for the last three years of the Society, 1883 to 1886. In these three years, the leading speakers were regularly a Mr Oswald, together with Mr Bill and Mr Dalzell. They illustrate three different partisan standpoints, yet have a good deal in common in their general view of politics. Debates were sometimes partisan, with a Liberal majority, but the Society was not, as has elsewhere been implied, simply another Liberal Party organ.[128] From time to time throughout its history partisan positions had been taken, notably in the reform debate in 1865, but in general and right to the end of its life speakers showed a substantial independence from set party lines. Mr Oswald, the dyed-in-the-wool Tory, was the exception.

Nothing is known of Mr Oswald's social background for he did not appear in the local directory. He was an absolutely loyal Tory, who simply treated every question as a party matter, to the repeated rage of the Liberal, but broader-minded, Mr Bill. Oswald's automatically partisan reaction meant that he rarely bothered to involve himself in justifications of his views. In reviewing the 'Past Session of Parliament' in 1883, for example, he simply supported the Lords wholeheartedly, condemning the Liberal House of Commons and 'concluded by saying that the Govt had by their shilly shallying manner of doing business had so delayed business that the Conservative party would have to be called in to do the work that the Liberals were to cowardly to undertake'.[129]

On reform, once again he followed the party line, introducing a motion 'That in the opinion of this meeting no measure of reform can be considered complete, that is not accompanied with a Redistribution of Seats.'[130] He lost, and the vote was very typical of the usual ratio of Liberal support in these meetings:

for Mr Bill's Amendment	32
for Mr Oswald's Resolution	8

His contributions to all the debates on reform simply repeated this argument.

Unfortunately Mr Oswald was curiously silent or absent throughout the record-breaking six month debate in 1885 on 'The Right of a Working Man to Represent Birmingham in Parliament' – a subject on which there was no official party line for him to voice. He did attack the caucus with the argument that 'Its leaders only adopted it in order to get the Loaves and Fishes of Office',[131] and of course he made the most of similar arguments in the debate after the Aston Riots had brought Liberals and Conservatives to blows.[132] Surprisingly, he opened a debate on 'The Proceedings of the Trades Congress' by declaring that unions had been highly beneficial to the workers, and urging their extension, but the impression this gave of possible dissent from his party line was diminished by his continuation of the subject the next week with the statement that as a Conservative he denied the right of unions to speak on political questions.[133]

By contrast to this rigid partisanship, Mr Bill, the rose engine turner was more revealing, and of a much more complex political philosophy.

On most partisan questions he was a Liberal, perhaps more passionately so in these meetings because he was frequently stung to an angry
defence of the Liberals by Oswald's bias. Oswald once accused him of
being a Radical and a Chartist and whether or not this was literally
true he did display a sense of history and of shared radical experience.[134]
Applauding the Redistribution Bill in 1884 'he concluded an eloquent
speech by reading the Soul Stirring Hymn of the Old Reform Union
in 1832'.[135] When the Lords became the burning issue, he looked back
and argued for the right of the Commons to abolish the Lords, on the
grounds of precedent – 'they had done it once, and could if they choose
do it again'.[136] But Cromwell's action had been arbitrary and unjust,
objected Oswald the next week, so Bill hit back with an account of
'Cromwell and the Long Parliament' and the legitimacy bestowed
then as now 'by the overwhelming voice of public opinion'.[137]

In a debate on the relative merits of orators, politicians and statesmen, Bill's heroes proved to be Bright and George Dawson (the local
Unitarian prophet of the Municipal Gospel): 'he held that orators did
not do much good unless they put it into practical use by becoming
politicians and statesmen'. The following week he listed 'G. Edmonds,
Thos Attwood, G. M. Muntz & the Revd H. Hutton all as men who in
Birmingham had make their mark, he claimed for these men a higher
rank than to any party politicians'.[138] One can only imagine how
curious the Populists would have found the inclusion of politicians in
this debate; aside from this last comment of Bill's there is no complaint
against them, and indeed no pejorative use of the word occurs in any
of my British sources.[139] Politicians and statesmen were much of a
muchness apparently (though a large majority voted for the greater
benefits conferred by orators, at the end of the debate).

Bill took the expected party line on the actual reform measures
proposed in 1884. He was bitter against the Lords, and willing for
strong action to end their veto power, or even to abolish the second
chamber altogether: 'In strong terms he characterised the hereditary
constitution of the House of Peers as baneful in its character and
inimical to the freedom of the people of England.'[140] The grounds for
criticism here, the freedom of the people, were echoed in many of his
speeches. Mr Bill was very conscious of the rights of Englishmen to
'Freedom of thought, liberty and honest Government', a notion which
had long been an inspiration to English radicals.[141] There was evidently
nothing incompatible, or even incongruous, to Mr Bill in coupling the
grandeur of such ends as freedom and the fulfilment of 'the will of the

people' with the modest means of marginally reformed parliamentary democracy. The nebulous thought of the rightful freedom of the Englishman meant much to these Sunday evening debaters; curiously the *Mail* never used the theme in its columns – a wasted opportunity to use a tradition which did still live among the working class.

The *Mail* evidently was in touch with its readership in its repeated support for working class representation. Bill had spoken against the party line in 1868, and he was still solidly for labour representatives in 1885.[142] He believed it essential that workers should be in the Commons, and in some numbers, and that they should be independent of both parties. Then they would see that government expenditure was cut and the national debt reduced.[143] His justification for this belief was best summed up in his objection to the candidacies of Lord Randolph Churchill and Colonel Burnaby:

> 1st they did not represent the interests of the Electors
> 2nd they were not so capable or as fit as our present representatives
> 3rd they were belonging to the class that eats the taxes of the people &
> therefore would not defend the taxpayers, & Birmingham would stultify
> itself if it returned these men to the Commons.[144]

But, for all the class consciousness suggested in this passage, Bill generally expressed a strongly individualist social philosophy. He acclaimed the views of Malthus in a debate on poverty, and was the only participant to argue the hard line that much of the misery of the poor was self-inflicted: 'The spread of education would cause the poorer class to consider this evil & they would be more prudent in future & not indulge in such early marraiges and such hasty results', he said severely.[145] He hoped to see no government expenditure on relief of this misery. But he approved of cooperative action through trades unions and heatedly defended their right to intervene in political affairs on the grounds that political questions 'affected the interests of the working classes'.[146] And he gave stronger support to 'Mr George and his Mission to England' than any other speaker, asserting that 'whoever in his opinion ruled the land ruled the people'.[147]

Mr Bill's combination of political radicalism and social individualism, subjective identification with the working class and yet inhumanity towards its lower levels, is a perfect example of the type described by John Vincent:

> There was, too, among working men, still a significant number who were
> self-employed and owners of property. Many were rated for the relief of
> the poor: and so far as the aristocracy of labour entered into sympathy with

the really destitute, it was by the same act of imagination that middle class reformers did so.[148]

Bill was an elderly man by 1884, and so perhaps one of a dying breed, but is a clear example of why a simple division of Victorian England, for the purposes of understanding its politics, into upper, middle and working classes was still inappropriate, even as late as the 1880s.

Bill generally accepted party policies. When he went beyond them in political matters he had little constructive to suggest, and nothing really radical. For example, his demand for labour representation was radical, but was never supported by any suggestion that he understood its potential for undermining the general principles or institutions of parliamentary government, or, as was the way of the American distrustful, that he saw this as a means of restoring a corrupted political process to its old glory. For British radicals the past gave warning of how abuses had gone too far and driven Englishmen to the defence of their liberties. It did not offer the vision of perfection lately lost which the Populists found in the origins of their polity; history, for Mr Bill, represented a gradual process, as much defensive as positive.

Nothing gave Mr Bill a deep enough sense of deprivation to turn him against his party. He talked of popular sovereignty, but eulogised his party leaders; he certainly respected ability, if he had no time for privilege. He was, in short, largely satisfied with things as they were, and not impelled by any burning vision of political purpose or political rights. And if, by the 1880s, he was a representative of the older generation, he carried the majority of the room with him time and time again.

Certainly the most interesting member of the Debating Society was Mr Dalzell, the carpet pin manufacturer. Through thirty years of debates he fought losing battles. He described himself as 'an old Radical' and had been in a Birmingham deputation at the Hyde Park demonstration in 1867.[149] He found pride and satisfaction, in 1886, that the country was near to achieving 'the dream of the Chartist Reformers'.[150] Yet he also called himself 'a conscientious Tory', and more often than not, though certainly not with the Pavlovian reaction of Mr Oswald, supported their policies.[151] He felt it necessary to account for this unusual affiliation by suggesting at one time that 'the Tories bring forward the talented working man' and at others that it might be out of disappointment with the caucus: 'he said he was a radical & a beleiver in Manhood Suffrage yet he denounced the present action of the Liberal party as being the result of prejudice & ignorance & a disgrace to them'.[152]

Conscientious Tory he may have been, but Mr Dalzell was no simple deference voter, nor would he have gone along with Tory Democracy's hierarchical theory of political organisation. He held stronger views than any of the other speakers on politics, power and their social bases, and he came the closest to feeling grievances that transcended party. In local politics, and following the sad case of the Aston Riots, for example, 'he held that the Tories were as bad as the Liberals, that there was in fact Six of one & half a Dozen of the other'.[153]

Dalzell was quite prepared to criticise the Commons – easier of course for a Tory to do, but his complaints were not just partisan. The Commons was all 'Aristocratic Younger Sons and Rich Middle Class Men and only one honest working man', he said, leading into an argument that 'the people's charter should be carried out in its entirety & that all members of parliament should be paid for their services'.[154] On working class representation, he and Mr Bill gave unqualified support to the same side. He was also unhappy about party politics, not only in what he believed to be regimentation in the local Liberal organisation, but also in national politics; though his counter-proposition here did sound more like the tradition-minded working man to whom Conservative party propaganda was appealing, for 'he again urged that party spirit should be done away with & only the patriotic party should rule'.[155] But in his general suggestions and his support for specific reform proposals he does not fit that pattern. The House of Commons should indeed be the representatives of the people: 'He deprecated the power of the aristocracy and the higher classes inasmuch as they plunged countries into difficulties without consulting the House of Commons & the people.'[156] Not only should the Commons be well filled with workers representing their own, but in policy matters it should follow, not lead, the people. In a discussion of the obstructive tactics of the Irish in Parliament, he argued that 'the Govt should not make public opinion, but should carry it out when uttered'; and the next year he held that 'every question that have to be settled by the legislature should be well ventilated & agatated by the people outside'.[157] To this end he supported franchise reform, though he was impatient with the caution of the Liberal measure: 'in speaking of the franchise demonstrations he said that they where only agatating a Bastard question for he believe in nothing short of manhood suffrage pure and simple'.[158] But at the end of the year he 'rejoiced that the Franchise Bill had become law & beleived the principle of the Redistribution Bill giving one man & one vote to a large extent was a grand reform, while the power taken from small boroughs, & placed in the hands of the great centres of industry was the Greatest of reforms that had been brought before the legislature'.[159]

Mr Dalzell was, though, no simple believer in the vote as an automatic panacea. Immediately after the passing of the 1867 Reform Act, he had argued strongly in the affirmative on the question 'after the passing of the Reform Bill – will the Reform League be necessary in this country or meet with national support?' and he held out thereafter for the Ballot and for Manhood Suffrage.[160] Perhaps part of his apparent bitterness towards the Liberals was because, looking back in 1885 and reviewing the history of the Reform League, he 'described the action of the Middle classes who then betrayed them'.[161]

He did not trust either the aristocracy or the middle class to represent any but their own interest, and he sometimes showed a clear sense of a working class interest against them. Men like Chamberlain, he argued to the Society, were as tyrannical as the aristocrats: 'He asked them to consider how men like Mr Chamberlain had amassed their colossal fortunes, they had done so out of the Blood, Brains & Strength of the Working men of this country.'[162] He joined Mr Bill in opposing Mr Oswald's sympathy for the landed aristocracy, saying that, though he was not in sympathy with much of Henry George's work, 'yet he held very strongly to the opinion that the land belonged to the people'.[163] Yet, when the Lords were the subject of hot debate, he opposed the Liberals' attack on them, not, as did Mr Oswald, simply from party dogma but on grounds of constitutional theory:

> What had caused England to be respected was the glorious Constitution of the country and that was composed of King, Lords and Commons & each had their part to play, & united made up the grandeur of the British Constitution...He objected to the destruction of the House of Lords as he believed it to be the greatest bulwark of English liberty.[164]

A couple of weeks later he reportedly reinforced this argument with a history of 'some of the great and stirring times in which they had stood by the people when an attempt had been made to trample on their liberty', but unfortunately none of the details are recorded.[165]

What is one to make of this man who was alternately a devout traditionalist and a fiery radical? Perhaps the variety of his views was just an idiosyncratic mix, evolved from his personal experiences of politics. But he was a shrewder observer than most of his colleagues on the gulf between reform achievements and their effect on actual working class power, and in his bitterness against middle class betrayal he seems to show the sense of injustice of the distrustful. He may have been typical of many for whom the two political parties simply did not offer congenial total programmes, and perhaps he supported the Tories because they had at least betrayed none of the political ideals they professed to hold. But, if they may have seemed principled in their political methods, no more than the Liberals could they express his social philosophy.

In one way, though Dalzell must have been of an age with Bill, they were generations apart. They were agreed on many of the specifics of parliamentary reform and they were moved by the same symbolism of English liberty, but Dalzell was a man of very different social philosophy. He had a sympathy for all the working class and a real sense of oppression and exploitation of his type of person by both the other social classes. He declared that trades union action against the 'greed of the capitalists' was too mild, since after years of effort the workers were as badly off as ever.[166] He argued for the 'principles of cooperation and the necessity of the nationalization of land', and, with evidence from conditions in London and China, against Bill's Malthusian position.[167]

But yet he believed that 'however grand the ideas of the Socialists were, they were impracticable'.[168] He was really a British Socialist born before his time. His social philosophy would have made him very much at home in the constitutional movement for the material betterment of the working class which emerged later from the fragmented socialist groups he knew. His pleasure at the near achievement of 'the dream of the Chartist reformers' in 1886 suggests that his political radicalism was modest enough to be content with the secondary priority which socialists gave to politics as a fulfilling activity in itself.[169]

The men of the Sunday Evening Debating Society bring to life the somewhat arid picture presented by the *Mail.* The successful career of the *Mail* did at least suggest that there must be in Birmingham a substantial readership who were well informed on topical political matters and prepared to turn out for the frequent political events organised by the Liberals. What could only be guessed at was the extent to which there were differences between the mass readership and the caucus leadership in their satisfaction with, or their criticism of, the political system.

The artisans and tradesmen of the Society show that the 'respectable' working class were men of equal political capacity to their equivalents in Kansas. They were interested and knowledgeable, and they were self-confident citizens. While the majority were clearly Liberal supporters, they were also clearly not mere sheep, blindly turning out in support of a party line. The majority rejected with scorn Mr Oswald's unthinking partisanship, and preferred to keep a careful and critical watch on their leaders. But though there was a good deal of unanimity on political ideals, this did not grow out of a common feeling of material injustice, a common social philosophy, or any overwhelming sense of grand purpose for political action. These political radicals were altogether remarkably well-satisfied with their place in society and in politics, nor had their experience within the political community since 1867 deeply disillusioned them with the realities of power. Nothing in their own experience or their own political culture moved them to reject the existing facts of political inequality or to move to independent action outside existing organisations or institutions.

Comparisons

Contextual differences between the radical Liberalism of Birmingham and the politics of the Populists, and indeed between Birmingham and the rest of Britain, were substantial. Nevertheless, one feature of the Birmingham case makes it particularly apt for the purposes of this study. The working class political community of Birmingham was a politically conscious group, exposed intensively and over a long period to a radical philosophy of the proper nature of democratic government and of their own place in such government. On a superficial view, its members seemed to hold and actively support beliefs about politics akin to those of the Populists and foreign to the traditions of their own polity. But a closer look behind this appearance must lead to the unqualified conclusion that differences from the Populists and similarities with their fellow Britons were the major characteristics of these workers' political culture.

Two general points are supported by this comparison. Clearly political beliefs are themselves important and independent factors in the explanation of political behaviour (or indeed of political apathy). Neither grievances nor differences in social and political structure *alone* account for the very different political tendencies of these two groups of nineteenth-century citizens. Further, the nature of political beliefs is itself problematic until they are understood from the perspective of their proponents themselves. It is a commonplace in our own lives that 'democracy' can mean all things to all men, yet it is still too easily assumed for analytical purposes that a political doctrine or a set of political attitudes will mean the same and result in the same political behaviour the world over. The differences discovered below the surface of public rhetoric in these cases illustrate the potential of cultural explanations of political behaviour but at the same time offer a caution against superficial analyses such as those based on isolated and ahistorical attitude surveys.

Comparison between countries and across time also suggests some more specific points. In the British case, it is notable that the radicalism of the Liberal Association in the last century raised fears that were strikingly similar to the alarm of some observers of political distrust today. The cry of critics then, political opponents and academics alike, was that British politics was becoming Americanised; whether this was from a simple fear of corruption or a more sophisticated analysis of democratic theory, it was never intended as a compliment.[170] Nor is it today, when it is raised by the appearance in Britain of changing attitudes rather than a new philosophy. In both cases the analogy with America is accurate *if* the philosophy or attitudes discerned in Britain are indeed what they appear at first to be; both then would rightly imply striking innovation in the British polity. Importing the principle of popular sovereignty would have undermined traditional parliamentarism in the 1880s; importing a permanent distrustfulness of political authority appears equally to run counter to all the informal norms of the British polity today. The evidence suggests no such simple likeness between the two countries.

On the behavioural level, differences between Liberals and Populists are clear. The Populists broke out of an entrenched two party system and for a while were able to act independently and forcefully in national politics, against all the odds. Moreover, though a small group of leaders played a crucial role in the movement, there was clearly massive grass roots spontaneity. By the side of the vitality of the early months of Kansas Populism, the Birmingham Liberals' performance looks modest. They, too, acted in support of political reform, but their actions were always in response to leadership initiatives. Socially and intellectually this leadership was far more distant from the masses than was the Populist leadership, and practically it had a far stronger hold on all the local channels of communication. There is virtually no evidence of initiative from below in the Management Committee minutes or the local press of Birmingham.[171] Where political beliefs were spontaneously expressed, as in the Sunday Evening Debating Society, it was in contexts which themselves only rarely directly generated political activity.[172] Political action in Birmingham seemed divorced from debate about the nature of politics even when it was directed to political reform. Beliefs and action in Kansas were closely related and reinforced each other continually.

Comparisons of beliefs are inevitably harder to make than of actions, for the evidence is indirect. It should no more be expected that the rank and file Liberals should have a coherent and neatly argued political philosophy than it was of the Populists. But, in the Populists' case what appeared to be something of a jumble of ideas and myths and precedents did give them a consistent set of cues to focus their critique of politics, and a sense of solidarity, legitimacy and power to direct their demands and actions. The Liberal masses lustily cheered the rhetoric of 'the people', but apparently it meant no more to them than a guaranteed oratorical cue for applause. They supported the caucus organisation, but there is no evidence that they did so as a matter of political principle. Their radical democracy was not a component of a whole social philosophy, as it was for the Populists. It was not fermented by immediate and pressing economic demands, nor did the Liberals expect consequences from political action of such grandeur as did the Populists. The reform campaign of the *Birmingham Daily Mail* stood in strange isolation, with no apparent roots other than the Parliamentary timetable, as an end in itself not as the means to some social improvement. At the Hope and Anchor there was a somewhat broader perception, but this at once reveals how narrowly based was the consensus of the reformers. Mr Bill and Mr Dalzell shared their purely political aims, but the society each wanted to create through political action was very different. The debaters were more conscious of the *social* solidarity of class than of the *political* solidarity of 'the people'. Some might argue that this is a fine semantic distinction and that Populist talk of 'the people' masked an equal class interest – yet their intention seems genuinely to have been more inclusive.

There was a tremendous, if naive, optimism among the Populists that all the people, using the immense power of a purified politics, would usher in a golden age. In theory, the Liberals were asking for much greater political change than were the Populists – they were radicals, not just reformers. Popular sovereignty would have revolutionised, not merely purified politics in Britain. But, behind the radical rhetoric, the Liberals' motivation seemed to come from vague hopes of injustice rectified, liberty defended and the ancient guarantee of the redress of grievances confirmed. They were critical of anomalies, where the Populists used stronger language. These were noble aims, no doubt, but they were also very traditional aims which had long been held within the framework of parliamentary institutions and legitimations. They were more often demanded in versions of the Chartists' six aims than in the terminology of American popular sovereignty, and it is these traditional demands and not his more radical philosophy which seem to have been in the minds of supporters of Chamberlain. The difference between Liberals and Populists was between cautious negativism and positive purpose; as Pelling observed of the Labour Representation Committee, the British 'were politicians from fear of adversity, rather than through hope of improvement'.[173]

Even the expression of the Liberals' beliefs was drab beside the lively sense of history found in Kansas. The Populists found historical villains and heroes enough to inspire their criticism of politics and to symbolise their ideals and one might expect the long history of the British polity to be even more fruitful. Yet it provided nothing of importance for the Liberals.

Its isolation from social grievances and historical precedents was not the only weakness of the political culture of the English workers as a motivating force. Another was that, instead of the unanimity of the Populists, there were two different positions in Birmingham. Chamberlain argued for the leadership, not on the grounds of norms abused in the existing system, but on practical grounds of the new situation resulting from the admission of large numbers of the working class to politics; in presenting a practical solution to a new situation he simultaneously required radical change in the norms and values of the political system. In this he was far from the reforming distrust of Populism. And the essential critical half of the distrust equation did not exist at all in this argument: Chamberlain's structural proposals did not build up from any specific grievances but derived their direct challenge to the institutions of parliamentary government straight from a philosophy developed before he became seriously involved in politics.

But Chamberlain was out of kilter with his rank and file support. They cheered his speeches and supported him faithfully, but their understanding was evidently rather different. They did have complaints against the personnel and the institutions of politics, but these fragments were not the seeds of distrust and were not comparable with the comprehensive political grievances that drove the Populists to their radical democratic demands, and to action outside established political institutions. For example, rank and file Liberals were much concerned with the matter of labour representation. But this concern was generated by a diffuse feeling that this was somehow appropriate, rather than by an overwhelming distrust of those currently representing them. Neither the electoral process nor the party system was a particular cause for complaint. They were only fired with anger against the House of Lords, but yet would have been content with its emasculation within the system, and their faith in the Commons was astonishing when compared with the fury of the Populists against the realities of Congressional abuse of power. When the Liberals talked at all of general principles, it was not in their leaders' language of popular sovereignty, but in the traditional terms of the defence of liberty and the righting of wrongs.

The overall impression of the rank and file view of politics is of no more than mild scepticism, both about the actual operation and the ultimate potential of politics. Their expectations were less and so, inevitably, was their disappointment. This led them to hope for modest reforms within the system, but in practice resulted in a willingness to let things, at all levels of the system, continue much as before. This is certainly not a picture of political distrust; neither criticisms nor ideals were prominent in their political discussion, nor did they add up to the funfair-mirror-image view of ideals distorted in realities which is the characteristic of the distrustful.

Neither did the Birmingham Liberals confirm the contemporary fear of a dangerously radical class of artisans, for their radicalism, for all its rhetoric, was a rather incoherent and passive thing. Nor, on the other hand did they fit the classic picture of the deferential worker, for they were not uncritical, nor deluded by aristocratic breeding or theatrical show. They were shrewd, self-respecting and politically aware, yet largely unmoved by their own admired leader's exposition of their rights and their political deprivation. This seems a baffling combination, which perhaps only makes sense as the kind of deference to ability which allowed respect for and trust in superior ability without any loss of personal confidence or feeling of deprivation of the rights of citizenship. Deference towards talent offers no threat to parliamentarism, and above all it presumes basic trust, growing out of rational commitment not emotional loyalty.

I have not attempted a systematic search for the causes of political distrust. However, it is clear that those reasons which lead people to distrust or to criticise their political systems are also influential in mediating the outcomes of such attitudes. Behind the Populists' proposals for political reform lay a deep distrust of the political situation, and behind this in turn lay hardship and suffering; this chain of circumstances is significant. It was the seriousness and persistence of their economic grievances which eventually escalated into criticism of politics itself – and the Liberals did not have this motivation. It was the conviction that politics could solve their problems which inspired the Populist crusade for reform, and the Liberals, with their different political culture, would probably not have chosen this route to a solution in any case. The Populist perception of a close connection between the social and the political not only encouraged the growth of political distrust by suggesting political reasons for social problems, but also encouraged political action as a solution.

The public campaign for political reform in Birmingham was curiously unsupported by any immediate social or political grievances. But even in times of serious economic discontent in Britain such grievances were not expressed through political channels. Hobsbawm has charted the connection of phases of industrial discontent with the growth, in erratic and sudden leaps, of the union movement in Britain. In times of recession, when the making of a living was at its most precarious, union activity tended to decline; workers then engaged not in direct instrumental politics to alleviate their hardship, but in a purely expressive politics of reform: 'It has been observed that franchise campaigns, even after 1850, tended to revive in times of slump, when industrial forms of activity were inadvisable.'[174]

The crucial fact about the political culture of British workers at this time was that it did not make politics the mighty and rightful road to the solution of social problems. The British worker feared to threaten the employer at times of severe deprivation and so turned to 'safe' politics. The Populists did not perceive this distinction. True, the latter were self-employed workers on the whole, but this does not account for their preference for political action over unionisation. Both examples and experience of non-political action were available to them; some of their supporters were already involved in the Knights of Labor, and union organisation in America was probably more advanced at that time than in Britain;[175] the concept and models of union action were there, but they formed a political party because they perceived the political weapon as both the most powerful and the most appropriate for the solution of their problems.

In one sense it is true that the revolution of rising expectations of benefits from government has gone further and faster in Britain than in the United States. Workers' protection and welfare measures were initiated earlier and the right to the full protection of a welfare state has never been universally accepted in the United States as it has in Britain.[176] But a second kind of expectation of government might be summarised as normative, as opposed to materialistic: this is a diffuse and general expectation, carrying no specific policy imputation. In this sense, Americans' expectations were always utopian, those of the British modest. Despite the prevalent individualism, American government was established with the most ambitious positive aims: as the preamble to the constitution runs, 'to form a more perfect union, establish justice, insure domestic tranquillity, provide for the common defence, promote the general welfare, and secure the blessing of liberty'.

The Populists saw the failure of government as temporary and its potential to fulfil these high aims as not disproven. They need only reform government and social welfare would automatically follow. They were radical for Americans in their willingness drastically to expand the actual scope of government policy, but they already had an unlimited expectation of its potential.

Some of the habitués of the Hope and Anchor wanted to see modest extensions of social intervention by the British government, but there was no widespread feeling for such policies. Nor was there any sign of an idealistic vision of the potential of government to shower blessings on its citizens. Partly this negativism reflected a general social conservatism: 'The members of the working class as a whole, cynical about the character of society as they knew it, were yet fearful of change which they thought would more likely be for the worse than for the better.'[177] But the tradition of radicalism, which had influenced their expression of demands in a negative way, was also partly responsible for this narrow view of the potential of government. Americans demanded much from their government, the British little.

There was, in any case, no agreement on what the good society would be. The Liberals' political radicalism was a thing apart from the social philosophies of its proponents; and Mr Bill and Mr Dalzell were illustrations of how irreconcilable these social philosophies were. The disunity of social philosophy left no hope of agreement on what the precise functions of government should be and no chance of allying political demands directly with an agreed analysis of social ills, as the Populists had done so effectively. The Populists drew support from both parties, by finding members of each who shared not only a social situation but an analysis of ills and solutions. The British working class lacked this agreement on social and economic solutions, and lacked the conceivable alternative of a purposeful political movement transcending differences in social philosophy with some unifying abstract vision of the power of politics.

That classic explanatory variable of difference between the two countries, social class, had some connection with these differences in political culture. Social and political radicalism in Britain had not always been so dissociated, but, as class perspectives became gradually more distinctive, a new social ideal, indigenous to the working class, marked their sense of separation within society. Perkin describes this social ideal as a simple version of the labour theory of value, essentially claiming the right of the workers to 'the whole produce of labour', from which it followed that the 'ideal citizen was the productive, independent worker, and its ideal society an equalitarian one based on labour and cooperation'. But this ideal made no particular political prescription; it 'could mean a merely political democracy or a socialist utopia'. And it shifted the old radical preoccupation with politics from its place of first priority – it 'transformed the merely political Rights of Man into the social revolutionary Rights of Labour'.[178]

By the latter part of the century, to the fact that the social and the political had become disconnected in radical thought was added their effective institutional separation. In mid century the unions, and at the end of the century the socialists too, pre-empted the expression of working class social and economic demands. Meanwhile, the Liberals continued to carry the banner for popular political power. Hybrid movements, which in various ways combined economic and political demands, like Lib–Labism, Hyndman's Social Democratic Federation or guild socialism fell between these two stools; the political principles upon which radicals could agree had been monopolised as their own by the Liberals, but Liberals could never be the spokesmen for the developing social radicalism of the working class.

The same dissociation of the social and the political reappeared at the end of the century in British Socialism, where economic radicalism was not coupled with any sense of urgency about the reform of political institutions. In theory, the indirect effect of Labour Party organisation on traditional parliamentarism should have been as drastic as the effect earlier predicted for Chamberlain's caucus organisation. In fact, of course, Labour has proved no more successful in transferring the exercise of sovereignty from Parliament to the people. The doctrinal view that economic revolution would automatically destroy super-structural political institutions was not the primary reason. What became the dominant strain of the Labour movement made its priority the maximisation of material benefits for the citizens, not the human fulfilment of democratic participation. Sidney Webb, for example, could never have agreed with the choice of bad government with democracy over good government without it. In a series of Fabian lectures on 'The Machinery of Democracy' in 1896, Webb took the old radical rhetoric of democracy and gave his understanding of it: 'Its best definition is "the government *of* the people, *by* the people, *for* the people." It connotes actual control, but not necessarily by means of election. . .The right of each man to an equal and identical share of government does not, even if valid, apply to its machinery.'[179] And in his next lecture he explained why he was content with this drastically curtailed version of Lincoln – he believed that it was wrong 'to imply that one person in society can do the work of governing as well as any other. This idea largely prevails in the United States.'[180]

The views of the Birmingham workers suggest that Webb was actually more in touch with working class political culture than was Chamberlain, with his 'American' philosophy. Even the radically inclined Sunday Evening Debaters were generally prepared to let those with proven capacity make their decisions for them in Parliament. They were willing for a political division of labour, and such deference was entirely compatible with Webb's conclusion that 'that form of government was most democratic which proved in practice to give the community the most effective control over its administrative and legislative machinery'.[181] There was nothing in popular political culture to challenge either traditional or Fabian constitutional theory by placing above such institutional concerns any compelling moral con-cern for democracy, so nothing to respond with either feeling or under-standing to Chamberlain's rhetoric.

John Vincent has described the political style of social radicalism as that of men who need politics for bread, and of political radicalism as of those who need it for circuses – a graphic summary of instru-mental and expressive politics.[182] The factor determining which style any individual will follow, he suggests, is not deprivation or objective class identification but the social structure of his work situation. The worker may find himself in a community of interest or in an individual-istic situation – miners and factory workers are typical of the first, the self-employed or the employee of a small firm of the second. Both the Birmingham workers and the Populists should then be 'men who needed politics chiefly to supply the circuses of their lives'.[183] But political styles do not fit so neatly with social characteristics as Vincent's scheme requires. British union men and Socialists do seem clear cases of politics for bread, with their political demands being practical measures overflowing from the primary arena of industrial conflict. But the radical Liberals in Birmingham appear to have been a classic case of cross-pressured confusion, for many must, like Mr Dalzell, have combined political radicalism with the social philosophy of the 'industrial' type. For the moment they voted their old Liberal loyalty, but later, when they were offered the choice of a party expressing their social philosophy, they were lost to the Liberals. A purer case of Vincent's individualists might seem to be the Populists, whose social and political concerns did not, any more than did those of the British Socialists, pull them in different partisan directions. Yet their case also defies this simple categorisation, for the Populists viewed politics as both instrumental and *also* an expressive act with moral connotations for the individual and for society – doubly functional in answering human needs for both bread and circuses.

For British workers, politics was not only *not* the prime instrument for social change, but also was *not* elevated to symbolic importance for its own sake. The Populists saw voting as more than a right or a duty; it represented the noble tradition of American citizenship and was an act of human self-fulfilment. For the good Nonconformists of Birmingham it was perhaps equally inspiring to be reminded that 'to vote is to perform a public duty'; Nash quoted this in his lecture and coupled it with Carlyle's tag, 'Duties are ours, events are God's'.[184] But it is hard to imagine that this would rouse the whole political community to stirring deeds and independent action, as did the conviction of the Populists. The Liberal rank and file applauded the idea of government of the people, but it seems that they were content, whatever Chamberlain may have meant by his phrase, to agree that 'government of the people means government for the people'.

The British outcome was what Moorhouse described as their 'pragmatic acceptance' of political reality. But this acceptance cannot be accounted for entirely by showing how the ruling class controlled and excluded them from political institutions and communications. The Populists felt so strongly about that kind of monopolisation of politics that they rejected existing channels of participation and developed their own. Though neither their party nor their press succeeded in gaining a permanent foothold in American politics, the point here is that they tried. They did not turn to non-political solutions and they did not accept a two party system which at that time had a longer record of control than did the British parties.

Structural factors cannot explain this difference. The Populists had the nerve to attempt to break the monopoly of power because of deeply internalised norms of the power of the people as a unified political force, and of the right of the people to act in this way. The British working class, too, before and during their 'incorporation' into politics, had a political culture; they were not a *tabula rasa* on which the ruling class were able to impose a political culture to suit their own interests. But their beliefs about politics suggested no essential linkage with their social aims, no utopian expectations of the power of politics, no political solidarity to give courage and confidence to independent political action, no moral fervour to participation, and no symbols, myths or precedents in history to present an unarguable case for both the legitimacy and the possibility of effective political action. Instead they had modest and defensive aims combined with a willingness to trust traditional ways of reaching political decisions.

The Populists were social individualists, yet felt a very real solidarity in political matters. 'We the people' was not merely a constitutional preamble but a real community with might and right on its side. Solidarity and group consciousness in Britain was first of all social, with no real political equivalent. Norms of equality and mutuality and of cooperative community flourished in the working class, but had relatively little influence as yet on political action. There was nothing that would encourage discontent to turn into political distrust, and even where one catches hints of this kind of view, nothing to direct its resolution into political action.

All these differences are drawn together by the tendency which I discovered during my study of these two groups, to think always of the Populists as the 'grass roots' and the Birmingham Liberals as the 'rank and file'. For in their beliefs and their political action the Populists displayed an initiative and spontaneity fitting for the roots of the system – whose function is not only to spread widely and freely so as to anchor the plant and bind the soil but also to draw in life to nourish the flowers and fruit. The first of these functions, of anchoring and balancing, is reminiscent of the social self-respect allowed the peasant as the feet in the medieval analogy of the body politic – supportive but not directive.

The second function is new and positive, for the roots are the source of vitality for the whole – life, growth and direction depend on their full development. The political metaphor of 'grass roots' probably appeared in the American language in the 1880s, in the period of major political change of which the Populist movement was an integral and striking part; in England the term has only recently been acknowledged, and even then reluctantly as an Americanism.[185] The military analogy of the rank and file has very different implications: the rank and file follow, accepting orders out of a sense of the legitimacy of their source and of the duties of their own position. They respond, but are not to initiate, are skilled in performing their own specialised task, but are dependent and routinised. The rank and file are as essential to an army as the feet are to the body – indeed there is little difference in the implications of these two models of civic action. For all the structural and philosophical changes between medieval and nineteenth-century British politics, it seems that the common man still understood and accepted much the same place for himself.

5. Distrust and democracy

Continuously in America, and intermittently at least in Britain, distrust has been a widespread response to politics. The probing of modern attitude surveys and the historical evidence of the words and deeds of ordinary citizens have endorsed each other; comparable evidence points to some general conclusions about the meaning of this sentiment to the distrustful themselves. Distrust is not alienation, though it retains something of the sense of wrongful deprivation classically inherent in that word. Nor is it anomie, whose connotations of norm-lessness, social inadequacy and passivity have all been shown to be inappropriate. The distrustful are often inarticulate, yet they do have a coherent and consistent set of political norms, do identify abuses accurately and do propose fitting, if not new or guaranteed, solutions. The differences in content between the two nations are closely related to differences in their political environments. The outburst in America in the 1960s was a return to normal rather than a dramatic collapse of normative integration – the distrustful there are not philosophical extremists but are true to the mainstream of the American political tradition. Where the Americans are reformers, the British are radicals in their challenge to traditional parliamentary democracy. Lacking the support of the dominant political tradition, distrust in Britain is still far from achieving the coherence and force which it has had in America. But the evidence does suggest a gradual evolution of both concern and philosophy.

Such differences in meaning suggest that we might expect rather different consequences in these two nations today, for all the superficial similarities in the rhetoric of distrust. Other political and social con-trasts reinforce this expectation. With the benefit of hindsight, it is clear that there were several categories of crucial influence on out-comes in the nineteenth century: the social and economic grievances of the distrustful, their own political capacities, and the responses of government and other political institutions, as well as the nature of their political ideals. The same categories throw some light on the prospects for politics today; I shall use them in this chapter to compare the present experience of each country with its past, and the two nations with each other.

Consequences for America

The American is the easier of the two national studies to interpret, since it is plain that distrust has been a permanent feature of the American polity since its establishment. The systematic post-war evidence suggests that there have been peaks and dips in its incidence, at least over the last thirty years. The historical evidence of overt, and sometimes dramatic, expressions of distrust suggests that the 1950s, in this as in other respects, were atypical years in their political calm and acquiescence. There were, even then, citizens who expressed the classic feelings of distrust, but they were mainly a residual group, ill-equipped for social involvement of any kind. In their attributes this group conformed more closely to the sociological picture of the anomic, though the expression of political distrust implied at least the possession of an embryonic normative structure of political beliefs. By contrast, in the Populist era as well as in the 1970s, not only was the incidence of distrust much higher but the social attributes of many of the distrustful were significantly different. They appeared to be composed of two distinct groups – that same residual group of the underprivileged and disadvantaged, together with numbers of highly competent, politically experienced and active citizens.

The fear in the 1950s was that rising disaffection would mean an intensifying critical consciousness among democratically insensitive groups. Action, if it came, could then only be destructive. But action, if and when it arises out of a distrustful analysis of the situation, is likely to come from that second group of democratic idealists, and their demands are for reform, not for radical change or structural demolition.

It is not only the benefits of hindsight that make the nature and effectiveness of action easier to assess in the case of the 1890s than of the present. Then, the intensity of specific grievances and the intensity of the purely political critique together created a situation in which the Populists were able, briefly, to over-ride partisan commitments of great emotional strength and factional differences on issues. They formed a movement with a broad enough base to operate with some effect in both state and federal politics. But such a coalescence of distrustful groups did not occur even at the peak of its recent incidence, around 1970. Where distrust has generated action recently, this has been fragmented and fleeting – and its causes and effects consequently much harder to establish.

The farmers' critique of government escalated into political distrust from shared grievances: they found a temporary unity which could transcend sectional and ideological differences in their support of the three issues of Land, Transportation and, particularly, Money. By comparison, the first weakness of the distrustful today is the absence of shared grievance. Indeed, even more damaging to the possibility of effective action is their polarisation into incompatible groups – cynics of the right and cynics of the left.[1] Before the 1972 Presidential election there was much talk of a new alliance of the 'alienated':

> The most famous strategy, that of 'the alienated voter,' aimed at bringing together the Wallace and McGovern factions in 1972 – more or less on McGovern's terms to be sure. What these factions had in common was anti-partisanship, or, more precisely, opposition to the traditional leadership of the Democratic Party...But each faction had its own reason for rejecting traditional party leadership, and they were very different reasons ...The problem, very simply was that the Wallace and McGovern factions were miles apart ideologically.[2]

As the Democrats found to their cost later that year, to win one of these groups of cynics was to lose the other. While 82 per cent of distrustful cynics of the left voted for McGovern in November, only 24 per cent of cynics of the right did so.[3]

The Populists were not only more united on issues, their issues were somewhat less transient. Free Silver had been salient to many of the electorate since the 1870s, but effectively excluded from electoral debate through the control of both major parties by goldbug factions. With the final settlement of this issue in 1896, and with general economic change, the remnants of the party faded swiftly away. But they had at least had six years' run for their money, after three decades of concern. Secrecy and deception in the political process, typified by the appearance in common political parlance of the 'credibility gap', was a prime focus of normative criticism through both the Johnson and Nixon administrations. But the cathartic effect of Richard Nixon's exposure and resignation seemed to meet the widespread eagerness for reassurance that 'the system worked' (however much luck was really responsible) and thus it stalled the most obvious accusation of abuse of democratic norms. War-related issues faded away with the withdrawal from Vietnam. Economic problems do remain salient. If they dominate elections once more, old partisan divisions may be revived and distrust silenced through the satisfaction of finding an appropriate electoral choice. The reactivation of the old New Deal alliance of liberals, blue collar workers and the poor is envisaged by some strategists, and may have contributed to the 1976 Democratic victory, with some of those cynics who were on the right on the social and racial issues of the 1972 election rejoining those on the left – not in a new movement but back within traditional party politics.

Yet the possibility of a long-term reversion to traditional patterns seems less likely when a second point of comparison is taken: the political capabilities and attributes of the distrustful. The deep partisan loyalties of the Populists were broken very suddenly in 1890. A similar process may be more solidly based today. In the 1950s, the classic study of *The American voter* could still claim that declared party identification was the best and most stable indicator of future voting behaviour – a psychological attribute fixed beyond likely question remarkably early in life. Since then, the decline of strong, securely internalised party identification has been precipitous: by 1974 the proportion of declared independents had risen to 34 per cent of the electorate from a level of 22 per cent in 1950.[4]

There was a sharp upturn in the numbers of independents in the mid sixties, at the same time as there was a sharp rise in the incidence of distrust and of interest in politics. The probability that these parallel developments were associated is enhanced by findings that both the decline in partisanship and the rise in disenchantment and concern were concentrated in the same group of the better educated.[5] These are the New Independents – a far cry from the floating voters of the 1950s whose contributions to the democratic process had to be tortuously justified as accidentally beneficial. Their general political and social competences predispose these New Independents to act. Their coherent criticisms and solutions suggest the possibility of purposeful action, accurately directed at the sources of abuse.

In these respects the distrustful of today seem similar to the Populists, yet a third party, so inevitable to the Populists, has not materialised. Clearly a major part of the explanation must be the current ideological polarisation. But there are other possibilities too; notably that people today may prefer alternative ways of acting, or that active but different responses have actually been overlooked through emphasising the Populists' single-minded party orientation.

The first of these possibilities, that the distrustful now opt for other ways of acting, is certainly not true of their preference: the sentiments are identical in the winning confidence of Populist picnics singing their chorus of 'let us vote/and trust' and in the more clinical datum of the 94 per cent of the Senate's sample who saw the exercise of the vote as the means to the restoration of democratic politics. And both groups chose similar alternative means to the recovery of their democratic rights – by taking non-partisan stands on issues, by institutional and party reform and by general demands for participation.

But, if the possibilities have been perceived in very similar terms, the situations have actually generated very different patterns of action. While there has been no equivalent of the People's Party, there have been innovations in American politics which can be associated with the rise of political distrust. They are well summarised by Samuel Huntington, in an unenthusiastic appraisal of the politics of the 1960s:

> The predominant trends of that decade involved challenges to the authority of established political, social and economic institutions, increased popular participation in and control over those institutions, a reaction against the concentration of power in the executive branch of the federal government and in favour of the reassertion of the power of Congress and of state and local government, renewed commitment to the idea of equality on the part of intellectuals and other elites, the emergence of 'public interest' lobbying groups, increased concern for the rights of. . .minorities and women, and a pervasive criticism of those who possessed or were even thought to possess excessive power or wealth. The spirit of protest, the spirit of equality, and the impulse to expose and correct inequities were abroad in the land.[6]

Generally, the behaviour linked with distrust has been well within the bounds of democratic modes of action, by any standard of democracy. Observers have been right to see the distrustful as a threat to the dominant power-holders in society, but wrong to see them as a threat to the political values of the system. Indeed, to claim that they have been either destructive radicals or confused incompetents effectively diverts attention away from the possibility that their critique of politics might be well-founded. Yet this was the tone of comment on the Populists and a reaction which has been revived with the revival of distrust today. Thus Huntington sees the politics of the 1960s as a 'democratic distemper', an ungovernable alternative to 'the time-honored traditional politics of compromise'.[7] For him, the activities of the distrustful are threatening despite their being couched in the language of democracy: 'The vulnerability of democratic government in the United States comes. . .from the internal dynamics of democracy itself in a highly educated, mobilized and participant society.'[8] With greater honesty at least than those writers of the 1950s who simply re-defined democracy to a standard of minimal participation, Hunting-ton's solution to governing America now is to admit the desirability of a degree of undemocratic government: 'democracy is only one way of constituting authority, and it is not necessarily a universally applicable one'.[9] It is an irony indeed that the achievement of relatively high levels of education and sophistication in the electorate, which the Populists believed would make effective democracy possible, has led to claims that it makes democracy impossible.

Huntington saw a gleam of hope in the possibility that the distrust-ful, through trying to change politics, would speedily discover their own ineffectiveness. From this discovery he anticipated a decline in participation and a return in 'a cyclical process of interaction' to passivity, and presumably to contentment.[10] But this surely presupposes that the distrustful will join Huntington in laying the blame for involvement and failure solely on themselves. The error here is that of the original concept of efficacy, the failure to distinguish two separate aspects of political perception – of oneself and of the system. Both the Populists and the present distrustful in fact have levelled, with some accuracy and some justification, specific criticisms at the system, and blamed themselves only for apathy. Distrust cannot be simply passed off as a by-product of non-political facts, of the baby-boom after the Second World War and 'the new disrespect for authority on the part of youth'.[11] It is equally plausible to suggest that if the system is rigid and unresponsive to democratic attempts at change, distrust of institu-tions will be reinforced; conceivably the distrustful may come to despair of its values as well as of its current state. A recent study of university students found a chain of events quite different from that envisaged by Huntington, one in which the failure of political action intensified rather than deflated distrust. As distrust intensified, students became more willing to 'select strategies that incorporate nontraditional tactics'.[12] Although surveys have shown no general intention yet among the distrustful to act outside conventional political modes, the situation may change if the validity and intensity of these feelings is ignored.

Whether reformist action in conventional ways can anyway be effective is a separate and complicated question. For all the similarities between the two periods, the past precedent of the Populists gives little guidance on how effective action might be today. It is not just the methodological difficulty of using historical evidence for prediction in vastly different circumstances – the effectiveness of the Populists them-selves remains problematic. Some historians have found them to be the progenitors of a stream of reforms implemented over the next several decades; others conclude that they failed at the point of compromise with the old parties in 1896. The dispute here is not primarily over facts, but over the appropriate criterion for judgement. Thus, their demands can simply be matched against legislative achievements. An alternative standard is of their faithfulness to their own principles; and this must be part of the judgement of the effectiveness of the distrustful, who are concerned with the means of politics and the principles of action, not simply with the achievement of their ends at any cost. By this criterion the Populists were successful, Henry Demarest Lloyd's denunciation notwithstanding. They perceived their options only in terms of conventional political action and in this they were consistent with their understanding and affirmation of democratic politics. Given this tight limitation of options, they faced a choice between cooperation with the despised political parties which dominated the system or annihilation. Their contemporary critics interpreted this co-optation into old politics as an unscrupulous sell-out for power. This seems an unwarrantedly uncharitable judgement. The evidence equally allows the presentation of their actions in 1896 as the reluctant choice of men who did not see politics as a zero-sum game in which their only alter-natives were to win or lose. That was the political ethos of Senator Ingalls, which they had roundly condemned in 1890.[13] Whether action confined to conventional modes of democratic politics can ever be adequate to defeat abuses of those same modes remains a dilemma for the distrustful. The case of the Populists emphasises the pitfalls but offers no solution.

The responses of government, parties and other elements in the polity may have a profound effect on both the attitudes of the distrustful and the options open to them. In the 1890s the Populists were taken seriously – the old parties moved swiftly to crush them and by forcing them into an impossible position before their convention in 1896 effec-tively closed most of their options, aided greatly by the fortuitous change in economic circumstances. Their normative critique was simply evaded – adjustments to political institutions in line with their programme came by degrees, after the Populists themselves had ceased to be a threat and often not for the purest democratic reasons.[14]

The current reaction is less clear, in part because it is to a diffuse mood of distrust rather than to a unified and distinctive political movement. There has been action, of varying degrees of decisiveness, on some of the fomenting issues – the ending of the draft, the moves to impeach and the resignation of Nixon, the outbreak of candidacies for office on platforms of honest government, for example. When demands are met distrust does decline – witness its fluctuations within the black community; at the height of optimism over the war on poverty and the passage of civil rights legislation in the mid 1960s distrust was markedly lower among blacks than others, but since then it has risen at a dramatic pace to levels exceeding those in the white population.[15]

In the 1890s, when significant social groups felt that neither of the major parties offered an appropriate choice on matters of central concern to them, there was eventually a realignment of party positions and of party loyalties. The end result was a new aggregation of social groups under the traditional party labels. The polarisation of the distrustful today on crucial issues would require a complex realignment if all were once more to be reabsorbed, yet a continued failure to offer substantial minorities appropriate choices, by this or more novel means, will surely contribute to the cycle of increasing distrust described above. By contrast with the swift reaction of the old parties to the Populists, the response now to the volatility of the electorate is inertia. In 1976, it was not so much an understanding of this volatility as a change in the salience of issues which left old party stands and old partisan loyalties still matching for substantial numbers of the electorate. But, with the notable exceptions of the blacks and southerners, there was no consequent return to voting. So long as nearly half the electorate find no strong reason for voting, the parties can hardly be said to be responsive to their preferences.

The indictment of inertia in the face of real discontent has wider application than just to the parties. Muskie's Senate subcommittee, for example, while taking distrust seriously enough to commission the first ever official survey of public attitudes, reacted to its findings with little more than polite expressions of sympathy. The reaction was in line with the evidence of the survey, of a marked difference in both social and political perception between the electorate and their representatives at all levels of government, with the public far less likely to feel that the quality of life in America was improving, and far more likely to be critical of political leadership. Indeed, the two groups apportioned blame for what they did see wrong with America very differently, with the leadership being strongly critical of the electorate and vice versa. Burnham has given other evidence of what he calls 'the emergence of a manifest elitist illusion among top American leadership of both parties':

> It has been very characteristic of both the Johnson top leadership...and of former President Nixon and his aides to blame the public at large for failing to support their disastrous blunders and, in the case of Nixon personally, to regard adult American citizens as 'children.' Quite appropriately, and in a very Greek way, this *hubris* has produced its *nemesis* and has led to *ate*: Pride meets its appointed Fate, and Destruction follows. For the realities have been quite otherwise.[16]

To the extent that he recognised this tendency and deliberately took the opposite position (and in this sense only) Jimmy Carter can fairly be called a Populist. As I argued earlier, there is no continuous sectional interest or ideological position which can be associated with the label. The only continuity is the philosophy of strongly participatory democracy, and in this respect Populism is one of the central themes of American political thought. Carter stood precisely with the distrustful Populists of the 1890s in his constant campaign assertion of the necessity of bringing government closer to the people, and of the people's capacity to rise to the responsibility. It remains to be seen whether he shares their inability to implement these good intentions. When pressed on the grounds for his optimism, in a famous interview, he certainly seemed to rely on the same intuitive feeling that past corruptions could somehow be overcome, given good will on all sides:

> PLAYBOY: It sounds as if you're saying Americans accepted indecency and lies in their Government all too easily. Doesn't that make your constant campaign theme, invoking the decency and honesty of the American people, somewhat naive and ingenuous?
> CARTER: I say that the American people are basically decent and honest and want a truthful Government...I don't think it's simplistic to say that our Government hasn't measured up to the ethical and moral standards of the people of this country. We've had better governments in the past and I think our people...are just as strong, courageous and intelligent as they were 200 years ago.[17]

It was easier, twenty years ago, for the school of democratic elitists to blame the electorate and to be reassured by their apathy. But the changing political context has been instrumental in bringing out coherence and accuracy in the political perceptions of the electorate. It is the argument of this book too that 'the realities have been quite otherwise' and that the lessons of the Populists in the last century have more relevance to the politics of today than the lessons of the 1950s. The 'democratic distemper', both then and now, has indeed been democratic and has been accurate in its analysis, principled even if often fumbling in its reaction. The catalyst of a democratic crisis is more likely to be a determinedly blind political elite. The solution is not to plead for a 'stable democracy' or a revitalisation of any past state of politics; what is needed for a start is a serious debate *between* both sides of the American public, citizens and their leaders, on the realities and possibilities of politics. Two separate debates currently run, with each side stigmatising the other as undemocratic and essentially hostile. Thus Huntington speaks anxiously of a serious loss of authority, but fails to acknowledge that, in a polity whose citizens have traditionally and strongly held norms of participatory democracy, authority and legitimacy will be recognised only where leaders can be seen honestly to be attempting to govern by those norms. If it is necessary that 'in many situations, the claims of expertise, seniority, experience and special talents may override the claims of democracy as a way of constituting authority', then this public must be convinced, not merely informed.[18]

The public are in fact more self-critical than their leaders seem to be. The Populists took much blame upon themselves, admitting that they had failed in the exercise of that eternal vigilance which was the price of liberty. For them, the actual anti-democratic behaviour was by the political elite, but through sins of omission or commission all were equally culpable. Likewise, substantial numbers of the public today assert the duty of the citizen to give up some of his own time to informing himself about government and politics, surely a ground for optimism rather than alarm.

The expression of political distrust comes naturally to those socialised into American political culture, but action is dependent on additional motivations and circumstances. Even with intense issue grievances and anger roused by an unresponsive political system, action remains exceedingly vulnerable. One reason has become plain: distrust is not an entirely independent feeling – the Americans are not such natural philosophers that political criticisms of this kind are unrelated to general contentment. Since distrust is rooted in issue grievances, it is highly responsive to changes in the political and social context. While Populism went further and survived longer than any of the fragmented moves taken recently, it too lacked the unity and staying power to continue in a changed situation.

Political culture plays a crucial role in providing the rationale for action. But the second weakness in distrust as a basis for action lies in the content of this same political culture. For its practical guidance is either as vague as the classic slogans which excited the Populists or else has failed before in the American experience. Indeed, it contains enough contradictions and dilemmas to dismay if not to paralyse the activist. Of course there must have been men among the Populists who were riding the wind for personal political advantage. But there is nothing conclusive in the act of fusion in 1896 to prove that the humanity and principle of the early political idealism of the movement had been drowned six years later in a wave of unmitigated opportunism. The democratic norms of the ordinary citizen, even coupled with humanity and principle, were and are not an adequate plan for action. They provide striking grounds for criticism and a moving call for action, together with a promise of effectiveness – but they do not tell precisely how to set about reform, nor how one might implement 'government of the people, by the people and for the people'. The crucial weakness of popular political culture is the simplicity of an understanding of democracy which is based upon a handful of rousing slogans. The problem is reflected, too, in the difficulties of the average person in moving from the affirmation to the application of democratic principles. In politics, as in other social concerns, the majority operate with a more particularistic and immediate frame of reference than do the most highly educated minority. And so, though politics is invested with utopian potential, the means seen to fulfil the potential are only those that failed before. As the Populists logically concluded, the only hope then is that new reformers and organisations will prove more resistant to corruption than did their predecessors.

But it is more than condescending to argue, as some of the more outspoken of the democratic elitists did, that this gulf between norms and application renders the ordinary citizen unfitted for participation in politics. The same difficulties are repeated in the educated and the elite, where there is also no final agreement on the means of implementing good government. For the real problem lies in the concept of democracy itself and its openness to endless reinterpretation. The data from both countries presented in this study make clear that ordinary citizens may have a different understanding of the implications of democracy from political elites and academics, but that they cannot therefore be dismissed as either ill-informed or outside the democratic tradition. The study of political distrust forces the attention back to the assumptions upon which varieties of democratic theory are predicated.

Consequences for Britain

No confident assertion of continuity and consistency is possible in the British case. The differences from America are substantial. In comparing Birmingham artisans with the Populists I emphasised differences; superficial similarities in rhetoric and programme were less significant than the contrasts in their concepts of democracy and their views on the role of the ordinary citizen in the polity and the potential of politics as a weapon for social change. Today there is a closer resemblance between the critique and the ideals of the British and Americans. But they differ still: Americans, as they did before, declare more passionately a sense of lost democratic rights, but the British now direct specific criticisms at more fundamental levels – at the principles of their parliamentary institutions, not simply at abuses in their operation. The two nations do now share a framework for their criticisms in the norms of radical democracy; this gives common ground for the identification of wrongs and for the proposal of similar reforms which both would achieve by similar means.

It is not only differences in content which are likely to lead to different consequences in Britain. In addition, in comparison with America today, the issue grievances in Britain are less clearly identifiable but probably less transient, the inhibitions upon action stemming from the capacities and norms of the distrustful are still greater, and, though the traditional ways of Britain seem more hostile to radical democracy, institutional and elite responses have been more sympathetic. The contribution of specific grievances to the rise of distrust in Britain is closely bound up with changes in the political culture, and I shall treat these together here, looking first at developments in British political culture and then at changes and responses in the politics of Britain.

The political culture of the superior working man of the 1880s seemed best described as fragmented in its grounds for analysis and criticism of politics, passive in its implications for action. In the first respect there has been a marked change in the intervening century; the discussion of politics is now shaped to a much greater degree by a unified normative framework, emphasising the right to participation and control and assuming the need for watchfulness in place of the trusting latitude given to earlier generations of representatives. Yet, if speaking out against abuses has thus become easier, action still seems much less likely than in America.

Populist political culture already in the nineteenth century encouraged criticism, and added a very real sense of the duty to follow
on with action, the confidence of might and right on their side and a
promise of the effectiveness of a purified politics in satisfying demands.
The Birmingham Liberals, despite their sense of self-respect as capable
citizens, deferred to their leaders, and in any case did not see politics as
the prime arena for achievement of their social and economic demands.
While they did share a subjective sense of class identity, this was not a
source of political strength like the Populist sense of the collective power
of the people. A class in itself perhaps, but not a class for itself, for the
overlapping of interests through traditional relationships and shared
respectability prevented the crystallisation of clearly defined inter-class
antagonism. In its understanding of the role of the citizen in the polity,
in its sense of the uses and power of politics and in the lack of a strong
collective political identity, the British political culture of today is
closer to its nineteenth-century predecessor than to its American
counterpart, and it is this that seems likely to inhibit action by the distrustful.

The British did in the nineteenth century, and do today, feel reason-
ably self-confident about their own political capacity. In Rosenbaum's
sample, self-declared efficacy was somewhat but not strikingly less than
that of the Americans. But they had actually been less active than their
American counterparts and several of their attitudes, in addition to the
lesser opportunities for participation, contribute to an explanation of
this difference. While the British did endorse the suggestion that the
citizen had a duty to observe and criticise his governors, they were far
less likely than the Americans to acknowledge the necessity for the
sacrifice of time and energy to this end. If elitism in government is to
be rejected, as it was by this group, and participation is to be the new
order of the day, then its cost must be recognised. It seems that ideals
might founder as easily on this point as Oscar Wilde's socialism, for
'Socialism takes too many evenings'. Even the relatively undemanding
duty of voting was seen as less important by the British than the
Americans – they felt less duty to vote, fewer believed that their vote
would have any effect and yet, more than the Americans, they believed
that voting was the only way they could participate.

This ambivalence towards the vote reflects another comparative
weakness of British political culture. For it is surely hard for a single
individual to feel genuinely that his vote alone does matter. Hence the
logical conclusion of at least one political scientist that voting must be

an entirely irrational act. The feeling of political efficacy must come from being a member of a political group with a real solidarity and collective purpose. This was the strength of the Populists, that, united, the people must triumph; political candidates in America today still make effective use of a symbolic identification with the people. Social class has been the collective identity in British politics and is the necessary explanation of much political behaviour. But in association with political distrust it is less potent than the American's 'people'. For one thing, it is a less inclusive concept; for the Populists the people comprised almost the whole population, only disqualifying that small minority of financiers and eastern elites so long as their actions were wholly inimical to the public good. Class, on the other hand, is a divisive concept and its division cuts right across the expression of political distrust, making a polarisation deeper and more permanent than the ideological polarisation of the Americans. While there are correlations in Rosenbaum's data both between distrustful attitudes and Liberal or independent politics, and between Liberal Party membership and middle class social position, distrust in fact is not particularly associated with any one social class. The attitudes are rather evenly spread across all levels of society, but the active distrustful are not: they are the better educated middle class, the group who are disproportionately likely also to be Liberals or independents. The data thus suggest that the distrustful in Britain as in America fall into two groups. But in Britain these are the active middle class, easily fitting the tradition of Liberal political radicalism and a party offering no ideological conflict with their social views and social position, and the largely inactive lower class, inactive in this case not only from their possession of lesser political skills but from their possession of a social ideology which suggests the primacy of other arenas of action. The nineteenth-century evidence suggested the possibility of such a split arising; the twentieth-century evidence confirms that it has materialised.

Despite their usefulness in the explanation of political behaviour, classes have never become primarily political entities in Britain. Class interests are fundamentally economic interests and political organisation in Britain has never been the first resort for the satisfaction of the most basic economic demands. A third major point of difference between American and British political culture is still their different understanding of the scope and power of politics.

There has been substantial change in Britain since the 1880s, for then there was criticism of government, but couched within a very modest and traditional framework, characterised by both low substantive and low normative expectations of government. By the 1970s the substantive expectations had become far more extensive; despite the survival of the old suspicion of the immediate interference of government in the private lives of ordinary workers, an extensive social welfare role for government is now taken for granted. Yet, in the most central economic matters, government is still not seen as the ultimate and legitimate resort of the aggrieved. There is, even here, a change from the pattern described by Hobsbawm for the nineteenth century or Runciman for the depression era, when workers responded to economic crisis by muting their demands or turning to what they perceived as a less threatening mode of action, political radicalism. Lately, economic demands have not abated in hard times. Instead they have escalated by questioning as never before the moral justification of 'a wider structure of social inequality which has no rationale whatsoever'.[19] Indirectly, the impact of assertive militancy regardless of economic circumstances has been and will be great on the operation of British politics. But the point to make here is that, by the union protagonists, disputes over wage levels and differentials are still not seen as primarily political: 'In other words, grievances arising out of inequality do not tend to become so highly politicized that established political institutions and processes are themselves challenged.'[20] The Populists saw their most effective weapon against similarly intense economic grievances as political action. Confronted with a succession of government-imposed prices and incomes controls over the last few years, the British union movement has still been intent on asserting the principle of free collective bargaining as the prime method of obtaining economic justice.

But government has changed the rules of the game. Previously its massive involvement in the economy was mainly in the direction of making inequalities tolerable through the welfare state. But incomes policies must either fix or deliberately alter existing economic inequalities, in each case by political decision. Furthermore, they educate people to look at the whole pattern rather than to bargain in terms of differentials with nearby groups – a change liable to overturn the traditional patterns of near-sighted relative deprivation. But, so long as the dissociation of social and political radicalism continues, it will be as crucial an inhibition on the translation of political distrust into effective political action as the absence of clearly directive personal norms. For, even where grievances have escalated into political distrust, the reaction will not be to throw resources and energies into political reform but to discount politics and to concentrate upon non-political industrial or social militancy. Political distrust in such circumstances will be a dead-end, a marginal feeling rather than the central grievance which it seems to be in the American polity. Yet, if it is believed that fundamental social decisions *should* be political decisions, one observer's anxious conclusion should be a sign of hope and a challenge to those with political power; that Britain may be on the way to 'breaking down the insulation of the British political system from issues and grievances stemming from inequality – the insulation which the national political culture has hitherto provided. In other words, it would carry the very real threat of extending economic into political instability.'[21]

The immediate effect of such dissociations of the social and political, and between the working and middle class, is a fragmentation of the energies of the distrustful, which are either directed out of politics or in opposite partisan directions. In the long term, there is a possible second source of the heightening of political salience to the working class by way of change in precisely that industrial arena where their present activity is most concentrated, namely through moves towards industrial democracy. Here, too, hard evidence of the spontaneity and authenticity of the demand is hard to come by. There is survey evidence and there is a sympathetic and probably over-optimistic assessment by Anthony Wedgwood Benn:

> Here in Britain the demand for more popular power is building up most insistently in industry, and the pressure for industrial democracy has now reached such a point that a major change is now inevitable, at some stage ...The claim is for the same relationship between government and the governed in factories, offices and shops as was finally yielded when the universal adult franchise brought about full political democracy, or what it might be more helpful to re-name 'voter's control'.[22]

The hope is that this growing demand may yet be the basis for the development of active concern with national as well as workshop politics. The argument envisages that the worker is more likely to participate at the workshop level, where decisions are more comprehensible and can be seen directly to affect him, than at the complex and distant level of national politics. And this participation would itself be an educational process, for workers would both learn of the inter-relatedness, and thus the relevance to them, of the different levels of politics, and would gain the experience and self-confidence to demand their rights elsewhere. But, if there is a real demand for industrial democracy, the official response has been as grudging as that to demands for more devolution of decision making from Westminster; the proposals of the Bullock Commission on Industrial Democracy would put shop stewards onto the board, but do little to bring rank and file workers into direct exposure to the perils and possibilities of shared control.[23]

Nonetheless, if changes are slow and reluctant, their cumulative effect on the political environment is likely to have consequences for interest and participation. And a most impressionistic view of the last decade of political debate in Britain suggests that there has been a rising incidence of, and a greater response to, discussions of institutional and electoral reform. This has been manifested in many ways: perhaps earliest in the debate on reform of the House of Commons to increase control of the executive, conducted principally by academics and by back-benchers disillusioned with their role and power in Parliament. Similarly, responsibility for the brief experiment of broadcasting the proceedings of Parliament must be partially attributed to the same frustration among Members, and to a new awareness of similar concern among their electorate. Electoral reform has been kept in the public debate by the perpetual losers under the present system, the Liberal Party, and by the debate over representation in the European Parliament; two thirds at least of the population continue to support reform in principle, although a recent poll reported that 40 per cent also doubted that a new voting system would result in better government.[24] And, of course, potentially the most far-reaching constitutional change of all, to some form of devolution, is still under discussion.

Most developments occurred parallel to, rather than being reliably attributable to, the rise of political distrust. But distrust has been conspicuous enough in Britain itself to call forth various direct responses to it from politicians. Contrasting reactions came from two members of the Labour Party: in 1971 Roy Hattersley (moved by a letter from a constituent which added to a specific complaint a comment that the electorate had, once more, been ignored) wrote an article on American populism, decrying its reliance on 'common wisdom' and its constant complaint of unresponsive government. As with nineteenth-century Members of Parliament discussing the new electorate, perhaps his conclusion was more to reassure himself than to convince others: 'In fact, the people are not populists, and never have been. They prefer politicians with confidence in their own judgement and courage to face the electoral consequences if that judgement proves wrong. Politicians who are blown by every gust of public opinion diminish politics and patronise the people.'[25] A year earlier, Benn had responded to a similar impression of disaffection in the electorate, with his tract on the New Politics: 'The main theme of this pamphlet is that the new citizen wants and must receive a great deal more power than all existing authority has so far thought it right, necessary or wise to yield him.'[26] Somewhat polemically, he argued that a change could be traced from the consensus of the early days of universal suffrage (when legitimacy was given to an essentially authoritarian system of government and popular control was limited to the casting of a single vote every five years) to a vacuum of legitimacy: 'It is arguable that what has really happened has amounted to such a breakdown in the social contract, upon which parliamentary democracy by universal suffrage was based, that that contract now needs to be re-negotiated on a basis that shares power much more widely, before it can win general assent again.'[27] Benn's solution was exactly the responsiveness to public opinion which Hattersley deplored: some 'comprehensive opinion-testing mechanism' like the referendum, or even 'a national institute of public opinion which acted as the independent agent for assessing and reporting the national view *before* Parliament reached its final decision'.[28] The 1975 referendum on the Common Market was certainly not introduced for such democratic and principled reasons; its position in relation to traditional constitutional doctrines was never formally tested, but it has, however unintentionally, established a precedent of major importance for the future. As Benn was well aware:

> The Labour government has restored the right of decision to the British people. The British referendum in 1975 represents as great an extension of political democracy as did the Reform Act of 1832. That Reform Act broke the power of a small parliamentary elite, itself elected by a mere 2 per cent of the population, to govern Britain in their own narrow interests, and started us on the path to full adult suffrage. This referendum directly challenges the claim of even a democratically elected House of Commons to give away for ever, the independence of our country and the liberties of our people, both of which it merely holds in trust for the electorate which elected it.[29]

The British case has thus proved different from the American, not only in the traditional content of its political culture but also in its development; over the last century this has been slowly changing and crystallising. In particular, the radical democratic critique, which was salient only to a few members of the political elite in the 1890s, has gained in coherence and has accumulated wider support. It was an ironic finding of my study of Birmingham workers that the most vaunted radical democrats of British history should prove not to have been distrustful. But the logic of the connection between distrust and radical democracy was not thus disproven, for the Birmingham Liberal membership turned out not to have been radical democrats either. The radical democrats were the Chamberlain wing of the Liberal elite and their political philosophy was shared neither by their rank and file nor by the Labour movement.

Since that time a more participatory definition of democracy has been more widely applied as a standard for the evaluation of the operations of the polity, and institutional innovations consistent with these principles have become a more familiar part of general political debate. The evidence is often shaky and certainly only suggestive of future trends rather than conclusive of a new mood in the minds of the general public. It does seem firm enough at least to endorse Dennis's assertion that in some ways the British were becoming like the Americans. But it seems even less justified than in the American context to deduce any imminent political crisis in Britain. For the picture of change is not one of the sudden collapse of the conventional picture of a consensual culture of deferential, committed and contented citizens into an anarchy of anti-political, or at least anti-democratic, turbulence.

There are, but their presence is hardly a novel phenomenon, groups who reject the political process and seek their ends by other means. These have not been the concern of this study, nor were they the subject of the data from which those cataclysmic prophecies were drawn. The rising incidence of distrust reflects a less dramatic change. The political culture of the 1880s was deferential, though not in the sense in which many classic studies have used that term. It was the deference of men who did not lack political self-confidence but saw practical advantages in extending the division of labour to politics. They were willing to turn over responsibility to leaders of proven capacity, and perhaps the more willing because of their low general expectations of politics. For at least the large lower class there was, however, no deep emotional commitment to the forms and purposes of government, such as was distilled by the Populists from American political tradition. But deference of any kind is the antithesis of distrust, which too is an attitude of self-respecting citizens but is a lack of confidence in the absolute reliability of any leadership, however capable. The last bastion of deference has been the middle class and it is particularly its decline there that has been behind the rapid escalation of articulate distrust. There, distrust displaces deference in a group with the capacity and political experience to seek for alternatives and to overcome the conceptual vacuum which previously effectively inhibited the mobilisation of distrust.

And for all the weakness of British political culture in generating such a mobilisation thus far, and for all the antipathy of traditional British parliamentarism to the norms of radical democracy, there does seem to be a more serious and sympathetic response to widespread political discontent from the British political elite than the inertia and intransigence found in America. It may well be said that the British are now belatedly proposing reforms which were introduced for similar reasons in America eighty odd years ago, whose contribution to democratic politics has often proved dubious. And it is true that such innovations as devolution, the referendum and electoral reform have been used as partisan tactics rather than being principled reforms. Yet the final impression of the current situation is of relative flexibility in Britain, compared with relative rigidity on the American part. It is a vital flexibility in the context of the collapse of the myth of deference as a generalisation of cultural consensus and internalised normative legitimacy. Pragmatic acceptance rather than normative commitment to the political system was relatively unimportant so long as politics were relatively unimportant. But now government has claimed away from the free-bargaining process the role of final arbiter of income distribution and thus of social inequality, surely the central issue in British society. It is surely not coincidental that as governments of both major parties politicised this issue in the 1960s criticism of politics itself began to escalate. For whatever the means of reaching a political decision on this most fundamental social matter may be, they must be seen as fully legitimate by the whole public – the development of political forms which can be accorded general normative commitment becomes essential.

Finally, it is useful to return to the deductions which Dennis and his colleagues made from their evidence of distrust among English children. It is clear that there has been no rapid transformation of a stable polity in a brief and dramatic period. Rather there has been a gradual accretion and clarification of the parts of a full radical democratic critique of the British polity, and this is a process which is by no means complete. Dennis was right to suggest that there had been a steady evolution of the political order, merely quite wrong to perceive the substance of that evolution as the enhancement of 'a homogeneous political culture and wide public regard for strong government'.[30] Dennis was also correct in his comment that the growth of distrust presents the political system with new sources of stress. But the tension which results is a tension within the bounds of democratic politics, not a tension between democracy and anarchy. It is, too, a tension whose impact on the polity is likely to be substantially weakened by the survival of many features of the political culture which still inhibit political action.

Though I quarrel with Dennis on almost every point of his predictions, in one respect the attempt to understand current developments in the light of historical patterns of culture has led me to endorse all the conventional wisdom about Britain. For there is no evidence to suggest any moment of dramatic change, any single incident sparking off a sudden change in political consciousness. Gradualism is still the hallmark of this changing political culture – the process of which there was the occasional hint a century ago is still half-formed and incomplete by comparison with the American model toward which it seems to be moving. As yet, the responses of those in power to the developing mood have been marginal and fragmentary, but much more in line with the demands of the electorate than elite reactions in America. Whether, as in many past political developments, the polity will change gradually too, to incorporate new positions and norms, remains to be seen.

Conclusions

A historical and comparative perspective greatly extends understanding of the meaning and consequences of political distrust in Britain and America. In more general terms, the evidence presented here also illuminates the relationship between political ideals and political history. For the concept of democracy believed by the ordinary citizen has, in each of these cases, contributed to the course of political events. Sartori's comment that political behaviour is a product of the actor's notion of what democracy 'is, can be, and should be', summarises what has been, until perhaps the last decade or so, a crucial difference between these nations:[31] in America the emphasis has been on what democracy is and *should* be, while Britain has been characterised by a more pragmatic and less urgent emphasis on what democracy is and *can* be. The long acceptance of the British political *status quo* has been, for a substantial segment of the community, from convenience rather than commitment. There has been a permanent undercurrent of criticism; it has remained an undercurrent partly because of the marginality of politics to many people and also from the absence of norms and indeed of language in their political culture to ease its expression.

The effect of a limited language has been only one example of the more general point that political culture is far from a passive 'bed-rock'. Constantly open to change itself, it can have a crucial impact on the development of critical attitudes, on the probability of their expression and on action in their name. In neither country has it been the sole causal factor involved; for example, effective action has indeed been inhibited by inarticulateness and the vagueness of directive norms, but these disadvantages have been reinforced by ideological and social cleavages among the distrustful, by the lack of social skills and active political experience of many and by the fact that distrust has been generated originally by unsatisfied grievances which have proved a transient and shifting foundation for the long job of political reform.

There has been a tendency, particularly in America, to take all these admitted weaknesses as grounds for the dismissal of distrust as a politically important phenomenon. My evidence suggests that distrust should not be used as an excuse for redefining democracy and narrowing its sphere in modern politics.

The simultaneous appearance in Britain of rising incidences of distrust and of familiarity with the norms of radical democracy may be more than coincidence. I have defined distrust neutrally and indeed there is no logical reason why this discrepancy between ideals and reality should not be identified in anything from a feudal to a totalitarian state. Why should not a convinced monarchist be critical of the current incumbent and demand a return to his idealised state of the monarchy, for example? No doubt, in many such polities the structural inhibitions on the expression of distrust would be considerable (in the extreme case its definition as the capital crime of treason might give the latently distrustful pause); but inhibitions on criticism may even be internalised as part of the complex of monarchist norms without contradiction – as, for example, in Luther's requirement of submission even to tyrants because 'His divine wrath needs them to punish the wicked and preserve outward peace.'[32]

But the norms of radical democracy themselves encourage the

expression of criticism, in both direct and oblique ways, to an extent that is not even true of other varieties of democracy, such as democratic elitism or parliamentary democracy. Radical democracy makes the people 'the ultimate and only sovereign in the polity', and insists that the exercise of this sovereignty be through direct and sustained participation.[33] Delegates are thus not elected to a deliberative assembly but are instructed; they are continually answerable to their constituents, who in turn are required to be continually informed and watchful. Here is the direct encouragement of radical democracy to the expression of political criticism, for it does indeed make 'eternal vigilance the price of liberty'.

The other connection of radical democracy with political distrust is more subtle. To the extent that the norm of the sovereignty of the people, exercised through direct personal participation, is internalised, then it must encourage a personal sense of blame and guilt for political failings. For responsibility is located where sovereignty is located. And perhaps distant political corruption is easier to ignore than are one's own failures. Thus the Populists took a fair share of the blame for the decadence of American politics on their own shoulders, acknowledging that 'the voters' motives and purposes determine the character and quality of government', and that much of the problem was that 'the American people have not stopped to think for years'.[34] And the same appeal to conscience was tellingly made at the height of the Watergate revelations, when the only remaining question was how much further up the political hierarchy responsibility could be traced; a membership appeal from the public interest lobby, Common Cause, revealed:

> Dear Fellow Citizen:
>   The identity of one person responsible for Watergate has never been disclosed.
>   That person is you.[35]

The radical democrat, unlike those of most other persuasions, must in the end blame himself – and the remedy lies in his own hands; throwing the rascals out and electing new men is not enough – self-reformation is a necessary component of political change. Thus, a political philosophy which places a personal responsibility upon each individual makes political distrust a duty – as 80 per cent of modern samples in Britain and America agreed, 'every person has a duty to criticise the government when it does something wrong even if the matter does not concern him directly'.

Radical democracy, strictly interpreted, allows no room for leadership, since it values equally the contribution of every citizen. The Populists had their leaders and ignored the contradiction, the more easily because, at least in the early days in Kansas, leaders were closely in touch with popular opinion – leading only in the sense of providing the centralised structure to coordinate the diffuse outburst of feeling. One solution to the paralysing ideological division of the distrustful today might be the emergence of a leader who could make distrust itself the most salient issue, overriding particular grievances. In America, both Carter and Ford attempted to do just this in 1976, hoping to appeal across party lines as the honest and trustworthy candidate. To the extent that either was believed, it seems likely that they thereby neutralised that position, leaving voters after all to decide on other, more divisive grounds. In Britain, the challenge to parliamentarism is a challenge to leadership, but thus far it has not found its own leader. True, Wedgwood Benn has tried to make the issue his own, but from a highly partisan position; and it is ironic that his 'populist' tract on the New Politics should be prefaced with a quotation with a highly patronising flavour: 'As for the best leaders, the people do not notice their existence. . .when the best leaders' work is done, the people say "we did it ourselves".'[36]

To the extent that radical democracy in its fullest form, government by 'a body of individuals bound together and guided forward by a unified and authoritative will', is ultimately unattainable, then it appears that frustrated political distrust of the kind which I have described will be endemic wherever the norms are held.[37] Its ideal polity depends upon two essential features: a community of rational, independent citizens and a society based upon a fundamental harmony of interests. Past political experience offers small encouragement to optimism on either count. The Populists were optimists, on similar grounds (though in more modest form) to many of the theorists of alienation and anomie. For Marx and Durkheim the elimination of alienation and anomie was to come through structural change, since their source was in structural failing. For later sociologists the solution lay in psychological change, primarily in adaptation to structural inevitabilities. The Populists saw neither social structure nor human nature as fixed; thus hope lay in both changing politics and changing people, just as blame was laid on both.

The Populists were optimists, but their optimism was muted by comparison with many greater philosophers; their historical sense and their political experience combined to suggest the vulnerability of their ideals. Once source of their doubts is clearly to be seen in their totally inadequate discussion of organisation and their failure to solve the dilemma of those who can only answer the corruption of party with the formation of another party. For they knew that structural reform and new political movements had been tried before and had provided at most only a temporary solution to the problems of implementing democratic government; each time the formal arrangements for a better polity succumbed to organisational weakness, and, since they never entirely separated the two, to human weakness. Thus, John Davis's life-cycle theory of parties, that 'political parties never advance' and yet that 'all progress in America is made by and through new parties'.[38]

Since the late nineteenth century, both the organisational problem and our knowledge of it have increased. The problem has grown because of the greater scope of government and the complexity and technical nature of policies, and from the related fact that the contacts with government which are most frequent and most significant to our daily lives are no longer with the institutions of representative government, but with the bureaucracy.[39] It was logical for the Populists to form a political party, because electoral pressure on their representatives was what counted; the rationality of such an initiative today is not so obvious – the shrewder farmers acknowledged this themselves as they turned to pressure group action and close connections with the county agents of the federal government in the twentieth century.[40] That the ordinary citizen with a variety of concerns still puts his emphasis on voting to rectify political failure may reflect only his failure to understand the full implications of organisational growth. Yet, bureaucracy has certainly become the public scapegoat in a way that it was not in the 1890s; what has not yet emerged is any serious attempt to reconcile this with political ideals. And if organisation theorists are right, this may prove the most resistant problem of all, for the imperatives of bureaucratic organisation appear entirely incompatible with the requirements of democracy.

But structural reform at least offers an immediate, if limited, hope of progress. Progress on the other front, of changing people, takes longer but, if it succeeded, would offer the more solid ground for hope. The Populists saw the current and evident incapacity of many to fulfil the duties of citizenship as a temporary lapse, which education and awareness could in the long run correct. This was a most fundamental difference from the commentators of the 1950s, who also blamed human weakness but saw a permanent flaw in the character of the masses, to be legislated against but lived with. The doubt of human perfectibility has been at the heart of constitutional debate in America since its independence and is the crucial problem for radical democracy. Madison's classic passage in *The Federalist* presented the dilemma to the Founding Fathers:

> But what is government itself but the greatest of all reflections on human nature? If men were angels, no government would be necessary. If angels were to govern men, neither external nor internal controls on government would be necessary. In framing a government which is to be administered by men over men, the great difficulty lies in this: you must first enable the government to control the governed; and in the next place enable it to control itself.[41]

It is not surprising that the Populists took Jefferson as their hero, for he initiated their side of the argument. While the emphasis of federalist thought was on the means of control of the governed, the Jeffersonians argued both for an immediately enlarged role for the people and for positive efforts to develop the attributes essential for a self-controlling democratic citizenry. But the familiar pressures of political necessity forced the Founding Fathers, too, into expedient but inadequate structural solutions: 'They did not believe in political parties as such, scorned those that they were conscious of as historical models, had a keen terror of party spirit and its evil consequences, and yet, almost as soon as their national government was in operation, found it necessary to establish parties.'[42]

The achievement of any absolute ideal of radical democracy is thus bound up with the inter-related problems of organisational and human weakness. If the distrustful have indeed been making impossible demands, the need to take them seriously would be diminished. But in fact they have been thinking in relative terms, not of an absolute and extreme ideal. Their version of democracy is one of many variants of that concept, embodying essential democratic propositions but emphasising the participatory dimension as the means of fulfilment of popular sovereignty. In such a polity distrust would remain a duty, but citizens need not be so greatly frustrated, for the distrustful are not making non-negotiable demands for the implementation of a 'repulsive' utopia, 'essentially *consensual and uniform*'.[43] This might be the logical extreme of their arguments, but there is no evidence of such a vision of the future in the less logical, even sometimes culpably superficial, minds of either Populists or recent distrustful. They have been demanding a move along a democratic continuum, not a leap to a finite end – institutional reform which could be both educative and fulfilling in itself and instrumental in bringing about a more just society. So long as they continue to see politics as an arena of compromise and gradual betterment, rather than as a place to fight to the death, then their differences over the nature of democratic government are only of degree and are potentially reconcilable.

The dilemma of democracy which is the central concern of this political distrust is the ancient question of who guards the guardians. The answer of the distrustful is that the people must and can. My evidence does not answer the ultimate questions – it neither shows that power necessarily corrupts nor that democratic citizens can approach an ideal of responsibility and disinterest. But it does show that democracy, in the eyes of the majority of its proponents, is premised upon political equality but is not *thereby* made an unattainable ideal. Its implementation in modern societies poses many other and substantial problems, but at the normative level the problem is one of the reconciliation of alternative interpretations of democracy, not one of the conversion or exclusion of anti-democrats or the control of permanently unfitted masses. Ordinary citizens are, in their own way, both as flawed and as competent as the political elite. The fact is that the long-held elitist suspicion that the people are a threat to democracy has long been matched by the perception of the people, less elegantly expressed but as well-founded, that the elites are a threat to democracy. They have no magical solution to this dilemma; only limited proposals based on the assumption that political equality includes an equality of watchfulness in which each group and individual will be vigilant for the failings of others – Demosthenes' wisdom translated into an everyday maxim – and involving structural guarantees against the abuse of power and for the enhancement of popular participation. The actual proposals of the distrustful may be sadly inadequate for their purposes; the lessons of past experience are not encouraging. Nonetheless, the contribution of the distrustful should be measured not only by the inadequacy of their actual achievement but also by the honesty with which they have taken the democratic premises of political equality and popular sovereignty and have attempted to change the world to fulfil their ideals, rather than lowering their ideals to conform with the world.

Notes

A work is cited with details of author, title but not subtitle, and short imprint only once in the notes for each chapter. Succeeding references to the same work are further abbreviated. Full details of all works cited in the notes will be found in the list of works cited.

The following abbreviations are used throughout the notes:

AJS   *American Journal of Sociology*
APSR   *American Political Science Review*
ASR   *American Sociological Review*
BJPS   *British Journal of Political Science*
BJS   *British Journal of Sociology*
POQ   *Public Opinion Quarterly*

PREFACE

1 Gallup Poll, reported in the *Washington Post*, July 12, 1973, summarises thirty years' responses to the question 'If you had a son, would you like to see him go into politics as a life's work?' The answer was 'No' from 68 per cent in 1945, 64 per cent in 1973.

2 James Sterling Young, *The Washington community, 1800–1828* (New York, 1966), p. 59 and Chapter 3.

3 Alexis de Tocqueville, *Democracy in America* (2 vols, New York, 1965), I, pp. 207–8.

4 James Bryce, *The American commonwealth*, 3rd edn (2 vols, New York, 1895), II, p. 66.

5 M. Ostrogorski, *Democracy and the organization of political parties* (2 vols, New York, 1908), II, pp. 240 and 574.

6 Gabriel Almond and Sidney Verba, *The civic culture* (Princeton, N.J., 1963), p. 102. The British responses were scattered over more items; the government still headed the list, but they also supported the people themselves, the physical attributes of the country, social legislation, world standing, the economic system, and there were more than twice as many 'Don't knows' as in the American sample.

7 Alexander Hamilton, James Madison and John Jay, *The Federalist* (London, 1965), p. 44.

8 Malcolm Shaw, *Anglo-American democracy* (London, 1968), pp. 124–5.

9 Jack Dennis, Leon Lindberg and Donald McCrone, 'Support for nation and government among English children', *BJPS*, 1 (1971), p. 40.

10 *Sunday Times* (London), July 15, 1973.

CHAPTER 1. ALIENATION AND DISTRUST

1 See R. D. Jessop, 'Civility and traditionalism in English political culture', *BJPS*, 1 (1971), 1–24.

2 Major studies are either by Americans: Jack Dennis, Leon Lindberg and Donald McCrone, 'Support for nation and government among English children', *BJPS*, 1 (1971), 25–48; or derivative from American studies: e.g., Ian Budge, *Agreement and the stability of democracy* (Chicago, 1970) and Ian Budge *et al.*, *Political stratification and democracy* (London, 1972).

3 See Daniel Bell, ed., *The radical right*, revised edn (Garden City, N.Y., 1964); Victor C. Ferkiss, 'Populist influences on American fascism', *Western Political Quarterly*, 10 (1957), 350–73.

4 See the extensive literature generated by Theodore Adorno *et al.*, *The authoritarian personality* (New York, 1950); also Seymour Martin Lipset, *Political man: the social bases of politics* (Garden City, N.Y., 1963), Chapter 4, 'Working-class authoritarianism'.

5 Most influential were Philip E. Converse, 'The nature of belief systems in mass publics', in *Ideology and discontent*, ed. by David Apter (New York, 1964), and Herbert McClosky, 'Consensus and ideology in American politics', *APSR*, 58 (1964), 361–82.

6 Angus Campbell *et al.*, *The American voter* (New York, 1960), Chapters 10 and 11.

7 Franz Neumann, *The democratic and the authoritarian state* (New York, 1957), p. 186. See also Alex Inkeles, 'Participant citizenship in six developing countries', *APSR*, 63 (1969), 1120–41.

8 Lipset, *Political man*, p. 27.

9 McClosky, 'Consensus and ideology', p. 373.

10 Gabriel A. Almond and Sidney Verba, *The civic culture* (Princeton, N.J., 1963, p. 479.

11 *Ibid.*, p. 479.

12 *Ibid.*, p. 487.

13 *Ibid.*, p. 483.

14 This unequal treatment is justified by the state of the literature. See particularly an important critical study of the philosophy, hypotheses and evidence of political alienation, but one which accepts the label of 'alienation' without question: James D. Wright, *The dissent of the governed* (New York, 1976).

15 See Steven R. Brown, 'Consistency and the persistence of ideology', *POQ*, 34 (1970), 60–8; Robert W. Jackman, 'Political elites, mass publics and support for democratic principles', *Journal of Politics*, 34 (1972), 753–73; Eugene Litwak, Nancy Hooyman and Donald Warren, 'Ideological complexity and middle-American rationality', *POQ*, 37 (1973), 317–32; Norman R. Luttbeg, 'The structure of beliefs among leaders and the public', *POQ*, 32 (1968), 398–409.

16 Luttbeg, 'The structure of beliefs', p. 406.

17 Norman H. Nie with Kristi Andersen, 'Mass belief systems revisited', *Journal of Politics*, 36 (1974), p. 566. See also, Philip E. Converse, 'Change in the American electorate', in *The human meaning of social change*, ed. by Angus Campbell and Philip E. Converse (New York, 1972).

18 Nie, 'Mass belief systems revisited', p. 570.
19 Gerald Pomper, 'From confusion to clarity', *APSR*, 66 (1972), 415–28; Richard W. Boyd, 'Popular control of public policy', *APSR*, 66 (1972), 429–49.
20 And if they are given a chance by their leaders; see V. O. Key's point that 'Fed a steady diet of buncombe, the people may come to expect and to respond...to buncombe', in *The responsible electorate* (Cambridge, Mass., 1966); and Benjamin I. Page and Richard A. Brody, 'Policy voting and the electoral process', *APSR*, 66 (1972), 979–95.
21 Litwak, 'Ideological complexity', p. 328.
22 Nie, 'Mass belief systems revisited', p. 578.
23 From a letter from Charles D. Willard to Theodore Roosevelt, quoted in George Mowry, *The era of Theodore Roosevelt* (New York, 1958), p. 52.
24 The evidence is summarised and tested in Wright, *Dissent of the governed*, Chapters 3–9.
25 Graeme Duncan and Steven Lukes, 'The new democracy', *Political Studies*, 11 (1963), pp. 168–9. See also: Peter Bachrach, *The theory of democratic elitism* (Boston, 1967); Carole Pateman, *Participation and democratic theory* (Cambridge, 1970).
26 Quoted by Duncan and Lukes, 'The new democracy', p. 65.
27 Edward A. Shils, *The torment of secrecy* (London, 1956), p. 133.
28 *Ibid.*, p. 136; Shils does admit that all of these 'in proper measure are virtues quintessential to the well-being of a democracy'.
29 *Ibid.*, p. 31.
30 Robert A. Dahl, *A preface to democratic theory* (Chicago, 1963), Chapter 2, with quotation from p. 34.
31 Donald MacRae, 'Populism as an ideology', in *Populism*, ed. by Ghita Ionescu and Ernest Gellner (London, 1969), p. 155.
32 Samuel H. Beer, *British politics in the collectivist age*, revised edn (New York, 1969), p. 40.
33 Peter Worsley, 'The concept of populism', in *Populism*, ed. by Ionescu and Gellner, p. 246.
34 A review of the state of knowledge and the problems, which remains current, is by Martin Fishbein, 'Attitudes and the prediction of behavior', in *Attitude theory and measurement*, ed. by Martin Fishbein (New York, 1967).
35 See Lester Milbrath, *Political participation* (Chicago, 1965), and Sidney Verba and Norman Nie, *Participation in America* (New York, 1972).
36 Converse, 'Change in the American electorate', pp. 322–37.
37 William A. Gamson, *Power and discontent* (Homewood, Ill., 1968), p. 48.
38 Murray B. Levin, *The alienated voter* (New York, 1960), p. vii.
39 Inkeles, 'Participant citizenship', *APSR*, 63 (1969), p. 1125.
40 Ada W. Finifter, 'Dimensions of political alienation', *APSR*, 64 (1970), p. 396.
41 Melvin Seeman, 'On the meaning of alienation', *ASR*, 24 (1959), 783–91.
42 Seeman himself has acknowledged and endorsed these developments; see his 'Alienation and engagement', in *The human meaning of social change*, ed. by Campbell and Converse, 467–527.
43 Studies examining the multidimensional 'political alienation' based on Seeman's typology include, in chronological order: Levin, *The alienated*

voter; Dwight G. Dean, 'Alienation and political apathy', *Social Forces*, 38 (1960), 185–9; Dwight G. Dean, 'Alienation: its meaning and measurement', *ASR*, 26 (1961), 753–8; Arnold M. Rose, 'Alienation and participation', *ASR*, 27 (1962), 834–8; William Erbe, 'Social involvement and political activity', *ASR*, 29 (1964), 198–215 (Erbe summarises alienation as 'an extended family of variables. . .that somehow indicate that an individual is not in complete harmony with his social and cultural surroundings'); Marvin E. Olsen, 'Two categories of political alienation', *Social Forces*, 47 (1969), 288–99, whose two categories are each composed of a grouping of several dimensions from Seeman's typology; Ada Finifter, 'Dimensions of political alienation'.

44 Gamson, *Power and discontent*, p. 48. See also: Joel D. Aberbach, 'Alienation and political behavior', *APSR*, 63 (1969), 86–99; Joel D. Aberbach and Jack L. Walker, 'Political trust and racial ideology', *APSR*, 64 (1970), 1199–1219; Paul R. Abramson, 'Political efficacy and political trust among black schoolchildren', *Journal of Politics*, 34 (1972), 1243–69; John E. Horton and Wayne E. Thompson, 'Powerlessness and political negativism', *AJS*, 67 (1962), 485–93.

45 Angus Campbell, Gerald Gurin and Warren E. Miller, *The voter decides* (Evanston, Ill., 1954), p. 187. The scale is discussed in detail, pages 187–94. Later findings are reported in Campbell, *The American voter*, and Philip E. Converse, 'Change in the American electorate', pp. 322–37.

46 Converse, 'Change in the American electorate', p. 334. An early critic on this ground was Robert E. Lane, in *Political life* (New York, 1959), p. 149. The two dimensions are also merged in the concept of 'civic competence' in Almond and Verba's *The civic culture*, see p. 181, and see Edward N. Muller, 'Cross-national dimensions of political competence', *APSR*, 64 (1970), 792–809, for a criticism of the same error. See also the criticism of the Michigan scale by David Easton and Jack Dennis, 'The child's acquisition of regime norms: political efficacy', *APSR*, 61 (1967), 25–38.

47 See, for example, Eric A. Nordlinger, *The working class Tories* (Berkeley, Cal., 1967), p. 115.

48 Gamson, *Power and discontent*, p. 48.

49 Fred I. Greenstein found small children entirely trusting, lacking any frame of reference to evaluate cynical allusions; but this seems only to apply to well-integrated cultural groups. See his *Children and politics* (New Haven, 1965), Chapter 3. Easton and Dennis in 'The child's acquisition', find trust existing well before the development of any cognitive political skills. Studies of ghetto children in Detroit and poor whites in Appalachia find cynicism present early; see, for example, Schley L. Lyons, 'The political socialization of ghetto children', *Journal of Politics*, 32 (1970), 288–304.

50 J. Herbert Hamsher, Jesse D. Geller and Julian B. Rotter, 'Interpersonal trust, internal–external control, and the Warren Commission Report', *Journal of Personality and Social Psychology*, 9 (1968), 210–15.

51 John Fraser, 'The mistrustful-efficacious hypothesis and political participation', *Journal of Politics*, 32 (1970), 444–9; Brett W. Hawkins, Vincent L. Marando and George A. Taylor, 'Efficacy, mistrust and political participation', *Journal of Politics*, 33 (1971), 1130–6.

52 Horton and Thompson, 'Powerlessness and political negativism'; Frederic Templeton, 'Alienation and political participation', *POQ*, 30 (1966), 249–61.

53 Leo Srole, 'Social integration and certain corollaries', *ASR*, 21 (1956), 709–16; other major discussions of anomie are: Robert K. Merton, 'Social structure and anomie', and 'Continuities in the theory of social structure and anomie', in his *Social theory and social structure*, revised edn (Glencoe, Ill., 1957), 131–94; Herbert McClosky and John H. Schaar, 'Psychological dimensions of anomy', *ASR*, 30 (1965), 14 40; Leo Srole *et al.*, 'Commentary: a debate on anomy', *ASR*, 30 (1965), 757–67.

54 Srole, 'Social integration', p. 714; Arthur G. Neal and Salomon Rettig, 'Dimensions of alienation among manual and non-manual workers', *ASR*, 28 (1963), 599–608.

55 McClosky and Schaar, 'Psychological dimensions', p. 19.

56 The most influential source of this distinction is Angus Campbell, 'The passive citizen', *Acta Sociologica*, 6 (1962), 9–21.

57 For example, Lipset, *Political man*, p. 116.

58 Seeman, 'On the meaning of alienation', p. 784.

59 Karl Marx, *Economic and philosophical manuscripts*, in *Early writings*, translated and edited by T. B. Bottomore (New York, 1964), p. 131.

60 Marx, *Early writings*, p. 129.

61 *Ibid.*, p. 156.

62 Karl Marx, *Bruno Bauer, die Jüdenfrage*, in *Early writings*, p. 13.

63 Neumann, *The democratic and the authoritarian state*, p. 163.

64 Karl Marx and Friedrich Engels, *The German ideology: I and III*, edited with an introduction by R. Pascal (New York, 1947), p. 22.

65 Seeman, 'On the meaning of alienation', p. 784 (italics his).

66 Steven Lukes, 'Alienation and anomie', in *Philosophy, politics and society*, Third series, edited by Peter Laslett and W. G. Runciman (Oxford, 1967), p. 145.

67 Emile Durkheim, *Suicide* (Glencoe, Ill., 1951), p. 246.

68 *Ibid.*, p. 247.

69 Thomas Hobbes, *Leviathan*, edited with an introduction by C. B. Macpherson (Harmondsworth, 1968), p. 161.

70 Durkheim, *Suicide*, p. 248.

71 *Ibid.*, p. 256.

72 *Ibid.*, p. 286.

73 *Ibid.*, p. 249.

74 *Ibid.*

75 *Ibid.*, p. 364.

76 *Ibid.*, p. 253.

77 Durkheim's solution to anomie is discussed most fully in his *The division of labour in society* (New York, 1964). See the Preface to the Second Edition; this quotation is from p. 26.

78 Durkheim, *Suicide*, p. 374.

79 Merton, *Social theory and social structure*, p. 136.

80 *Ibid.*, pp. 137 and 176.

81 Frank Parkin, *Class inequality and political order* (London, 1972), pp. 81–2.

CHAPTER 2. TWO VIEWS OF POLITICAL DISTRUST

1 Jack Dennis, Leon Lindberg and Donald McCrone, 'Support for nation and government among English children', *BJPS*, 1 (1971), p. 47.

2 *Ibid.*, p. 45.

3 *Ibid.*, p. 47.

4 Robert D. Putnam, *The beliefs of politicians* (New Haven, 1973), p. 233.

5 Two different schools of thought maintain this argument: British democratic elitists, whose methods and theory follow the Americans, for example Ian Budge, *Agreement and the stability of democracy* (Chicago, 1970); and those radicals who acknowledge the fact but deplore it as the deliberate product of elite control, for example, H. F. Moorhouse, 'The political incorporation of the British working class', *Sociology*, 7 (1973), 341–59.

6 Henry Pelling, *Popular politics and society in late Victorian Britain* (London, 1968), Chapter 1.

7 Gabriel A. Almond and Sidney Verba, *The civic culture* (Princeton, N.J., 1963), p. 498.

8 *Ibid.*, p. 456.

9 *Ibid.*, p. 102, and Table 5, pp. 248–9.

10 See Frank Parkin, *Middle class radicalism* (Manchester, 1968) and Philip Abrams and Alan Little, 'The young activist in British politics', *BJS*, 16 (1965), 315–33.

11 The following details are from an unpublished paper on the survey, by Nelson Rosenbaum:

'The respondents in this study were selected by means of a multi-stage, stratified, cluster-sampling design. A total of 993 subjects were selected in the Boston, Mass., SMSA and 962 in the Greater London Area. The procedure utilized in both areas was as follows: All school districts were listed and stratified into categories of higher and lower mean income-levels. Two districts were then randomly selected from each list, making a total of four primary sampling units in each area. In each of the four districts selected, all public and private educational institutions enrolling students in the 12–19 age-range were listed and stratified according to four age-level categories (12–13, 14–15, 16–17, and 18–19). Some schools appeared on more than one of the resulting 16 lists since they enrolled students in more than one age-level. Individual institutions were then selected at random from each of the lists. Permission to conduct research was secured from individual principals and deans or, when necessary, from central educational authorities. In cases of rejection, substitution was by random selection from the lists. Within each institution, it was attempted to select classes for testing at random. But this was not always possible due to administrative difficulties. Within each class, all students were administered the questionnaire on which this study is based. The final samples constitute a good cross-section of the London and Boston adolescent populations. The data was collected by means of a questionnaire developed and pre-tested on a group of 100 London adolescents in February 1972. It was administered to the London adolescent sample in April–May 1972, and to the Boston adolescent sample in November–December 1972.'

12 M. Kent Jennings and Richard G. Niemi, 'Patterns of political learning', in *Political opinion and behavior*, ed. by Edward C. Dreyer and Walter A. Rosenbaum, 2nd edn (Belmont, Cal., 1970), p. 160.

13 Robert Coles, 'The politics of middle class children', *New York Review of Books*, 22 (March 6, 1975), p. 13; see also companion articles in the issues of February 20 and March 20, 1975.

14 Fred I. Greenstein, *Children and politics* (New Haven, 1965), p. 31.

15 Eric A. Nordlinger, *The working class Tories* (Berkeley, Cal., 1967), p. 115.

16 Richard Rose, *Politics in England* (London, 1965), p. 47.

17 Dennis, 'Support for nation and government', pp. 39–42.

18 Though the standard of democracy is here created by the series of questions asked by the researcher, not by the spontaneous emphases of the respondents, in a comparative survey it is an entirely valid measure of differences between two countries, within the arbitrary limits which it establishes. What it does not measure is the definition which the respondents would create in a free situation, and cross-national differences between these.

19 Almond and Verba, *The civic culture*, p. 493. Subject orientations are defined on p. 19: 'The subject is aware of specialized governmental authority; he is affectively oriented to it, perhaps taking pride in it, perhaps disliking it; and he evaluates it as either legitimate or as not. But the relationship is toward the system on the general level, and toward the output, administrative, or "downward flow" side of the political system; it is essentially a passive relationship.'

20 *Ibid.*, p. 490.

21 *Ibid.*, Table 2, p. 109.

22 Jennings and Niemi, 'Patterns of political learning', pp. 177–9.

23 Almond and Verba, *The civic culture*, p. 455; Table 2, p. 186, summarises the incidence of levels of subjective civic competence.

24 The full text of the statements summarised in Table 4 and used here was as follows:

(i) Democratic ideals

People should not be allowed to vote unless they can do so intelligently.
Despite all the talk about democracy, it will always be necessary to have a few people in the government actually running things.
Politics should be left to the politicians.
I don't care about the government's methods as long as it gets things done.
Every person has a duty to criticise the government when it does something wrong even if the matter does not concern him directly.
Only people with a proper education should be eligible for election to political office.
When you come right down to it, so many other people vote in national elections that it isn't very important whether the individual votes or not.
Every person, no matter what his background, should have an equal chance to participate in the making of political decisions which affect him.
Every person should devote himself to staying informed about politics and government even if it means giving up some spare time.

(ii) Assessment of government

How much attention do you think people in the federal government pay to what the people think when they make decisions on policy issues?

In general, do you think that almost all of the people running the federal government are smart people who know what they are doing or do you feel that some of them don't seem to know what they are doing?

How much say do you think that people like your parents and yourself have about what the government does?

Do you feel that people in the federal government waste a lot of the money we pay in taxes, waste some of it, or don't waste very much of it?

Suppose you or your parents needed help with some problem from the federal government – for example, a tax question or a housing matter. How much do you think you could rely on the government to provide the help you needed?

To what extent do you think the people running the federal government are honest in their dealings with the public?

How much attention do you think most Congressmen (MPs) pay to the people who elect them when they decide how to vote in Congress (Parliament)?

(iii) Additional to Table 4

Do you think that officials in the federal government give everyone an even break or do you think they give special favours and privileges to some people?

Would you say the federal government is pretty much controlled by a few interest groups looking out for themselves or that it is run for the benefit of all the people?

How much say do you think people like your parents and yourself should have about what the government does?

25 *Annual register: world events in 1972* (London, 1973), p. 1.

26 'Harris Polls and the general election on 28th February 1974' (London, 1974). Pages 17–20 of this report reprint an article by Louis Harris from the *Daily Express*, February 26, 1974, in which he linked the pre-election surge in Liberal support with the presence of substantial political disaffection: 'the Liberal surge in the closing days of this campaign will make this a watershed election in British political history. . .Fundamentally, this is a people in revolt against the old ways of politics. It is a people who sense a wider gulf between themselves and their leaders than ever before' (p. 17).

27 William A. Gamson, *Power and discontent* (Homewood, Ill., 1968), p. 48.

28 John Fraser, 'The mistrustful-efficacious hypothesis and political participation', *Journal of Politics*, 32 (1970), 444–9; Brett W. Hawkins, Vincent L. Marando and George A. Taylor, 'Efficacy, mistrust and political participation', *Journal of Politics*, 33 (1971), 1130–6.

29 See Sidney Verba and Norman H. Nie, *Participation in America* (New York, 1972), Chapter 8. Almond and Verba, *The civic culture*, pp. 379–87, has a more general discussion on the political effects of varying levels of education. They point out, as my data confirms here, 'that the orientations that distinguish the educated from the relatively uneducated tend. . .to be

affectively neutral. So far we have not shown either that educated individuals necessarily support the political system more, or that they are more hostile to it' (p. 382).

30 The status variable is a tripartite classification of high, middle and low status, based on father's occupation. Education is scaled by the type of school attended and the estimated standard of performance.

31 These examples are from the *Guardian* (weekly edition), November 6, 1971, p. 21; and the *Mobile Register*, September 28, 1973, p. 4–A: 'But public distrust of government. . .can be unhealthy, even when convincingly defended on the ground of justification'.

32 *Sunday Times*, July 15, 1973; quotation from a report on both surveys by David McKie, 'What We Think of Our Rulers', *Guardian* (weekly edition), July 28, 1973, p. 9.

33 Figures reported from the BBC survey are from tables made available by the Opinion Research Centre, London. The poll was taken by the ORC from 6–10 June, 1973. The Granada figures are from *The state of the nation: Parliament*, edited by Duncan Crow (London, 1973), p. 201.

34 Arthur H. Miller, Thad A. Brown and Alden S. Raine, 'Social conflict and political estrangement, 1958–1972' (paper prepared for the Midwest Political Science Association convention, Chicago, May 3–5, 1973).

35 Mass Observation, *Puzzled people* (London, 1948), p. 151

36 Great Britain. Parliament. *Royal Commission on the Constitution 1969–73*. Cmnd 5460–1 (2 vols, London, Her Majesty's Stationery Office, 1973). The survey data is presented in detail in the *Research papers 7*; hereafter I shall refer to the Commission by the chairman's name – Kilbrandon; United States Senate. Subcommittee on Intergovernmental Relations of the Committee on Government Operations. *Confidence and concern: citizens view American government: a survey of public attitudes*. Committee Print (3 vols, Washington, D.C., Government Printing Office, 1973). I shall refer to this in abbreviation as the Senate Survey.

37 Kilbrandon, I, para. 6.

38 *Ibid.*, para. 16.

39 See Kilbrandon, *Research papers 7*, pp. 111–12 for the full brief.

40 Senate Survey, I, p. iii. The Letter of Transmittal, from which this quotation is taken, and the Foreword are signed by Senator Edmund Muskie, the chairman, and Senator Edward S. Gurney, the ranking minority member, of the subcommittee.

41 *Ibid.*

42 A Harris Poll, taken in June 1973, asked the following: 'On the whole, the British system of government works pretty well', and the response was Agree 82%, Disagree 15%, Don't Know 3%. The astounding gap between these two surveys might be partly accounted for by collapsing at least the first two of the Kilbrandon categories to make an equivalent to Harris's Agree percentage of 48%. Given the larger, random sample and more subtle question, it might be suspected that Kilbrandon tapped the feeling involved more accurately. The Index of Dissatisfaction upon which some of the report's cross tabulations are based is less accurate as a measure of distrust, since for it the Table 1 data are incorporated into an index with six other items measuring quite specific satisfaction with named public services –

schools, hospitals, roads and so on. (See *Research papers* 7, page 2 and Appendix D, pp. 154–8, for details of the indices.) Its findings, however, are not markedly different; they show a normal distribution of scores, with 29% very satisfied, 33% fairly satisfied and 38% dissatisfied (p. 157).

43 *Ibid.*, p. 3.

44 *Ibid.*, Table 8, p. 8.

45 Slightly more of the satisfied were also well-informed, but again the difference was slight – see *ibid.*, Table 10, p. 11. The findings on political comprehension show that those rated as weak in their understanding of the drift of the questioning were not more or less dissatisfied in general, though they were more inclined to give 'Don't know' answers; see *ibid.*, Table 11, p. 12.

46 *Ibid.*, p. 23.

47 Kilbrandon, I, para. 324.

48 Kilbrandon, *Research papers* 7, p. 4.

49 For examples see the questionnaire, *ibid.*, pp. 114–29, especially questions 10, 11, 14, 15, 26–9.

50 *Ibid.*, Table 17, p. 20. The scale is described with more technical detail on p. 158. The terminology here is confusing: powerlessness, particularly in the American literature, has been an alternative name for the Efficacy Scale which measures feelings of personal ability to take political action. The scale in the Kilbrandon survey is clearly a measure of system evaluation, while personal efficacy is here labelled 'Confidence in political capability', as described in Table 14, pp. 16–17 of *ibid.*

51 *Ibid.*, p. 21.

52 *Ibid.*, Appendix A, pp. 111–12, gives the full brief from the Commission.

53 Kilbrandon, *Research papers* 7, p. 20.

54 *Ibid.*, p. 22.

55 *Ibid.*

56 *Ibid.*, p. 20.

57 36% agreed strongly with this statement and a further 31% agreed a little, *ibid.*, p. 20. The *Memorandum of dissent* (Kilbrandon, II, para. 51), shrewdly points out how much greater this endorsement might have been if the question had asked about 'people like yourself' – for who wants just 'ordinary people' to be their governors?

58 Kilbrandon, *Research papers* 7, Table 55, p. 74.

59 Kilbrandon, II, para. 76.

60 *Ibid.*, para. 47.

61 *Ibid.*, para. 79.

62 Kilbrandon, *Research papers* 7, p. 76.

63 *Ibid.*, Table 48, p. 67.

64 *Ibid.*, Table 49, p. 69.

65 See details of the reasons for non-voting, *ibid.*, p. 5. But note that, since the questionnaire in this case presented a multiple choice, the respondents may have picked out the best-sounding excuses.

66 *Ibid.*, p. 8.

67 Kilbrandon, *Research papers* 7, pp. 16–17. Compare the responses to Rosenbaum's much more general question, reported in Table 6.

68 Kilbrandon, *Research papers* 7, p. 16.

69 Kilbrandon, II, para. 61.

70 Kilbrandon, *Research papers* 7, p. 18.

71 *Ibid.*, p. 21.

72 *Ibid.*, pp. 28–9.

73 *Ibid.*, p. 69.

74 Kilbrandon, II, para. 78.

75 The *Memorandum of dissent* gives turnout figures from 1945–70. In 1945 it was 72.7%, rising in 1950 to 84.0% and showing a decline since then back to 72.0% in 1970. They compare this with changes in other industrialised democracies and show that Britain has shown the largest decline: − 12%. See Kilbrandon, II, footnote to para. 77. Britain looks bad partly because the United States is not included, with its 55% turnout in 1972. And the picture would have been very different with 1945 instead of 1950 as a baseline – Britain would then have shown only a decline of − 0.7%.

76 Kilbrandon, *Research papers* 7, pp. 98–9 and Table 65, p. 86.

77 Kilbrandon, II, paras. 79–80.

78 Kilbrandon, I, para. 318.

79 *Ibid.*, para. 396.

80 *Ibid.*, para. 418.

81 Senate Survey, I, p. 216.

82 *Ibid.*, p. 64.

83 *Ibid.*, II, p. 138. 74% of those feeling that the quality of life had improved held strongly positive feelings towards the role of government in this improvement, but only 18% of those feeling that the quality of life had not improved did so. See also *ibid.*, p. 148.

84 *Ibid.*, p. 429.

85 *Ibid.*

86 *Ibid.*, p. 431.

87 *Ibid.*, p. 432.

88 *Ibid.*, I, pp. 46–7.

89 'Given a chance to express themselves and their concern directly to the top executive officials in their community, their State and their country, Americans overwhelmingly choose Watergate as the issue they would raise in the White House, but pick taxes and school funds as the first gripes to hand their Governors, and street repair, traffic congestion and police performance as the major problems to lay before their Mayors', *ibid.*, p. viii. The question was open-ended and there was no guidance in assigning functions to levels of government; answers are reported in full in *ibid.*, II, pp. 383–4.

90 *Ibid.*, I, pp. 140–5.

91 *Ibid.*, p. 213.

92 *Ibid.*, pp. 214–15.

93 *Ibid.*, p. 231.

94 *Ibid.*, pp. 146–9. The leaders' reasons are given more fully on p. 315.

95 *Ibid.*, p. 149.

96 The suggestions of the public are tabulated in detail in *ibid.*, II, pp. 41–2.

97 *Ibid.*, I, p. iii.

98 The full statements and a summary of the responses are given in *ibid.*, I, p. 236.

99 *Ibid.*, p. 68.

100 The figures in this paragraph are from *ibid.*, p. 259. On the general scale of alienation the young are marginally more disenchanted, but the upper income group slightly less; no connection can be made on this basis between distrust and a likelihood of direct or unconstitutional action.

101 The actual turnout was 54.5% in 1972 and 43.4% in 1970. The claims of the sample are from the Senate Survey, ii, pp. 17 and 19.

102 A summary table of all reported political activity is in *ibid.*, i, p. 256.

103 *Ibid.*, p. 238.

104 *Ibid.*, i, pp. 234 and 260.

105 Summarised in *ibid.*, p. 262, with reasons tabulated on p. 263.

106 *Ibid.*, p. 93.

107 Similar credit was given to groups seeking ecological improvement and crime control, though protests about Vietnam and bussing were viewed with much greater ambivalence. See *ibid.*, pp. 94–5.

108 Kilbrandon, *Research papers 7*, p. 94.

109 *Ibid.*, p. 100.

110 Senate Survey, i, p. v.

111 *Ibid.*, p. xii.

112 Arthur H. Miller, 'Political issues and trust in government: 1964–1970', *APSR*, 68 (1974), 951–72.

113 Arthur H. Miller and Warren E. Miller, 'Issues, candidates and partisan divisions in the 1972 American presidential election', *BJPS*, 5 (1975), 403–8. For evidence of a similar division within the Democratic Party, see Gary R. Orren and William Schneider, 'Democrats versus Democrats: party factions in the 1972 presidential primaries' (Unpublished paper, Department of Government, Harvard University, 1974), pp. 91–2.

114 Especially data reported by the Survey Research Center, University of Michigan: Donald E. Stokes, 'Popular evaluations of government', in *Ethics and bigness*, ed. by Harlan Cleveland and Harold D. Lasswell (New York, 1962), 61–72; Philip E. Converse, 'Change in the American electorate', in *The human meaning of social change*, ed. by Angus Campbell and Philip E. Converse (New York, 1972), 322–37; Miller, 'Social conflict and political estrangement'; Miller, 'Political issues and trust in government'.

115 For example, Charles Edward Merriam and Harold Foote Gosnell, *Non-voting* (Chicago, 1924), p. 125; George Horace Gallup, *The Gallup Poll: public opinion, 1935–1971* (3 vols, New York, 1972).

116 Gallup Poll findings, reported in Hadley Cantril, ed., *Public opinion, 1935–1946* (Princeton, N.J., 1951) and the *Gallup Political Index* (London, 1961–73); for example, those who thought Britain not to be a democratic country and those who thought politicians were out for themselves were between 30 and 40 per cent in the 1940s; by the 1970s the first figure had fallen below 30 per cent and the second had risen above 40 per cent. From the mid 1950s to 1970, the numbers believing that 'people like yourself' have too little influence on the country's future rose from about 50 per cent to 70 per cent.

117 Richard Hoggart, *The uses of literacy* (Harmondsworth, 1958), pp. 230–1.

CHAPTER 3. GRASS ROOTS POLITICS IN KANSAS

1 This discussion relies heavily on Bernard Bailyn, *The ideological origins of the American revolution* (Cambridge, Mass., 1967).

2 Alexander Hamilton, James Madison and John Jay, *The Federalist* (London, 1965), p. 44.

3 Jimmy Carter, *Why not the best?* (New York, 1976).

4 See James Sterling Young, *The Washington community, 1800–1828* (New York, 1966), Chapter 3; these changes have however contributed to the increase in self-respect, the perceived desirability of a political career and the frequent deference which politicians are now accorded as individuals, even if general attitudes to the system remain little different from the Era of Good Feelings.

5 For example, Walter Dean Burnham, *Critical elections and the mainsprings of American politics* (New York, 1970), reviews the literature on critical elections and discusses the possibility of another occurring.

6 The voluminous literature on Populism is thoroughly listed and discussed in the bibliographical essay in Sheldon Hackney, ed., *Populism* (Boston, 1971), and criticised in the first two chapters of Walter T. K. Nugent, *The tolerant Populists* (Chicago, 1963), and in C. Vann Woodward, 'The Populist heritage and the intellectual', in his *The burden of Southern history*, revised edn (New York, 1968). I shall not attempt to repeat either exercise here, but make reference only to a few conspicuous examples. A good example of the 'extremist' attribution is Victor C. Ferkiss, 'Populist influences on American fascism', *Western Political Quarterly*, 10 (1957), 350–73.

7 For example, by Angus Stewart, 'The social roots', in Ghita Ionescu and Ernest Gellner, eds, *Populism* (London, 1969), 180–96.

8 C. Vann Woodward, 'The ghost of Populism walks again', *New York Times Magazine*, June 4, 1972, p. 60.

9 John D. Hicks, *The Populist revolt* (Lincoln, Neb., 1961). There was no attempt to supersede this general account, first published in 1931, until the publication of Lawrence Goodwyn's *Democratic promise* (New York, 1976).

10 Edward A. Shils, *The torment of secrecy* (London, 1956), for example pp. 102–3, 133–6; also influential in expounding this view were essays in *The radical right*, ed. by Daniel Bell (Garden City, N.Y., 1964).

11 *Lincoln Beacon* (Lincoln, Kansas), February 13, 1890.

12 Richard Hofstadter, *The age of reform* (New York, 1955), Chapters 1–3.

13 *Ibid.*, p. 5.

14 Ferkiss, 'Populist influences', p. 356.

15 For example, J. Rogers Hollingsworth, 'Populism: the problem of rhetoric and reality', *Agricultural History*, 39 (1965), p. 84.

16 Kenneth Barkin, 'A case study in comparative history: Populism in Germany and America', in Herbert J. Bass, ed., *The state of American history* (Chicago, 1970), 373–404.

17 Hofstadter, *Age of reform*, p. 24.

18 Norman Pollack, *The Populist response to industrial America* (Cambridge, Mass., 1962), p. 143. For Pollack, unlike earlier commentators, 'radical' was not at all a pejorative term.

19 O. Gene Clanton, *Kansas Populism* (Lawrence, Ks., 1969), p. 242.

20 Lloyd Free and Hadley Cantril, *The political beliefs of Americans* (New Brunswick, N.J., 1968), p. 36.

21 Richard M. Scammon and Ben J. Wattenberg, *The real majority* (New York, 1970), p. 195.

22 Recent studies which have been particularly useful include: Michael Paul Rogin, *The intellectuals and McCarthy* (Cambridge, Mass., 1967); James Edward Wright, *The politics of Populism* (New Haven, 1974); and, giving great detail on Kansas, Nugent, *Tolerant Populists*, Clanton, *Kansas Populism*, and Peter H. Argersinger, *Populism and politics* (Lexington, Ky., 1974). This last not only has important conclusions on the reasons for the demise of Populism, but provides the essential narrative background to my analysis.

23 Woodward, 'The Populist heritage', p. 115.

24 *Kansas Farmer* (Topeka, Ks.), June 18, 1890, p. 8. It is convenient, though strictly inaccurate, to refer to the state's political activists before that date as 'Populists', and it is also important to note that references throughout this study to 'Populists' are to this united and single-minded group in Kansas in 1890. Political theory and practice diverged increasingly as the movement developed and simultaneously split into regional and issue factions, so that it soon became misleading to generalise about a homogeneous Populist movement.

25 See Hicks, *Populist revolt*: 1890 election results are on p. 179, and pp. 274–281 contain an account of the installation of Governor Lewelling and the subsequent, discrediting 'legislative war'.

26 The records of the Nebraska Farmers' Alliance do exist but reveal little about policy or principle, though much about financial and administrative minutiae. See the *Nebraska Farmers' Alliance papers, 1887–1901* and *Guide to the microfilm edition* (Lincoln, Neb., 1966). The Kansas State Historical Society collections contain the minute book of the Gove County Farmers' Alliance, Union no. 2628, for May 24, 1890 to July 4, 1891. They report only resolutions passed, which follow the line of those printed in the Kansas press.

27 William E. Connelley, *History of Kansas newspapers* (Topeka, Ks., 1916).

28 20 of 47 correspondents identified themselves as organisers or activists in the movement. The *Advocate* first endorsed third party action on May 8, 1890, p. 8. On April 23, 1890 the *Kansas Farmer* was suggesting that loyalty to the Alliance might have to take precedence over party loyalty. Resolutions from local sub-alliances supporting an independent Alliance ticket were first reported in April and completely replaced bipartisanship resolutions in May and June.

29 Both membership figures are estimates, the first from *Appleton's annual cyclopaedia, 1890* (New York, 1891), p. 301, the second from the daily *Capital* (Topeka, Ks.), October 15, 1890, where is also recorded a total of 2,886 sub-alliances in the state. See also June G. Cabe and Charles A. Sullivant, *Kansas votes: national elections, 1859–1956* (Lawrence, Ks., 1957).

30 *The Ignatius Donnelly papers*, microfilm edition, and Helen McCann White, *Guide to a microfilm edition of the Ignatius Donnelly papers* (St Paul, Minn., 1968). The history of Minnesota Populism is recorded in Martin Ridge, *Ignatius Donnelly* (Chicago, 1962).

31 Titles and political affiliations of newspapers were taken from F. G. Adams, *List by counties of newspapers and periodicals published in Kansas, January 1, 1891* (Topeka, Ks., 1891) and dates of publication from Connelley's *Kansas newspapers*. 93 Populist papers existed during this period, 51 of these for the whole 6 months from January to June, 1890. Of this latter group, 10 were used: one paper from each of the 7 Congressional districts, this first sample including the statewide *Advocate*, plus 2 further papers with influence outside their local areas, the *Kansas Farmer* and the *Ottawa Journal and Triumph*. The tenth paper, the *Washington Post*, was read as a check on the value of including a second paper from each district; I have used some items from its columns but found it largely repetitive of material already covered, since the local press filled a good deal of space by reprinting the same items from larger circulation papers. All the chosen papers, listed below, were weeklies: District I: *Hiawatha Journal* (Hiawatha, Brown County); District II: *Farmer's Friend* (Iola, Allen County), *Ottawa Journal and Triumph* (Ottawa, Franklin County); District III: *Winfield Telegram* (Winfield, Cowley County); District IV: *Advocate* (Meriden, Shawnee County, 1889; Topeka, Shawnee County, 1890), *Kansas Farmer* (Topeka, Shawnee County); District V: *Junction City Tribune* (Junction City, Geary County), *Washington Post* (Washington, Washington County); District VI: *Lincoln Beacon* (Lincoln, Lincoln County); District VII: *Galva Times* (Galva, McPherson County). Districts III, IV and V formed the backbone of the agricultural 'Populist belt' of Kansas. Districts I and II were the eastern areas of mixed agriculture, some mining and industry, and longer established, less precariously financed settlement; VI and VII were the great western spaces of the state, sparsely settled at this time, with towns like Galva and Lincoln on their eastern fringe and geographically still part of the wheat belt centre of the state.

32 Richard Jensen, *The winning of the midwest* (Chicago, 1971), p. 165.

33 See Argersinger, *Populism and politics*, Chapters 1 and 2; D. O. McCray, 'The administrations of Lyman U. Humphrey', *Transactions of the Kansas State Historical Society*, 9 (1905–6), pp. 425–6; W. F. Rightmire, 'The Alliance movement in Kansas – origin of the People's Party', *ibid.*, 1–8.

34 Clanton, *Kansas Populism*, pp. 64–5 and 242; Judge Doster of Kansas was the original 'rattle-brained fanatic', *ibid.*, p. 69. Hofstadter refers to the 'ragged elite' in *Age of reform*, p. 101.

35 Hicks, *Populist revolt*, p. 211.

36 Hofstadter, *Age of reform*, p. 95.

37 *Advocate*, January 16, 1890, p. 4.

38 From 'An open letter to our Kansas delegation in Congress', *Advocate*, March 13, 1890, p. 7.

39 *Ibid.*, June 11, 1890. Grammatical and spelling errors were common in all these newspapers, and even more frequent in the manuscript sources used. They appear in the text here exactly as in the original, and because of their frequency I have refrained from interruption by the repeated use of the conventional *sic*.

40 Robert H. Wiebe, *The search for order: 1877–1920* (New York, 1967), p. 27.

41 *Ibid.*, p. 33.

42 *Advocate*, April 30, 1890, p. 6. Emphasis is in the original.

43 Argersinger, *Populism and politics*, pp. 73–9.

44 *Lincoln Beacon*, February 13, 1890.

45 A typical reference to 'wolves' is *Farmer's Friend*, June 14, 1890; 'True Blue's' letter, *Kansas Farmer*, April 9, 1890, p. 4; *Kansas Farmer* editorial, April 23, 1890, p. 5.

46 *Farmer's Friend*, April 19, 1890, p. 1, editorial, quoting from the *Progressive Farmer*.

47 *Ottawa Journal*, June 5, 1890, p. 2; Letters, C. French to Donnelly, April 9, 1890, William E. Wright to Donnelly, February 7, 1891, Donnelly MSS; *Advocate*, June 4, 1890, p. 2, and February 6, 1890, p. 9.

48 *Ottawa Journal*, June 5, 1890, p. 2.

49 *Washington Post*, June 12, 1890, p. 4.

50 Letter, W. M. Bean to Donnelly, January 10, 1890, Donnelly MSS.

51 *Hiawatha Journal*, March 27, 1890.

52 *Galva Times*, March 14, 1890, p. 2; *Advocate*, April 9, 1890, p. 7.

53 *Advocate*, February 6, 1890, p. 9, from an article by L. L. Polk, national Alliance president, and Mrs Hart's article, *ibid.*, June 11, 1890, p. 11.

54 *Ottawa Journal*, March 20, 1890, p. 1.

55 *Advocate*, April 30, 1890, p. 6.

56 *Ibid.*, February 20, 1890, p. 1.

57 *Hury Kain* (Topeka, Ks.), December 30, 1893. Populist Judge Ballard published the journal in 1893–4. It guyed both the seriousness of the movement and the outsider's rural simpleton stereotype of the Populists, but for all its exaggeration it was very much in tune with the sentiments of the conventional Populist press. Its title page slogan, 'Ekel Meanness to All: Speshul Wickedness to Nun', parodied the Alliance's 'equal rights to all and special privileges to none'.

58 *Advocate*, February 6, 1890, p. 1.

59 *Ibid.*, March 13, 1890, p. 6, and June 4, 1890, p. 2.

60 *Ibid.*, March 6, 1890, p. 2.

61 *Ibid.*, April 9, 1890, p. 4.

62 *Ibid.*, June 11, 1890, p. 11.

63 *Ottawa Journal*, June 5, 1890, p. 2, by an anonymous author.

64 *Advocate*, January 16, 1890, p. 5.

65 For example, editorials in the *Kansas Farmer*, April 23, 1890, p. 9, and June 18, 1890, p. 4. The song appears in Leopold Vincent, ed., *Alliance songster* (Winfield, Ks., 1890).

66 Woodrow Wilson, *Congressional government* (Boston, 1925), p. 11.

67 *Farmer's Friend*, May 3, 1890, p. 1.

68 *Advocate*, February 20, 1890, p. 7; *Ottawa Journal*, April 10, 1890, p. 2.

69 *Advocate*, January 16, 1890, p. 4.

70 *Ibid.*, February 6, 1890, p. 6.

71 *Ibid.*, January 30, 1890, p. 8.

72 *Ibid.*, June 25, 1890, p. 6.

73 Kansas State Historical Society, *John Davis scrapbook C*, p. 50. From a cutting from the *Knights of Labor Journal* (Philadelphia), September 8, 1892, which gives extracts from the introduction by Davis to his projected book on 'the Reform Movement'.

74 *Ottawa Journal*, June 5, 1890, p. 2; W. Scott Morgan, *History of the Wheel and the Alliance and the impending revolution* (Hardy, Arkansas, 1889), p. 715. This book was being widely advertised for sale, conspicuously in the Populist press, throughout 1890.
75 *Advocate*, May 7, 1890, p. 11.
76 *Ibid.*, June 11, 1890, p. 11.
77 *Ibid.*, April 23, 1890, p. 11.
78 *Ibid.*, January 9, 1890, p. 7.
79 *Ibid.*, April 9, 1890, p. 4.
80 *Junction City Tribune*, March 20, 1890, p. 2.
81 *Advocate*, June 4, 1890, p. 2.
82 *Farmer's Friend*, April 19, 1890, p. 1.
83 *Galva Times*, March 28, 1890, p. 2.
84 Morgan, *Wheel and Alliance*, p. 774.
85 *Hiawatha Journal*, April 24, 1890, p. 2.
86 *Advocate*, February 20, 1890, p. 1.
87 *Ibid.*, February 6, 1890, p. 9.
88 *Ibid.*, May 14, 1890, p. 5.
89 For example, see the *Kansas Farmer*, April 23, 1890, p. 9.
90 *Advocate*, April 9, 1890, p. 1.
91 *Ibid.*, April 2, 1890, p. 1.
92 *Farmer's Friend*, May 3, 1890, p. 1; *Advocate*, April 23, 1890, p. 11; *Junction City Tribune*, January 16, 1890, p. 2.
93 Benedict Arnold 'demanded a large sum of money and some contemptible honors', *Advocate*, June 18, 1890, p. 2; see references to Red Coats, *Hury Kain*, January 13, 1894, and letter, Fred Elwell to Donnelly, January 7, 1890, Donnelly MSS.
94 *Advocate*, June 18, 1890, p. 4.
95 Letters, John Abercrombie to Donnelly, February 15, 1891, 'The Poles of Silver Lake' to Donnelly, April, 1891, Donnelly MSS.
96 For example, *Hury Kain*, January 13, 1894; Morgan, *Wheel and Alliance*, p. 774; *Advocate*, June 11, 1890, p. 11.
97 *Galva Times*, May 9, 1890, p. 2.
98 *Winfield Telegram*, May 16, 1890, p. 1
99 *Galva Times*, May 9, 1890, p. 2.
100 *Hiawatha Journal*, June 12, 1890, p. 2.
101 *Advocate*, June 11, 1890, p. 11.
102 *Ibid.*, November 15, 1889, p. 5.
103 Richard Hofstadter, *The American political tradition* (New York, 1948), p. 46.
104 *Advocate*, April 2, 1890, p. 7.
105 Marvin Meyers, *The Jacksonian persuasion* (Stanford, 1960), p. 7.
106 Ross E. Paulson, in his introduction to *Radicalism and reform* (Lexington, Ky., 1968), points to the changing meaning of such programmatic slogans, depending on their social and political contexts. For interpretations of Populism which do not take that point and come to opposite conclusions, see Hofstadter, *Age of reform*, pp. 62–3, and Matthew Josephson, *The politicos: 1865–1896* (New York, 1938), pp. 472–3.
107 *Farmer's Friend*, August 23, 1890, p. 5.

108 Donald MacRae, 'Populism as an ideology', in Ionescu and Gellner, *Populism*, p. 160.

109 *Advocate*, May 14, 1890, p. 5.

110 *Ibid.*, May 7, 1890, p. 11.

111 *Ibid.*, February 6, 1890, p. 9.

112 *Ibid.*, June 4, 1890, p. 2.

113 *Ibid.*, April 30, 1890, p. 6.

114 *Junction City Tribune*, March 20, 1890, p. 2.

115 *Advocate*, March 26, 1890, p. 3; September 21, 1889, p. 1.

116 *Kansas Farmer*, April 2, 1890, p. 11.

117 *Advocate*, June 25, 1890, p. 6.

118 *Ibid.*, February 20, 1890, p. 4.

119 *Winfield Telegram*, January 16, 1890, p. 1.

120 *Kansas Farmer*, February 26, 1890, p. 6.

121 Hicks, *Populist revolt*, p. 430, where he gives the full text of the platform.

122 For example, *Advocate*, October 12, 1889, p. 4; December 6, 1889, p. 8; February 13, 1890, p. 6; *Junction City Tribune*, February 6, 1890, p. 4; *Kansas Farmer*, March 19, 1890, p. 11.

123 The Cincinnati platform demand is given in Hicks, *Populist revolt*, p. 434; on women's suffrage see *Washington Post*, April 3, 1890 and *Advocate*, March 26, 1890, p. 7. The direct election of senators was included in the resolutions of the state convention of county presidents of the Alliance in March, *Kansas Farmer*, April 2, 1890, p. 7.

124 *Kansas Farmer*, April 9, 1890, Greenwood County Alliance resolution; *Advocate*, February 20, 1890, p. 4; *ibid.*, March 20, 1890, p. 3; see also *Junction City Tribune*, January 16, 1890, p. 2, on the petition as a strategy for raising legislative matters.

125 *Kansas Farmer*, March 19, 1890, p. 7.

126 *Farmer's Friend*, May 3, 1890, p. 1 – the extract is from C. C. Nelson, *The millionaire, the tramp and the pauper*; Letter, L. C. Dickey to Donnelly, February 1891, Donnelly MSS.

127 Unsigned letter to Donnelly, February 1891, Donnelly MSS.

128 *Farmer's Friend*, May 3, 1890, p. 1.

129 *Advocate*, January 23, 1890, p. 7; April 30, 1890, p. 10.

130 Letter, Eric Olsen to Donnelly, February 18, 1890, Donnelly MSS.

131 *Advocate*, May 7, 1890, p. 12.

132 *Ibid.*, June 4, 1890, p. 2.

133 Hofstadter, *Age of reform*, p. 108, quoting Lloyd.

134 *Advocate*, October 5, 1889, p. 6.

135 *Winfield Telegram*, June 5, 1890, p. 2.

136 *Advocate*, October 5, 1889, p. 6.

137 *Ibid.*, February 20, 1890, p. 4.

138 *Winfield Telegram*, February 27, 1890, p. 5.

139 *Lincoln Beacon*, March 6, 1890.

140 *Advocate*, May 7, 1890, p. 11.

141 M. Ostrogorski, *Democracy and the organization of political parties* (2 vols, London, 1908), II, p. 658.

142 Rightmire, 'Alliance Movement in Kansas'.

143 *Hiawatha Journal*, January 30, 1890, p. 2.

144 Letter, H. H. Frazer of Sulphur Springs, Cloud County, Kansas, to Donnelly, circa January 10, 1890, Donnelly MSS.

145 *Galva Times*, May 23, 1890, p. 1.

146 *Junction City Tribune*, July 19, 1890, p. 2; *Kansas Farmer*, June 18, 1890, p. 8; and see especially the editorial on this point in the *Washington Post*, May 22, 1890, p. 4.

147 See a letter from Michael Lynch, an Alliance lecturer, to Donnelly, April 3, 1890, Donnelly MSS, also the *Great West*, February 7, 1890, p. 2: 'We need a leader, bold, brave and true, like Washington or Lincoln'. Both writers might might have had flattery to Donnelly in mind – I came across no equivalent demand in Kansas.

148 *Kansas Farmer*, June 18, 1890, p. 8.

149 *Ottawa Journal*, May 15, 1890, p. 2.

150 *Hiawatha Journal*, April 24, 1890, p. 2.

151 *Advocate*, April 2, 1890, p. 4.

152 For example, *Farmer's Friend*, May 3, 1890, p. 1; May 10, 1890, p. 1; July 5, 1890, p. 4; the Ottawa leader was W. J. Costigan – *Ottawa Journal*, March 27, 1890, p. 2.

153 *Advocate*, May 28, 1890, p. 4.

154 *Ibid.*, June 11, 1890, p. 11.

155 *Ibid.*, May 14, 1890, p. 10.

156 *Hiawatha Journal*, March 13, 1890, p. 2.

157 *Winfield Telegram*, June 19, 1890, p. 2.

158 *Advocate*, March 26, 1890, p. 7.

159 Letter, W. G. Bowers to Donnelly, April 16, 1890, Donnelly MSS.

160 *Ottawa Journal*, June 5, 1890, p. 2.

161 *Kansas Farmer*, January 1, 1890, p. 11.

162 *Advocate*, May 7, 1890, p. 3.

163 Elizabeth N. Barr's account of the summer of 1890 in Kansas, quoted in Clanton, *Kansas Populism*, p. 73.

164 Charles D. Willard, in a letter to Theodore Roosevelt, quoted by George Mowry, *The era of Theodore Roosevelt* (New York, 1958), p. 52.

165 Jensen, *Winning of the midwest*, p. 166; Paul Kleppner, *The cross of culture* (New York, 1970), Chapter 4.

166 Bailyn, *Ideological origins*, p. 319.

167 Vincent, *Alliance songster*, p. 1.

CHAPTER 4. RANK AND FILE LIBERALISM

1 Letter, John Abercrombie to Ignatius Donnelly, February 15, 1891, Donnelly MSS. Census returns for 1895 record Abercrombie, his English wife and four children as residents of Alexandria. They had been in the state since 1876 and were settled in that district by 1878. Abercrombie's occupation is variously listed in censuses and directories as surveyor, civil engineer and farmer. He died in 1921.

2 For example, Henry Pelling, *Popular politics and society in late Victorian Britain* (London, 1968), pp. 62 and 165; Richard Hoggart, *The uses of literacy* (Harmondsworth, 1958), pp. 79 and 230–1.

3 For example, R. D. Jessop, 'Civility and traditionalism in English political culture', *BJPS*, 1 (1971), 1–24.

4 Neal Blewett, 'The franchise in the United Kingdom, 1885–1918', *Past and Present*, 32 (1965), 27–56.

5 The formal organisation is fully described in Birmingham Liberal Association, *Objects, constitution and laws* (Birmingham, 1880); the Executive Committee had six elected members from each ward and up to forty co-opted members; the General Committee added to this five further representatives from each ward to form an unwieldy body, known by this date as the Eight Hundred.

6 A typical contemporary critique was by Edward D. J. Wilson, 'The caucus and its consequences', *Nineteenth Century*, 4 (1878), 695–712. See also M. Ostrogorski, *Democracy and the organization of political parties* (2 vols, New York, 1908), 1, chapters 3–4.

7 Joseph Chamberlain, 'The caucus', *Fortnightly Review*, New series 24 (1878), pp. 722 and 726.

8 The political history of Birmingham is summarised in Asa Briggs, *History of Birmingham* (2 vols, London, 1952) and analysed in E. P. Hennock, *Fit and proper persons: ideal and reality in nineteenth century urban government* (Montreal, 1973).

9 Andrew Jones, *The politics of reform, 1884* (Cambridge, 1972), p. 3.

10 *Birmingham Daily Mail*, July 2, 1883, reported on p. 2 with editorial comment on p. 3.

11 *Ibid.*, April 7, 1884, p 2.

12 F. Schnadhorst, *The caucus and its critics* (Birmingham, 1884), p. 9.

13 Chamberlain, 'The caucus', p. 734 (author's italics).

14 See attendance records in Birmingham Liberal Association, Management Committee, *Minute book, June 15, 1882–September 9, 1884*, Manuscript in Birmingham Public Library Local History Collection; H. J. Jennings, editor of the *Birmingham Daily Mail*, reports in his memoirs, *Chestnuts and small beer* (London, 1920), p. 85: 'Once or twice I took an independent line, but the action had disagreeable consequences and threatened to be sacrificial'. See also his editorial in the *Mail*, August 11, 1883, p. 2.

15 Quoted in Jennings, *Chestnuts*, p. 87.

16 Briggs, *History of Birmingham*, II, p. 173.

17 See Ian R. Christie, *Wilkes, Wyvill and reform* (London, 1962), especially pp. 222–4.

18 The best account of this process is Harold Perkin, *The origins of modern English society, 1780–1880* (London, 1969), Chapters 6 and 7.

19 The controversies are summarised in Perkin, *Origins of modern English society*, Chapter 5. The labour aristocracy and its political consequences are considered in Pelling, *Popular politics*, Chapter 3; Royden Harrison, *Before the Socialists* (London, 1965), Chapter 1; E. J. Hobsbawm, 'The labour aristocracy in nineteenth century Britain', in John Saville, ed., *Democracy and the labour movement* (London, 1954).

20 J. R. Vincent, *Pollbooks* (Cambridge, 1967), Chapter 1.

21 Quoted by Vincent in *Pollbooks*, p. 53, from the *Journal of the Royal Statistical Society*, June, 1886.

22 Harrison, *Before the Socialists*, pp. 32–3.

23 Ostrogorski, I, p. 346.
24 H. J. Hanham, *Elections and party management* (London, 1959), p. 77.
25 Pelling notes that after this date 'the one constituency where opposition to Chamberlain seemed to have some strength – BIRMINGHAM EAST – was populated by workers who were engaged in large-scale industry'. See *The social geography of British elections, 1885–1910* (London, 1967), p. 181.
26 J. L. Garvin, *The life of Joseph Chamberlain* (4 vols, London, 1932), I, p. 174.
27 *Ibid.*, p. 148.
28 Geoffrey Best, *Mid-Victorian Britain, 1851–1875* (Frogmore, 1973), p. 282.
29 Alfred Marshall, 'The future of the working classes'; quoted in Harrison, *Before the Socialists*, p. 27.
30 Quoted from Mayhew's study of *London labour*, by Pelling in *Popular politics*, p. 57.
31 Walter Bagehot, *The English constitution* (Ithaca, N.Y., 1966), p. 249.
32 *Ibid.*, p. 281.
33 Charles Booth, *Life and labour of the people of London* (17 vols, New York, 1970), First series, I, p. 177. Booth splendidly represents Victorian ambivalence about the respectable working class – earlier, p. 51, he extolled them for their self-respect and social responsibility.
34 Bagehot, p. 181.
35 *Ibid.*, p. 171.
36 *Ibid.*, pp. 250–1.
37 *Ibid.*, p. 248.
38 *Ibid.*
39 *Ibid.*, pp. 247–8.
40 Birmingham Liberal Association, Management Committee, *Minute Book*, October 1, 1883.
41 *Mail*, July 21, 1884; editorial comments on demands for the abolition of the House of Lords, p. 2.
42 Garvin's estimate of literacy in the city in 1867 was that 'amongst the working-class citizens now about to be created by Household Franchise not far from half could not read a newspaper'. (*Joseph Chamberlain*, I, p. 90.) But the 1871 Census gave literacy rates for the nation of 80.6 per cent for males and 73.2 per cent for females. See Richard D. Altick, *The English common reader, 1800–1900* (Chicago, 1957), pp. 166–72. Given the social composition of the Birmingham working class, and the industrious nonconformist tradition of self-help, this would seem a reasonable estimate, especially as the political community at that time did not extend to the lower ranks of workers where illiterates would generally be found.
43 There are no circulation figures in the paper itself, or in local records. The Birmingham Post and Mail have no records. The history of the *Mail*'s middle-class sister paper, the *Birmingham Post*, records how that paper achieved a circulation of 23,000 by 1885 and went on from strength to strength: 'reorganisation in 1869 cleared the way for another extension of newspaper enterprise the next year, when an evening paper was published in response to the demand for news of the fighting in the Franco–Prussian War of 1870. The *Birmingham Daily Mail*, as it was first called, proved to be in the true line of succession of Feeney–Jaffray enterprise. Being addressed

to a mass readership, the evening paper soon outstripped its parents in circulation and became in due course the commercial pillar of the business structure.' H. R. G. Whates, *The Birmingham Post, 1857–1957* (Birmingham, 1957), p. 44.

44 Jennings, *Chestnuts*, p. 81.

45 *Ibid.*, p. 85.

46 Thomas Anderton, *A tale of one city* (Birmingham, 1900), p. 131.

47 Andrew Jones in *The politics of reform* emphasises the internal workings of the political elite in influencing the detail and timing of political proposals.

48 *Mail*, November 2, 1883, editorial on accusations of corruption made against local Liberals, p. 2.

49 *Ibid.*, November 10, 1883, p. 2.

50 *Ibid.*, September 15, 1883, p. 2.

51 *Ibid.*, September 21, 1883, p. 2.

52 H. F. Nash, *Man's political rights and duties* (Birmingham, 1882), p. 9. Nash's address was published as a pamphlet, on the enthusiastic motion of the Junior Liberal Association.

53 *Mail*, November 1, 1883, editorial comment on Lord Randolph Churchill's opposition to reform, p. 2.

54 Nash, *Man's political rights*, p. 9, and a similar comment in a *Mail* editorial, November 21, 1883, p. 2.

55 Birmingham Liberal Association, Management Committee, *Minute Book*, October 1, 1883.

56 *Mail*, September 19, 1884, editorial comment, p. 2.

57 *Ibid.*, July 28, 1883, p. 2.

58 *Ibid.*, August 22, 1883, p. 2.

59 *Ibid.*, July 4, 1884, p. 2.

60 *Ibid.*, July 9, 1884, p. 2.

61 *Ibid.*, July 21, 1884, p. 2.

62 *Ibid.*, September 15, 1883, editorial comment, p. 2.

63 *Ibid.*, September 15, 1883, p. 2.

64 Quoted in S. Maccoby, *English radicalism, 1853–1886* (London, 1938), p. 83.

65 *Mail*, October 7, 1884, p. 2.

66 Nash, *Man's political rights*, p. 2.

67 *Ibid.*, pp. 6–7.

68 Christopher Hill, 'The Norman yoke', in Saville, *Democracy and the labour movement*, p. 66.

69 Nash, *Man's political rights*, p. 7.

70 *Ibid.*, p. 10.

71 *Ibid.*, p. 12.

72 *Mail*, July 21, 1883, p. 2.

73 *Ibid.*, July 21, 1884, p. 2.

74 *Ibid.*, October 8, 1884, speech reported, p. 2.

75 *Ibid.*, August 4, 1884, p. 2.

76 *Ibid.*, March 25, 1884, p. 2.

77 *Ibid.*, August 4, 1884, p. 2.

78 H. F. Moorhouse, 'The political incorporation of the British working class: an interpretation', *Sociology*, 7 (1973), p. 354.

79 Murray Edelman, *The symbolic uses of politics* (Urbana, Ill., 1964), p. 173.
80 Quoted from a Birmingham Parliamentary deputation in the 1860s by Briggs, *History of Birmingham*, II, p. 165.
81 *Mail*, January 24, 1884, p. 2.
82 *Ibid.*, January 10, 1884, p. 2.
83 *Ibid.*, December 26, 1883, p. 2.
84 Vincent, *Pollbooks*, p. 50.
85 *Mail*, January 24, 1884, p. 2.
86 John Vincent, *The formation of the British Liberal Party* (Harmondsworth, 1972), pp. 13–14.
87 *Mail*, March 1, 1884, p. 2.
88 *Ibid.*, July 21, 1884, p. 2.
89 *Ibid.*, December 2, 1884, p. 2.
90 *Ibid.*, December 6, 1883, p. 2.
91 *Ibid.*, March 1, 1884, p. 2.
92 *Ibid.*, November 14, 1883, p. 2.
93 *Ibid.*, July 4, 1884, p. 2.
94 Birmingham Liberal Association, Management Committee, *Minute book*, June 25, 1884.
95 Joseph Chamberlain, 'A new political organisation', *Fortnightly Review*, New series 22 (1877), p. 134.
96 Nash, *Man's political rights*, pp. 12–13.
97 *Ibid.*, p. 12.
98 *Mail*, July 9, 1884, p. 2.
99 *Ibid.*, April 16, 1884, p. 2.
100 George Jacob Holyoake, *Sixty years of an agitator's life*, 2nd edn (2 vols, London, 1893), I, pp. 456–8.
101 See W. A. Dalley, *An historical sketch of the Birmingham Trades Council, 1866–1926* (Birmingham, 1927).
102 Hennock, *Fit and proper persons*, Chapter 2.
103 Quoted by Briggs, *History of Birmingham*, II, p. 194, and see pp. 192–4 for a history of working class candidacies.
104 *Mail*, September 15, 1883, p. 2.
105 Nash, *Man's political rights*, p. 12.
106 *Mail*, August 20, 1883, p. 2.
107 *Ibid.*, July 14, 1884, p. 2.
108 *Ibid.*, April 15, 1884, p. 2.
109 *Ibid.*, April 17, 1884, p. 2.
110 *Ibid.*, July 11, 1884, p. 2.
111 *Ibid.*, November 27, 1883, speech reported, p. 3.
112 *Ibid.*, July 2, 1883, speech reported, p. 2.
113 *Ibid.*, April 17, 1884, p. 2.
114 *Ibid.*, December 6, 1883, p. 2.
115 Garvin, *Joseph Chamberlain*, I, p. 110.
116 There is a general account of this society and similar organisations by Brian Harrison – 'Pubs', in H. J. Dyos and Michael Wolff, eds., *The Victorian city: images and realities* (2 vols, London, 1973), I, pp. 161–90.
117 Sunday Evening Debating Society, held at Mr Robert Edmonds', The Hope and Anchor Inn, Navigation St., Birmingham, *Minute books*, in the

Birmingham Public Library Local History Collection. *Minutes*, February 10, 1862. Navigation Street is right in the centre of the city, close to what was then one of two main line railway stations and on the border between the business and cultural and industrial areas. The Hope and Anchor Inn is no more.

118 *Kelly's directory of Birmingham, 1884* (London, 1884). In addition to listing residents and businesses street by street this contains two alphabetical listings, one of business and commercial firms, the other the Court Directory; the criteria for inclusion in the latter are not stated. Some businessmen can be identified in the commercial or residential lists, but many names are professionally unidentifiable except that their addresses suggest that they were in the upper income groups in the city. Their social prominence seems to have had a purely local significance. The three listed in the Court Directory were Jeremiah Thomas, Joseph Lampard and Charles Hibbs. In eight further cases the Court Directory contained names similar to those in Society records and it is obviously likely that one of these was the debater.

119 *Kelly's directory, 1884.* The six are George Bill, rose engine turner; Allen Dalzell, carpet pin manufacturer; Benjamin Bushell, iron fender manufacturer; Richard Crump, cooper; Geoffrey Nuttall, Liberal registration agent; Mr Bransby, washing blue manufacturer. The street listings for these six suggest that they had small workshop businesses operated from their home or backyard. Probable identification of a further eight names yields a brushmaker, a beer retailer or a moulder's tool maker (apparently related and near neighbours), the proprietor of a fancy repository, a black ornament manufacturer, a shopkeeper, a coach or general smith, a furniture broker and a cabinet and chair maker.

120 The rose engine turner was a skilled craftsman, a rose engine being an 'appendage to a turning lathe by means of which curvilinear or intricate patterns can be engraved'. The manufacture of carpet pins or tacks was typical of the metal manufacturing industries of Birmingham, no doubt similar to the origins of the Chamberlain family fortune in the manufacturing of screws.

121 *Minutes*, December 28, 1884.

122 *Ibid.*, February 10, 1884.

123 *Ibid.*, September 13, 1885. Sir Robert Giffen and Leone Levi both published extensive studies of income distribution, e.g. Giffen's 'The progress of the working classes in the last half-century', a lecture delivered to the Statistical Society in 1883 and published thereafter, and Levi's *Wages and earnings of the working classes* (London, 1867 – still in print in the 1880s) and *Work and play* (London, 1877).

124 *Minutes*, January 17, 1886.

125 *Ibid.*, January 1, 1882; spelling and punctuation always as in the original.

126 *Ibid.*

127 *Ibid.*, November 8, 1868.

128 Harrison, in 'Pubs', claims that by the 1880s the society had lost independence and simply reflected party positions. The strong partisan flavour of many debates at this time, however, seems to have followed the recent appearance of Mr Oswald as a regular debater; his unreflective party line

provoked a similar response. A much clearer example of blind partisanship was the wild swings in the votes during the 1865 debates on reform, which exactly followed the prevarications of the Liberal Party.

129 *Minutes*, August 26, 1883.

130 *Ibid.*, March 30, 1884.

131 *Ibid.*, April 20, 1884.

132 *Ibid.*, November 2, 1884.

133 *Ibid.*, September 23 and 30, 1883.

134 *Ibid.*, May 31, 1885.

135 *Ibid.*, December 7, 1884.

136 *Ibid.*, August 17, 1884.

137 *Ibid.*, August 24, 1884.

138 *Ibid.*, November 4 and 11, 1883. See Hennock, *Fit and proper persons*, for an account of local political dignitaries.

139 Cf. comments by Woodrow Wilson: 'It is interesting to observe that. . .the distinction we make between "politicians" and "statesmen" is peculiarly our own. In other countries where these words. . .are used, the statesman differs from the politician only in capacity and in degree, and is distinguished as a public leader only in being a greater figure on the same stage, whereas with us politicians and statesmen differ in kind. A politician is a man who manages the organs of the party outside the open field of government. . . while the statesman is the leader of public opinion, the immediate director . . .of executive or legislative policy, the diplomat, the recognized public servant.' *Constitutional government in the United States* (New York, 1908; reprinted 1961), p. 212.

140 *Minutes*, August 17, 1884.

141 *Ibid.*, July 6, 1884. And see E. P. Thompson, *The making of the English working class* (New York, 1963), Chapter 4.

142 *Minutes*, July 12, 1868, and August 20 to December 20, 1885.

143 *Ibid.*, September 13, 1885.

144 *Ibid.*, April 27, 1884.

145 *Ibid.*, December 17, 1883.

146 *Ibid.*, September 30, 1883.

147 *Ibid.*, January 20, 1884.

148 Vincent, *British Liberal Party*, p. 114.

149 *Minutes*, August 26, 1883, and May 12, 1867.

150 *Ibid.*, January 3, 1886.

151 *Ibid.*, February 18, 1884.

152 *Ibid.*, August 30, 1885, November 9, 1884, and see also March 9, 1884.

153 *Ibid.*, November 16, 1884.

154 *Ibid.*, August 22, 1885.

155 *Ibid.*, October 25, 1885.

156 *Ibid.*, September 16, 1883.

157 *Ibid.*, April 13, 1884, and August 2, 1885.

158 *Ibid.*, August 3, 1884.

159 *Ibid.*, December 14, 1884.

160 *Ibid.*, June 9, 1867.

161 *Ibid.*, September 13, 1885.

162 *Ibid.*, January 19, 1885.

163 *Ibid.*, March 2, 1884.

164 *Ibid.*, July 27, 1884.

165 *Ibid.*, August 10, 1884.

166 *Ibid.*, September 30, 1883.

167 *Ibid.*, September 23, 1883.

168 *Ibid.*, September 27, 1885.

169 *Ibid.*, January 3, 1886.

170 See Henry Pelling, *America and the British left* (London, 1956) for an account of changing attitudes among British radicals to the American example; its early inspiration faded during the century and by the 1880s Henry George was only one source of information about social problems which 'measures of constitutional reform were powerless to alleviate' (p. 55), raising the doubt that 'political democracy was enough to make people happy' (p. 58).

171 The *Minutes* between June 15, 1882 and September 9, 1884, record only two probable instances of action initiated outside the Management Committee. On February 2, 1883, a requisition from an unspecified source that the Eight Hundred be summoned to discuss the Bradlaugh case was reported, and a meeting duly called for February 8. On May 13, 1884, a letter from the Secretary of St George's Ward Liberal Association asked on behalf of his committee that the Executive Committee be called to petition Parliament to make King Edward VI's School 'More effective' by removing its government from the Charity Commissioners and giving it to the local authority. Again, it was agreed that the Executive Committee be summoned. All major policy initiatives, including the issue of political reform, and electoral matters, including the selection of a new candidate in 1885, were raised by the Management Committee itself.

172 There had been occasional cases of protest action as a direct response to debates in earlier years; for example, the Secretary of the Society corresponded with the government following a debate on mine safety – reported in the *Minutes*, February 10, 1862.

173 Pelling, *Popular politics*, p. 15.

174 E. J. Hobsbawm, 'Economic fluctuations and some social movements since 1800', *Economic History Review*, Second series, 5 (1952), p. 7.

175 Pelling, *America and the British left*, p. 64: 'now initiatives in this field often came to Britain across the Atlantic' and he points out that the Knights of Labor, however unsuccessful in the long run, had unionised unskilled labour well before similar attempts by the 'new unions' in Britain.

176 Though it should be emphasised that early policies of this kind were evidently not a response to changed expectations among their likely beneficiaries but were ahead of public opinion; see Pelling, *Popular politics*, Chapter 1.

177 *Ibid.*, p. 18.

178 Perkin, *Origins of modern English society*, pp. 231–6.

179 *Fabian News*, 6 (November, 1896), p. 35.

180 *Ibid.*

181 *Ibid.* (December, 1896), p. 39.

182 Vincent, *Pollbooks*, Chapter 3.

183 *Ibid.*, p. 50.

184 Nash, *Man's political rights*, p. 15.
185 According to Mencken the term 'grass roots' was in use in its political sense
in Ohio by 1885, although there is no printed record as early as this. In
English lexicography it first appears only in the 1972 Supplement to the
Oxford English dictionary: 'Used spec. to describe the rank-and-file of the
electorate or of a political party.' The earliest English usage recorded was
in 1948.

CHAPTER 5. DISTRUST AND DEMOCRACY

1 Arthur H. Miller and Warren E. Miller, 'Issues, candidates and partisan
divisions in the 1972 American presidential election', *BJPS*, 5 (1975), p. 405.
2 Gary R. Orren and William Schneider, 'Democrats versus Democrats: party
factions in the 1972 presidential primaries' (Unpublished paper, Department
of Government, Harvard University, 1974), pp. 91–2.
3 Miller and Miller, 'Issues', p. 405.
4 Walter Dean Burnham, 'American politics in the 1970s: beyond party?' in
The American party systems, ed. by William Nisbet Chambers and
Walter Dean Burnham, 2nd edn (New York, 1975), p. 318.
5 See Norman H. Nie with Kristi Andersen, 'Mass belief systems revisited:
political change and attitude structure', *Journal of Politics*, 36 (1974), 540–
591.
6 Samuel P. Huntington, 'The democratic distemper', *Public Interest*, 41
(1975), p. 9.
7 *Ibid.*, p. 17.
8 *Ibid.*, p. 37.
9 *Ibid.*, p. 36.
10 *Ibid.*, p. 19.
11 *Ibid.*, p. 33.
12 Martin D. Abravanel and Ronald J. Busch, 'Political competence, political
trust and the action orientations of university students', *Journal of Politics*,
37 (1975), p. 75.
13 Two of the most recent studies of Populism confirm this conclusion of the
sincerity of its democratic intentions and their inadequacy as practical
prescriptions for competing in American politics; see Peter H. Argersinger,
Populism and politics (Lexington, Ky., 1974), especially Chapter 10, and
Lawrence Goodwyn, *Democratic promise* (New York, 1976).
14 In the South, Populists even fought against these reforms of the political
structure, perceiving the potential for the *restriction* of democratic
participation paradoxically inherent in measures such as the secret ballot
and the direct primary – a restriction which in fact was effective not only in
the overtly oligarchic politics of the Deep South but also nationally. See
J. Morgan Kousser, *The shaping of southern politics* (New Haven, 1974)
and Walter Dean Burnham, 'The changing shape of the American political
universe', *APSR*, 59 (1965), 7–23.
15 See Arthur H. Miller, Thad A. Brown and Alden S. Raine, 'Social conflict
and political estrangement, 1958–1972' (paper prepared for the Midwest
Political Science Convention, Chicago, May 3–5, 1973), pp. 10–16.
16 Burnham, 'American politics', p. 347.

17 'Playboy interview: Jimmy Carter', Playboy, November, 1976, p. 77.

18 Huntington, 'Democratic distemper', p. 36.

19 John H. Goldthorpe, 'Social inequality and social integration in modern Britain', Advancement of Science, 26 (1969), p. 195. This article substantially influenced my discussion through its suggestion of the potential impact on politics of the extension of government into the area of wage and price control.

20 Ibid., p. 193.

21 Ibid., p. 202.

22 Anthony Wedgwood Benn, The new politics: a socialist reconnaissance (London, 1970), pp. 16–17.

23 Report of the Committee of Inquiry on Industrial Democracy, January 1977. Chairman, Lord Bullock. Cmnd 6706 (London, 1977).

24 Opinion Research Centre poll, reported in the Guardian (London), April 7, 1977, p. 6.

25 Roy Hattersley, 'Patronising the people', Guardian (London), December 28, 1971, p. 10.

26 Benn, New politics, p. 23.

27 Ibid., p. 11.

28 Ibid., pp. 23–4.

29 Anthony Wedgwood Benn, 'Community and independence', Guardian (London), May 7, 1975, p. 9.

30 Jack Dennis, Leon Lindberg and Donald McCrone, 'Support for nation and government among English children', BJPS, 1 (1971), p. 45.

31 Giovanni Sartori, Democratic theory (New York, 1965), p. 5.

32 From Luther's tract 'Secular authority'; in Martin Luther: selections from his writings, edited by John Dillenberger (New York, 1961), p. 389.

33 Samuel H. Beer, British politics in the collectivist age, revised edn (New York, 1969), p. 40.

34 Hiawatha Journal (Hiawatha, Kansas), April 24, 1890, p. 2; Advocate (Topeka, Kansas), April 2, 1890, p. 4.

35 Quoted in John F. Manley, American government and public policy (New York, 1976), p. 337.

36 Benn, New politics, title page; the quotation is attributed to Lao Tzu.

37 Beer, British politics, p. 40.

38 Kansas State Historical Society, John Davis scrapbook C, p. 50.

39 See Eugene Lewis, American politics in a bureaucratic age (Cambridge, Mass., 1977).

40 See Grant McConnell, The decline of agrarian democracy (New York, 1969).

41 Alexander Hamilton, James Madison and John Jay, The Federalist (London, 1965), p. 264.

42 Richard Hofstadter, The idea of a party system (Berkeley, Cal., 1969), p. viii.

43 Donald McCrae, 'Populism as an ideology', in Populism, ed. by Ghita Ionescu and Ernest Gellner (London, 1969), pp. 160 and 162

Works cited

PRIMARY SOURCES

Advocate. Meriden, Kansas 1889–90. Topeka, Kansas. 1890.

Birmingham Daily Mail. July, 1883–December, 1884.

Birmingham Liberal Association, Management Committee. *Minute book, June 15, 1882–September 9, 1884*. Manuscript in Birmingham Public Library, Local History Collection.

Donnelly, Ignatius. *The Ignatius Donnelly papers, 1889–91*. Microfilm edition. St Paul, Minn., Minnesota Historical Society, 1968.

Farmers' Alliance, Gove County, Kansas, Union No. 2628. *Minute book, May 24, 1890–July 4, 1891*. Manuscript in Kansas State Historical Society collections.

Farmer's Friend. Iola, Kansas. January–June, 1890.

Galva Times. Galva, Kansas. January–June, 1890.

Great Britain. Parliament. Royal Commission on the Constitution, 1969–73. *Report*. Cmnd 5460–1. *Research papers 7: Devolution and other aspects of government: an attitudes survey*. London, Her Majesty's Stationery Office, 1973.

Great West. St Paul, Minnesota. January–June, 1890.

Hiawatha Journal. Hiawatha, Kansas. January–June, 1890.

Hury Kain. Topeka, Kansas. 1893–4.

Junction City Tribune. Junction City, Kansas. January–June, 1890.

Lincoln Beacon. Lincoln, Kansas. January–June, 1890.

Nebraska Farmers' Alliance. *Nebraska Farmers' Alliance papers, 1887–1901*. Microfilm edition. Lincoln, Neb., Nebraska State Historical Society, 1966.

Ottawa Journal and Triumph. Ottawa, Kansas. January–June, 1890.

Sunday Evening Debating Society, held at Mr Robert Edmonds', The Hope and Anchor Inn, Navigation Street, Birmingham. *Minute books, 1850–1886*. 2 vols. Manuscript in Birmingham Public Library, Local History Collection.

United States Senate. Subcommittee on Intergovernmental Operations. *Confidence and concern: citizens view American government; a survey of public attitudes*. 3 vols. Washington, D.C., Government Printing Office, 1973.

Washington Post. Washington, Kansas. January–June, 1890.

Winfield Telegram. Winfield, Kansas. January–June, 1890.

SECONDARY SOURCES

Aberbach, Joel D. 'Alienation and political behavior', *American Political Science Review*, 63 (1969), 86–99.

Aberbach, Joel D., and Walker, Jack L. 'Political trust and racial ideology', *American Political Science Review*, 64 (1970), 1199–219.

Abrams, Philip, and Little, Alan. 'The young activist in British politics', *British Journal of Sociology*, 16 (1965), 315–33.

Abramson, Paul R. 'Political efficacy and political trust among black schoolchildren', *Journal of Politics*, 34 (1972), 1243–69.

Abravanel, Martin D., and Busch, Ronald J. 'Political competence, political trust and the action orientations of university students', *Journal of Politics*, 37 (1975), 57–82.

Adams, F. G. *List by counties of newspapers and periodicals published in Kansas, January 1, 1891.* Topeka, Ks., Kansas State Historical Society, 1891.

Adorno, T. W.; Frenkel-Brunswik, Else; Levinson, Daniel J.; and Sanford, R. Nevitt. *The authoritarian personality.* New York, Harper, 1950.

Almond, Gabriel A., and Verba, Sidney. *The civic culture: political attitudes and democracy in five nations.* Princeton, N.J., Princeton University Press, 1963.

Altick, Richard D. *The English common reader, 1800–1900.* Chicago, University of Chicago Press, 1957.

Anderton, Thomas. *A tale of one city.* Birmingham, 'Midland Counties Herald' Office, 1900.

Annual register: world events in 1972. London, Longman, 1973.

Appleton's annual cyclopaedia, 1890. New York, Appleton, 1891.

Apter, David, ed. *Ideology and discontent.* New York, Free Press, 1964.

Argersinger, Peter H. *Populism and politics: William Alfred Peffer and the People's Party.* Lexington, Ky., University Press of Kentucky, 1974.

Bachrach, Peter. *The theory of democratic elitism.* Boston, Little, Brown, 1967.

Bagehot, Walter. *The English constitution.* With an introduction by R. H. S. Crossman. Ithaca, N.Y., Cornell University Press, 1966. First published 1867.

Bailyn, Bernard. *The ideological origins of the American revolution.* Cambridge, Mass., Belknap Press, 1967.

Bass, Herbert J., ed. *The state of American history.* Chicago, Quadrangle Books, 1970.

Beer, Samuel H. *British politics in the collectivist age.* Revised edn. New York, Vintage Books, 1969.

Bell, Daniel, ed. *The radical right.* Revised edn. Garden City, N.Y., Anchor Books, 1964.

Benn, Anthony Wedgwood. 'Community and independence', *Guardian* (London), May 7, 1975, p. 9.

Benn, Anthony Wedgwood. *The new politics: a socialist reconnaissance.* Fabian Tract 402. London, Fabian Society, 1970.

Best, Geoffrey. *Mid-Victorian Britain, 1851–1875.* Revised edn. Frogmore, Herts., Panther Books, 1973.

Birmingham Liberal Association. *Objects, constitution and laws.* Birmingham, Birmingham Liberal Association, 1880.

Blewett, Neal. 'The franchise in the United Kingdom, 1885–1918', *Past and Present*, 32 (1965), 27–56.

Booth, Charles. *Life and labour of the people of London.* Reprinted from the edition of 1902–4. 17 vols. New York, AMS Press, 1970.

Boyd, Richard W. 'Popular control of public policy: a normal vote analysis of the 1968 election', *American Political Science Review*, 66 (1972), 429–49.

Briggs, Asa. *History of Birmingham.* 2 vols. London, Oxford University Press, 1952.

Brown, Steven R. 'Consistency and the persistence of ideology, some experimental results', *Public Opinion Quarterly*, 34 (1970), 60–8.

Bryce, James. *The American Commonwealth*. 3rd edn. 2 vols. New York, Macmillan, 1895.

Budge, Ian. *Agreement and the stability of democracy*. Chicago, Markham, 1970.

Budge, Ian; Brand, J. A.; Margolis, Michael; and Smith, A. L. M. *Political stratification and democracy*. London, Macmillan, 1972.

Burnham, Walter Dean. 'The changing shape of the American political universe', *American Political Science Review*, 59 (1965), 7–23.

Burnham, Walter Dean. *Critical elections and the mainsprings of American politics*. New York, Norton, 1970.

Cabe, June G., and Sullivant, Charles A. *Kansas votes: national elections, 1859–1956*. Lawrence, Ks., Governmental Research Center, University of Kansas, 1957.

Campbell, Angus. 'The passive citizen', *Acta Sociologica*, 6 (1962), 9–21.

Campbell, Angus, and Converse, Philip E., eds. *The human meaning of social change*. New York, Russell Sage Foundation, 1972.

Campbell, Angus; Converse, Philip E.; Miller, Warren E.; and Stokes, Donald E. *The American voter*. New York, Wiley, 1960.

Campbell, Angus; Gurin, Gerald; and Miller, Warren E. *The voter decides*. Evanston, Ill., Row, Peterson, 1954.

Cantril, Hadley, ed. *Public opinion: 1935–1946*. Princeton, N.J., Princeton University Press, 1951.

Carter, Jimmy. *Why not the best?* New York, Bantam, 1976.

Chamberlain, J. 'The caucus', *Fortnightly Review*, New series 24 (1878), 721–41.

Chamberlain, J. 'A new political organisation', *Fortnightly Review*, New series 22 (1877), 126–34.

Chambers, William Nisbet and Burnham, Walter Dean, eds. *The American party systems*. 2nd edn. New York, Oxford University Press, 1975.

Christie, Ian R. *Wilkes, Wyvill and reform: the parliamentary reform movement in British politics, 1760–1785*. London, Macmillan, 1962.

Clanton, O. Gene. *Kansas populism: ideas and men*. Lawrence, Ks., University Press of Kansas, 1969.

Cleveland, Harlan, and Lasswell, Harold D., eds. *Ethics and bigness*. New York, Harper, 1962.

Coles, Robert. 'Children and politics: outsiders', *New York Review of Books*, 22 (March 20, 1975), 29–30.

Coles, Robert. 'The politics of middle-class children', *New York Review of Books*, 22 (March 6, 1975), 13–16.

Coles, Robert. 'What children know about politics', *New York Review of Books*, 22 (February 20, 1975), 22–4.

Connelley, William E. *History of Kansas newspapers*. Topeka, Ks., Kansas State Historical Society, 1916.

Crow, Duncan, ed. *The state of the nation: Parliament*. London, Granada Television, 1973.

Dahl, Robert A. *A preface to democratic theory*. Phoenix Books. Chicago, University of Chicago Press, 1963.

Dalley, W. A. *An historical sketch of the Birmingham Trades Council, 1866–1926*. Birmingham, Birmingham Trades Council, 1927.

Dean, Dwight G. 'Alienation: its meaning and measurement', *American Sociological Review*, 26 (1961), 753–8.

Dean, Dwight G. 'Alienation and political apathy', *Social Forces*, 38 (1960), 185–9.

Dennis, Jack; Lindberg, Leon; and McCrone, Donald. 'Support for nation and government among English children', *British Journal of Political Science*, 1 (1971), 25–48.

Dreyer, Edward C., and Rosenbaum, Walter A., eds. *Political opinion and behavior*. 2nd edn. Belmont, Cal., Wadsworth, 1970.

Duncan, Graeme, and Lukes, Steven. 'The new democracy', *Political Studies*, 11 (1963), 156–77.

Dunning, W. A., ed. *Farmers' Alliance history and agricultural digest*. Washington, D.C., Alliance Publishing Co., 1891.

Durkheim, Emile. *The division of labour in society*. Translated by George Simpson. New York, Free Press, 1964.

Durkheim, Emile. *Suicide*. Translated by John A. Spaulding and George Simpson, and edited by George Simpson. Glencoe, Ill., Free Press, 1951.

Dyos, H. J., and Wolff, Michael, eds. *The Victorian city: images and realities*. 2 vols. London, Routledge and Kegan Paul, 1973.

Easton, David, and Dennis, Jack. 'The child's acquisition of regime norms: political efficacy', *American Political Science Review*, 61 (1967), 25–38.

Edelman, Murray. *The symbolic uses of politics*. Urbana, Ill., University of Illinois Press, 1964.

Erbe, William. 'Social involvement and political activity: a replication and elaboration', *American Sociological Review*, 29 (1964), 198–215.

Ferkiss, Victor C. 'Populist influences on American fascism', *Western Political Quarterly*, 10 (1957), 350–73.

Finifter, Ada W. 'Dimensions of political alienation', *American Political Science Review*, 64 (1970), 389–410.

Fishbein, Martin, ed. *Attitude theory and measurement*. New York, Wiley, 1967.

Fraser, John. 'The mistrustful-efficacious hypothesis and political participation', *Journal of Politics*, 32 (1970), 444–9.

Free, Lloyd, and Cantril, Hadley. *The political beliefs of Americans*. New Brunswick, N.J., Rutgers University Press, 1968.

Gallup, George Horace. *The Gallup Poll: public opinion, 1935–1971*. 3 vols. New York, Random House, 1972.

Gallup Political Index. London, Social Surveys (Gallup Poll), 1961–73.

Gamson, William. *Power and discontent*. Homewood, Ill., Dorsey, 1968.

Garvin, J. L. *The life of Joseph Chamberlain*. 4 vols. London, Macmillan, 1932.

Goldthorpe, John H. 'Social inequality and social integration in modern Britain', *Advancement of Science*, 26 (1969), 190–202.

Goodwyn, Lawrence, *Democratic promise: the Populist moment in America*. New York, Oxford University Press, 1976.

Great Britain. Parliament. *Report of the Commission of Enquiry on Industrial Democracy*. Chairman Lord Bullock. Cmnd 6706. London, Her Majesty's Stationery Office, 1977.

Greenstein, Fred I. *Children and politics*. New Haven, Conn., Yale University Press, 1965.

Hackney, Sheldon, ed. *Populism: the critical issues*. Boston, Mass., Little, Brown, 1971.

Hamilton, Alexander; Madison, James; and Jay, John. *The Federalist*. Everyman Library. London, Dent, 1965.

Hamsher, J. Herbert; Geller, Jesse D.; and Rotter, Julian B. 'Interpersonal trust, internal–external control, and the Warren Commission report', *Journal of Personality and Social Psychology*, 9 (1968), 210–15.

Hanham, H. J. *Elections and party management: politics in the time of Disraeli and Gladstone*. London, Longman, 1959.

'Harris Polls and the general election on 28th February, 1974'. London, Louis Harris International, 1974.

Harrison, Royden. *Before the Socialists: studies in labour and politics, 1861–1881*. London, Routledge and Kegan Paul, 1965.

Hattersley, Roy. 'Patronising the people', *Guardian* (London), December 28, 1971, p. 10.

Hawkins, Brett W.; Marando, Vincent L.; and Taylor, George A. 'Efficacy, mistrust and political participation: findings from additional data and indicators', *Journal of Politics*, 33 (1971), 1130–6.

Hennock, E. P. *Fit and proper persons: ideal and reality in nineteenth century urban government*. Montreal, McGill-Queens University Press, 1973.

Hicks, John D. *The Populist revolt*. Bison Books. Lincoln, Neb., University of Nebraska Press, 1959. First published 1931.

Hobbes, Thomas. *Leviathan*. Edited by C. B. Macpherson. Harmondsworth, Penguin, 1968.

Hobsbawm, E. J. 'Economic fluctuations and some social movements since 1800', *Economic History Review*, Second series 5 (1952), 1–25.

Hofstadter, Richard. *The age of reform: from Bryan to F.D.R.* New York, Vintage Books, 1955.

Hofstadter, Richard. *The American political tradition and the men who made it*. New York, Vintage Books, 1948.

Hofstadter, Richard. *The idea of a party system*. Berkeley, University of California Press, 1969.

Hoggart, Richard. *The uses of literacy*. Harmondsworth, Penguin, 1958.

Hollingsworth, J. Rogers. 'Populism: the problem of rhetoric and reality', *Agricultural History*, 39 (1965), 81–5.

Holyoake, George Jacob. *Sixty years of an agitator's life*. 2 vols. 2nd edn. London, T. Fisher Unwin, 1893.

Horton, John. 'The dehumanisation of anomie and alienation: a problem in the ideology of sociology', *British Journal of Sociology*, 15 (1964), 283–300.

Horton, John E., and Thompson, Wayne E. 'Powerlessness and political negativism: a study of defeated local referendums', *American Journal of Sociology*, 67 (1962), 485–93.

Huntington, Samuel. 'The democratic distemper', *Public Interest*, 41 (1975), 9–38.

Inkeles, Alex. 'Participant citizenship in six developing countries', *American Political Science Review*, 63 (1969), 1120–41.

Ionescu, Ghita, and Gellner, Ernest, eds. *Populism: its meaning and national characteristics*. London, Weidenfeld and Nicolson, 1969.

Jackman, Robert W. 'Political elites, mass publics, and support for democratic principles', *Journal of Politics*, 34 (1972), 753–73.

Jennings, H. J. *Chestnuts and small beer*. London, Chapman and Hall, 1920.

Jensen, Richard. *The winning of the mid-west: social and political conflict, 1888–1896*. Chicago, University of Chicago Press, 1971.

Jessop, R. D. 'Civility and traditionalism in English political culture', *British Journal of Political Science*, 1 (1971), 1–24.

Jones, Andrew. *The politics of reform, 1884*. Cambridge, Cambridge University Press, 1972.

Josephson, Matthew. *The politicos, 1865–1896*. New York, Harcourt, Brace, 1938.

Kelly's directory of Birmingham, 1884. London, Kelly, 1884.

Key, V. O., Jr. *The responsible electorate: rationality in presidential voting, 1936–1960.* Cambridge, Mass., Belknap Press, 1966.

Kleppner, Paul. *The cross of culture: a social analysis of midwestern politics, 1850–1900.* New York, Free Press, 1970.

Kousser, J. Morgan. *The shaping of southern politics: suffrage restriction and the establishment of the one-party south, 1880–1910.* New Haven, Conn., Yale University Press, 1974.

Lane, Robert E. *Political life.* New York, Free Press, 1959.

Laslett, Peter, and Runciman, W. G., eds. *Philosophy, politics and society.* Third series. Oxford, Blackwell, 1967.

Levin, Murray B. *The alienated voter.* New York, Holt, Rinehart and Winston, 1960.

Lewis, Eugene. *American politics in a bureaucratic age: citizens, constituents, clients and victims.* Cambridge, Mass., Winthrop, 1977.

Lipset, Seymour Martin. *Political man: the social bases of politics.* Garden City, N.Y., Anchor Books, 1963.

Litwak, Eugene; Hooyman, Nancy; and Warren, Donald. 'Ideological complexity and middle-American rationality', *Public Opinion Quarterly*, 37 (1973), 317–32.

Luther, Martin. *Selections from his writings.* Edited by John Dillenberger. Garden City, N.Y., Anchor Books, 1961.

Luttbeg, Norman R. 'The structure of beliefs among leaders and the public', *Public Opinion Quarterly*, 32 (1968), 398–409.

Lyons, Schley L. 'The political socialization of ghetto children: efficacy and cynicism', *Journal of Politics*, 32 (1970), 288–304.

McClosky, Herbert. 'Consensus and ideology in American politics', *American Political Science Review*, 58 (1964), 361–82.

McClosky, Herbert, and Schaar, John H. 'Psychological dimensions of anomy', *American Sociological Review*, 30 (1965), 14–40.

Maccoby, S. *English radicalism, 1853–1886.* London, Allen and Unwin, 1938.

McConnell, Grant. *The decline of agrarian democracy.* New York, Atheneum, 1969.

McCray, D. O. 'The administrations of Lyman U. Humphrey', *Transactions of the Kansas State Historical Society*, 9 (1905–6), 414–30.

Manley, John F. *American government and public policy.* New York, Macmillan, 1976.

Mann, Michael. 'The social cohesion of liberal democracy', *American Sociological Review*, 35 (1970), 423–39.

Marx, Karl. *Early writings.* Translated and edited by T. B. Bottomore. New York, McGraw-Hill, 1964.

Marx, Karl, and Engels, Friedrich. *The German ideology: Parts I and III.* Edited by R. Pascal. New York, International Publishers, 1947.

Mass Observation. *Puzzled people: a study in popular attitudes to religion, ethics, progress and politics in a London borough.* London, Gollancz, 1948.

Merriam, Charles Edward, and Gosnell, Harold Foote. *Non-voting: causes and methods of control.* Chicago, University of Chicago Press, 1924.

Merton, Robert K. *Social theory and social structure.* Revised edn. Glencoe, Ill., Free Press, 1957.

Meyers, Marvin. *The Jacksonian persuasion: politics and belief.* Stanford, Stanford University Press, 1960.

Milbrath, Lester. *Political participation: how and why do people get involved in politics?* Chicago, Rand, McNally, 1965.

Miller, Arthur H. 'Political issues and trust in government: 1964–1970', *American Political Science Review*, 68 (1974), 951–72.

Miller, Arthur H.; Brown, Thad A.; and Raine, Alden S. 'Social conflict and political estrangement, 1958–1972'. Paper prepared for the Midwest Political Science Association Convention, Chicago, May 3–5, 1973.

Miller, Arthur H., and Miller, Warren E. 'Issues, candidates and partisan divisions in the 1972 American presidential election', *British Journal of Political Science*, 5 (1975), 393–434.

Moorhouse, H. F. 'The political incorporation of the British working class: an interpretation', *Sociology*, 7 (1973), 341–59.

Morgan, W. Scott. *History of the Wheel and the Alliance and the impending revolution*. Hardy, Arkansas, Published by the author, 1889.

Mowry, George. *The era of Theodore Roosevelt*. New York, Harper, 1958.

Muller, Edward N. 'Cross-national dimensions of political competence', *American Political Science Review*, 64 (1970), 792–809.

Nash, H. F. *Man's political rights and duties: an address delivered to the members of the Birmingham Junior Liberal Club, on Thursday October 27, 1882*. Birmingham, Buckler Brothers, 1882.

Neal, Arthur G., and Rettig, Salomon. 'Dimensions of alienation among manual and non-manual workers', *American Sociological Review*, 28 (1963), 599–608.

Nebraska State Historical Society. *Nebraska Farmers' Alliance papers, 1887–1901: guide to the microfilm edition*. Lincoln, Neb., Nebraska State Historical Society, 1966.

Neumann, Franz. *The democratic and the authoritarian state*. New York, Free Press, 1957.

Nie, Norman, and Andersen, Kristi. 'Mass belief systems revisited: political change and attitude structure', *Journal of Politics*, 36 (1974), 540–91.

Nordlinger, Eric A. *The working class Tories*. Berkeley, University of California Press, 1967.

Nugent, Walter T. K. *The tolerant Populists: Kansas populism and nativism*. Chicago, University of Chicago Press, 1963.

Olsen, Marvin E. 'Two categories of political alienation', *Social Forces*, 47 (1969), 288–99.

Orren, Gary R., and Schneider, William. 'Democrats versus Democrats: party factions in the 1972 presidential primaries'. Unpublished paper, Department of Government, Harvard University, 1974.

Ostrogorski, Moisei. *Democracy and the organisation of political parties*. 2 vols. New York, Macmillan, 1908.

Page, Benjamin I., and Brody, Richard A. 'Policy voting and the electoral process: the Vietnam War issue', *American Political Science Review*, 66 (1972), 979–95.

Parkin, Frank. *Class inequality and political order: social stratification in capitalist and communist societies*. London, Paladin, 1972.

Parkin, Frank. *Middle-class radicalism: the social bases of the British Campaign for Nuclear Disarmament*. Manchester, Manchester University Press, 1968.

Pateman, Carole. *Participation and democratic theory*. Cambridge, Cambridge University Press, 1970.

Patterson, Samuel C.; Boynton, G. R.; and Hedlund, Ronald D. 'Perceptions and expectations of the legislature and support for it', *American Journal of Sociology*, 75 (1969), 62–76.

Paulson, Ross E. *Radicalism and reform: the Vrooman family and American social thought, 1837–1937*. Lexington, Ky., University of Kentucky Press, 1968.

Pelling, Henry. *America and the British left.* London, Black, 1956.
Pelling, Henry. *Popular politics and society in late Victorian Britain.* London, Macmillan, 1968.
Pelling, Henry. *The social geography of British elections, 1885–1910.* London, Macmillan, 1967.
Perkin, Harold. *The origins of modern English society, 1780–1880.* London, Routledge and Kegan Paul, 1969.
'Playboy interview: Jimmy Carter', *Playboy*, November, 1976, 63–86.
Pollack, Norman. *The Populist response to industrial America.* Cambridge, Mass., Harvard University Press, 1962.
Pomper, Gerald M. 'From confusion to clarity: issues and American voters, 1956–1968', *American Political Science Review*, 66 (1972), 415–28.
Putnam, Robert D. *The beliefs of politicians; ideology, conflict and democracy in Britain and Italy.* New Haven, Conn., Yale University Press, 1973.
Ridge, Martin. *Ignatius Donnelly: the portrait of a politician.* Chicago, Chicago University Press, 1962.
Rightmire, W. F. 'The Alliance movement in Kansas – origin of the People's Party', *Transactions of the Kansas State Historical Society*, 9 (1905–6), 1–8.
Rogin, Michael Paul. *The intellectuals and McCarthy: the radical specter.* Cambridge, Mass., MIT Press, 1967.
Rose, Arnold M. 'Alienation and participation: a comparison of group leaders and the "mass"', *American Sociological Review*, 27 (1962), 834–8.
Rose, Richard. *Politics in England.* London, Faber and Faber, 1965.
Sartori, Giovanni. *Democratic theory.* New York, Praeger, 1965.
Saville, John, ed. *Democracy and the labour movement.* London, Lawrence and Wishart, 1954.
Scammon, Richard M., and Wattenberg, Ben J. *The real majority.* New York, Coward-McCann, 1970.
Schnadhorst, F. *The caucus and its critics.* Birmingham, National Liberal Federation, 1884.
Schwartz, David C. *Political alienation and political behavior.* Chicago, Aldine, 1973.
Seeman, Melvin. 'On the meaning of alienation', *American Sociological Review*, 24 (1959), 783–91.
Shaw, Malcolm. *Anglo-American democracy.* London, Routledge and Kegan Paul, 1968.
Shils, Edward. *The torment of secrecy: the background and consequences of American security policies.* London, Heinemann, 1956.
Srole, Leo. 'Social integration and certain corollaries: an exploratory study', *American Sociological Review*, 21 (1956), 709–16.
Templeton, Frederic. 'Alienation and political participation: some research findings', *Public Opinion Quarterly*, 30 (1966), 249–61.
Thompson, E. P. *The making of the English working class.* New York, Vintage Books, 1963.
Tocqueville, Alexis de. *Democracy in America.* 2 vols. New York, Vintage Books, 1965.
Verba, Sidney, and Nie, Norman. *Participation in America: political democracy and social equality.* New York, Harper and Row, 1972.
Vincent, John. *The formation of the British Liberal Party, 1857–1868.* Harmondsworth, Penguin, 1972.
Vincent, John R. *Pollbooks: how Victorians voted.* Cambridge, Cambridge University Press, 1967.
Vincent, Leopold, ed. *Alliance songster.* Winfield, Ks., 1890.

Webb, Sidney. 'The machinery of democracy', *Fabian News*, 6 (October, November, December, 1896, January 1897).

Whates, H. R. G. *The Birmingham Post, 1857–1957*. Birmingham, Birmingham Post and Mail, 1957.

White, Helen McCann. *Guide to a microfilm edition of the Ignatius Donnelly papers*. St Paul, Minn., Minnesota Historical Society, 1968.

Wiebe, Robert H. *The search for order: 1877–1920*. New York, Hill and Wang, 1967.

Wilson, Edward D. J. 'The caucus and its consequences', *Nineteenth Century*, 4 (1878), 695–712.

Wilson, Woodrow. *Congressional government*. Boston, Houghton, Mifflin, 1925. First published 1885.

Wilson, Woodrow. *Constitutional government*. New York, Columbia University Press, 1961. First published 1908.

Woodward, C. Vann. *The burden of southern history*. Revised edn. New York, New American Library, 1968.

Woodward, C. Vann. 'The ghost of populism walks again', *New York Times Magazine*, June 4, 1972.

Wright, James D. *The dissent of the governed: alienation and democracy in America*. New York, Academic Press, 1976.

Wright, James Edward. *The politics of populism: dissent in Colorado*. New Haven, Conn., Yale University Press, 1974.

Young, James Sterling. *The Washington community, 1800–1828*. New York, Harcourt, Brace, 1966.

Index